ENCOUNTERS WITH THE SOUL

Barbara Hannah

ENCOUNTERS WITH THE SOUL:

Active Imagination
As Developed by C. G. Jung

SIGO PRESS

#7462471

Copyright © 1981 Barbara Hannah

SIGO PRESS, 1601 Ocean Park Blvd., 210, Santa Monica, CA 90405
Publisher, Sisa Sternback-Scott

ISBN 0-9384 3402-0 (pbk.)
ISBN 0-9384 3404-7 (hardcover)

Library of Congress Catalog Number: 81-5316

Cover and Illustration on p. vi: The Inward Gaze is one of 39 plates in the book *Light From the Darkness—The Paintings of Peter Birkhaüser*, with an introduction by Eva Wettenschlag and Kasper Birkhäuser and commentaries by Marie-Louise von Franz, published by Birkhäuser Boston Inc., 380 Green Street, Cambridge, MA 02139, price: $18.00.

Cover Design John Coy
General Editor: Sisa Sternback-Scott. Copy editor: Becky Goodman
Printed in Korea

Table of Contents

THE INWARD GAZE   Peter Birkhäuser

Commentary to *The Inward Gaze*
by Marie-Louise von Franz

If we look inward, the "other" looks at us too, but with a strange faraway eye. The unconscious begins to unveil its secret play of fantasy: images of seductive beauty and the most cruel abysses of nature. They are framed above by a transparent snake, a symbol of spiritual power.

Often Peter Birhauser was persecuted in his dreams by a strange "old woman," an unrecognizable, terrifying enemy. This is the dark side of nature, inertia and death, from which the creative artist has to wrestle free again and again. The figure who sees this vision is colorless—his consciousness is drained of life, and the whole play of colors has gone into the reality of his unconscious, where a frog rises from below, an old symbol of resurrection.

Introduction

When C. G. Jung went on the quest of finding his own myth after his break with Freud, he ventured into the realm of the collective unconscious, unguided and alone. In this unique confrontation he discovered, by trial and error, a new way of coming to terms with the contents of the unconscious within the unitary reality of creative fantasy. Jung later called this method "active imagination," and recommended it warmly to many of his patients. He described active imagination as the only way toward a direct encounter with the reality of the unconscious without the intermediary use of tests or dream interpretation. Although he discussed documents of active imagination in seminars, he did not publish any of them, probably because he realized how far removed these documents were from the collective, conscious views of his time.

A great change has taken place since then. In Europe as well as in the United States, innumerable techniques have cropped up for releasing some forms of unconscious fantasies in an awakened state of consciousness. All of them, however, are only forms of passive imagination, which nevertheless have a salutary effect. Nowadays, there is practically no mental hospital where painting, modeling, dance, music and writing are not used to help patients express their problems. At the end of his life, Jung remarked that passive imagination had been more or less understood by the world, unlike active imagination. In short, what is lacking is the active, ethical confrontation, the active entering of the whole person into the fantasy-drama. But in my experience, this is very difficult for people to understand in a *practical* way. Barbara Hannah's book is therefore a unique help for understanding this point through her well-chosen examples. *Her point-by-point comments on every turn*

1

within the stories and dialogues were often surprising and most helpful for me. The figures of the unconscious are powerful and weak, benevolent and insidious, and a very alert mind and heart are needed to avoid the mass of possible traps into which one can inadvertently step when dealing with them.

In a way, one must be potentially "whole" already in order to enter the drama; if one is not, one will learn to become so by painful experience. Active imagination is thus *the* most powerful tool in Jungian psychology for achieving wholeness—far more efficient than dream interpretation alone. Barbara Hannah's book is the first and only book I know of which can promote its understanding by illustrating, through various examples, the steps, the pitfalls and successes of this method of encountering the unconscious.

In contrast to the numerous existing techniques of passive imagination, active imagination is done *alone,* to which most people must overcome considerable resistance. It is a form of play, but a bloody serious one. Perhaps, therefore, the resistance many people have against it is sometimes justified, and one should not push anyone into it thoughtlessly. Very often, a situation of utter despair (as that which the World-Weary Man met) is needed to initially open the door. But I think that nobody who has once discovered active imagination would ever want to miss it, because it can literally achieve miracles of inner transformation.

Barbara Hannah not only comments on several modern examples of active imagination, but also on two most remarkable historical examples. We also know that many alchemists used an *imaginatio vera et non phantastica* in their work, which was a form of active imagination. This gives us the satisfaction of knowing that we are dealing here not with a weird innovation, but with a human experience which has been lived through before. It is actually a new form of one of the oldest forms of *religio,* in the sense of "giving careful consideration to the numinous powers."

Marie-Louise von Franz

CHAPTER 1

Confronting the Unconscious

The first point to establish for any reader who is not familiar with the psychology of C. G. Jung is that what we know of ourselves is *not* all that we are. If we observe ourselves and what happens to us with any care, our lives teach us this lesson every day. On the one hand why do we just miss the train we are particularly anxious to catch? Why do we lose or break an object to which we are especially attached? Why do we do and say so many things which we very much regret afterwards? Why do we wake up depressed for no apparent reason? And, on the other hand, why do we sometimes surprise ourselves by doing or saying something much better than we ever expected of ourselves, or wake up very cheerful for no cause of which we are are aware?

Once we have learned of the existence of this unknown side from our own experience of ourselves, theory is seldom, if ever, convincing; naturally, it becomes of the utmost importance to find out something about the unknown in ourselves. It was while Jung himself was engaged in this task—a veritable labor of Hercules—that he discovered the technique that he called "active imagination," which is the subject of this book.

I say, very carefully, *discovered*, not invented, for active imagination is a form of meditation which man has used, at least from the dawn of history, if not earlier, as a way of learning to know his God or gods. In other words, it is a method for exploring the unknown, whether we think of the unknown as an outside god—as an immeasurable infinite —or whether we know that we can meet it by contemplating our unknown selves in an entirely *inner* experience. As Christ said, "The kingdom of heaven is within you," not somewhere outside, beyond the sky.

The Easterner realizes this truth much better than we do. They speak of the universal and personal atman as one and the same thing, and they say of the purusha that he is a thumbling who dwells in the heart of every man and yet he covers the universe and is "smaller than small and greater than great." In the same sense, microcosm and macrocosm were terms which were generally understood by the Western world in earlier days.

Naturally, dreams are *the* messengers *par excellence* from the unconscious. But dreams use a symbolic language which is very diffi- cult to understand. This applies especially to our own dreams, which always tell us something we do *not* know, and which is usually the last thing we would expect. After his break with Freud, when he faced the unconscious alone, Jung had many dreams. At the time, however, he was unable to understand most of them; in fact, it was years before their meaning became apparent.

Earlier, when Jung was still experimenting with the Freudian tech- nique of dream interpretation, with its facile explanations that every dream is a wish fulfillment which is made incomprehensible by the censor protecting our sleep, and so on, he, like all the psychologists of that time, thought that when the analysis was over, the patient could keep in adequate touch with the unconscious by "understanding his dreams." It was only when he was confronted with so many of his own dreams which he could not understand that he learned how com- pletely inadequate the method really was, and was therefore obliged to search further. He says of this time that all he possessed to help his patients were "a few theoretical prejudices of dubious value. This idea—that I was committing myself to a dangerous enterprise not for myself alone, but also for the sake of my patients—helped me over several critical phases."[1]

[1]Carl Gustave Jung, *Memories, Dreams, Reflections* (New York: Pantheon Books, 1973), p. 179.

It may be difficult for the unprepared reader to understand why facing the unknown in ourselves is a "dangerous enterprise." Only experience can teach one what a terrifying enterprise it is to turn away from the familiar affairs of our conscious world and face the entirely unknown in the inner, unconscious world. When Jung first did so, he was horrified to note that the visions which he saw and heard were very similar to the fantasies he had seen overcome many of his patients at the Burghölzli Mental Hospital. At first, he feared that they might overcome him also, and he lived for many months with the fear of madness hanging over his head. This was caused by a repeated vision of great portions of Europe being bathed in a sea of blood. It was only in August 1914, on the outbreak of war (which involved all the countries he had seen submerged in blood), that he realized that his visions of 1913 had been a forewarning of the First World War and did not refer to his own psychology.

Thus freed from the terrible nightmare of possible madness, he was able to turn quietly and objectively to the contents of his visions. There, he discovered the empirical existence not only of the personal unconscious of which both Freud and Adler had also been fully aware, but of the collective unconscious behind it, with its archetypes and infinite possibilities. This inner world is just as real as the outside world, with which we are familiar; in fact, it is *more* real, for it is infinite and everlasting and does not change and decay as the outside world constantly does. To those who remember the world as it was before 1914, the present world is so utterly changed that it seems to be a different world altogether.

Jung once told me that the unconscious itself was not dangerous. There was only one real danger, he said, but that was a very serious one: *panic!* The fear that grips a person when something very unexpected confronts him, or when he begins to be afraid of losing his footing in the conscious world, can upset him so much that it is really no wonder that so few people embark on the task. Indeed, it is necessary to have very secure roots and to be well established in the outer world before it is wise to make any such attempt. We must remember that Jung was a married man with several children, with his own house and garden on the lake, and with unusual success in his profession, before he undertook his own "confrontation with the unconscious." He points out in *Memories, Dreams, Reflections* that Nietzsche undertook the same journey when he wrote *Thus Spake Zarathustra,* and was blown away like a leaf because he had no roots nor obligations in the outer world.[2]

The fear that makes us dread this journey into the unknown and which really makes it a "dangerous enterprise" is the fear of being swamped by the contents of the unconscious. In themselves, they are no more dangerous than the contents of the outer world, but just as we can lose our orientation in a difficult outer interview, which we could have managed easily had terror not overcome us, so we can do the same in our confrontation with the unconscious, with even more alarming consequences, because they are unknown. Properly used, the method of active imagination can be of the greatest help in keeping our balance and in exploring the unknown; but misunderstood and indulged in, rather than regarded as a scientific piece of *hard work,* it can release forces in the unconscious that can overcome us and even land us in a psychotic episode.

Above all, we must realize that active imagination is *hard work*— probably the most tiring piece of work we have ever encountered. We undertake it in order to open negotiations with everything that is unknown in our own psyche. Whether we know it or not, our whole peace of mind depends on these negotiations; otherwise, we are forever a house divided against itself, distressed without knowing why and very insecure because something unknown in us is constantly opposing us. As Jung writes in *Psychology and Alchemy:* "We know that the mask of the unconscious is not rigid—it reflects the face we turn towards it. Hostility lends it a threatening aspect, friendliness softens its features."[3]

It is therefore of the utmost importance to feel friendly to the idea that there is a great deal of a personal nature, and still more of an impersonal one, that we do not know and which continues to exert a compelling effect upon us. Once we realize—preferably from our own experience—that this is a *fact* which we cannot alter, there is really no reason not to feel friendly towards it. If fate obliges us to live with a companion or companions whom we would not have chosen for ourselves, it is obvious that life will go much more smoothly if we turn a friendly, rather than hostile, face towards them.

[2]Ibid., pp. 102f.
[3]C. G. Jung, *Psychology and Alchemy,* vol. 12, *Collected Works* (Princeton: Princeton University Press, 1968), par. 29.

I remember a very wise woman telling me that, on a long tour through countries she had always wanted to visit, she was forced to share a room with another woman who was completely uncongenial to her. At first she felt this would inevitably spoil the tour. Then she realized that she would waste one of the most interesting and pleasurable times of her life if she allowed her dislike to spoil it. Therefore, she set herself to accept her uncongenial companion, detaching herself from her negative feelings and from the woman herself, while being friendly and kind towards her. This technique worked marvelously, and she managed to enjoy the tour immensely.

It is just the same with elements from the unconscious that we dislike and which we feel are very uncongenial to us. We spoil our own tour through life if we allow ourselves to resent them. If we can accept them for what they are and be friendly towards them, we often find they are not so bad after all, and at least we are spared their hostility.

The first figure we usually meet in the confrontation with the unconscious is the personal shadow. Since she (or he) mainly consists of what we have rejected in ourselves, she is usually quite as uncongenial to us as the woman's traveling companion was to her. If we are hostile to the unconscious, however, it will become more and more unbearable, but if we are friendly—realizing its right to be as it is— the unconscious will change in a remarkable way.

Once, when I had a dream of a shadow who was especially obnoxious to me but which, from previous experience, I was able to accept, Jung said to me, "Now your consciousness is less bright but much wider. You know that as an indisputably honest woman, you can also be dishonest. It may be disagreeable, but it is really a great gain." The further we go, the more we realize that every widening of consciousness is indeed the greatest gain we can make. Almost all of our difficulties in life come from our having too narrow a consciousness to meet and understand them, and nothing helps us more in understanding these difficulties than learning to contact them in active imagination, as I hope our later examples will show.

As I mentioned before, active imagination—although it differs from its predecessors is being more empirical and scientific in character—is by no means a new method. One could even say that it is as old as the earliest efforts of man to relate to forces greater and more eternal than himself. When man tries to open negotiations with such powers, with the idea of coming to terms with them, he instinctively discovers some form of active imagination. If you read the Old Testament attentively from this point of view, you will find that it is full of such attempts. I remind you, as only one example among a multitude, of the way Jacob shaped his whole life on what he *heard* the Lord speak to him. It is true that, in Jacob's case, the will of the Lord was often revealed in dreams, but by no means was this always the case. Jacob no doubt had inherited a faculty for hearing what those forces said to him—whether they are named God or the unconscious in this special case, makes no essential difference—from his mother Rebecca. She went to "enquire of the Lord" when the twins struggled in her womb, and she shaped her rather dubious methods of dealing with her old husband and her sons on His reply. "Rather dubious methods" they certainly were, if we judge them from the standpoint of conventional morality; but if we consider that she was carrying out the Lord's will, they take on a very different character.

The Lord himself tells us: "I form the light, and create darkness, I make peace and create evil: I the Lord do all these things."[4] If he creates evil, he will certainly at times wish his creatures to do what we regard as evil, but this was far more evident in the days of Rebecca than it is today. The important thing is always "to obey the will of the Lord," to use the language of the Old Testament.

Good and evil are the pair of opposites that naturally come to mind after 2000 years of Christianity. And these opposites are causing most of our troubles today. This is aptly symbolized in the outer world by the Iron Curtain, and this is the step which we are forced by circumstances to take beyond the Christian teaching of constantly striving after the good, and repressing the evil. Although this suppression was necessary 2000 years ago, the appalling prevalence of evil today shows us what inevitably happens when one opposite is repressed for too long.

I remember vividly that when Jung was asked in a discussion if he thought there would be atomic war, he answered: "I think it depends on how many people can stand the tension of the opposites in themselves. If enough can, I think we shall just escape the worst. But if not, and there is atomic war, our civilization will perish, as so many civilizations have perished before, but on a much larger scale." This

[4]*Isaiah* 45:7.

shows the tremendous value which Jung set on standing the tension between the opposites and, if possible, uniting them in ourselves. For if we project the dark opposite beyond the Iron Curtain or onto the terrorists, for example, we are failing to contribute the grain that we might place on the positive side of the world scale of peace or war.

We can say that Rebecca's way of dealing with the puzzle set before her by those twins struggling in her womb already contains our main motive in turning to active imagination today. She could not understand what was happening to her and, as Jung often said, "the only unbearable suffering is suffering that we do not understand." So Rebecca asked herself, "If *it be so,* why *am* I thus?"[5] and went "to enquire of the Lord." In principle, this procedure was exactly the same as ours today when something unbearable happens to us, or when the apparent meaninglessness of life becomes more than we can stand. It is then that we turn to something or someone who knows more than we do, in order to understand or to learn what to do.

In the early days, when Jacob and Rebecca lived, man was still naive and simple enough to go straight to what he *knew* to be the fountain-head of knowledge—in the case of the early Jews, "the Lord"—and to ask what he wanted to know. At that time, he was still able to hear what his invisible counterpart said in reply. There are still people who have retained this naive simplicity, but I must say that they are very rare and seem to be becoming, alas, almost extinct. This characteristic follows the principle of the Elgonyi primitives in East Africa, who traditionally trusted their whole fate to the dreams of their medicine men. But they told Jung sadly, in 1925: "No, since the English came, we have not had any more big dreams, for you see, the District Commissioner knows what we should do." In these rational days, we all, whether we know it or not, trust more and more in the "District Commissioner" and everything he stands for. We have thus lost touch —for the most part completely forgotten—the superhumanly wise guidance that exists in the unconscious, which Jung even called "the absolute knowledge" in his essay on synchronicity.[6] Earlier, mankind usually gave a name to this absolute knowledge and called it "God," "the Lord," the "Buddha mind," ad infinitum.

[5]Italics mine.
[6]C. G. Jung, "Synchronicity: An Acausal Connecting Principle," *The Structure and Dynamics of the Psyche,* vol. 8, *Collected Works* (Princeton: Princeton University Press, 1968), par. 948.

Laurens van der Post even attributes the ruthless extermination of the Bushman race primarily to the fact that they "were impossible to tame." Or, in the language Jung used to describe the Elgonyi primitives, it was impossible to make them give up their dreams and trust to the "District Commissioner." Yet van der Post's whole account of Hans Taaibosch, in his enthralling novel, *A Mantis Carol,*[7] shows vividly how much the better part the Bushmen chose when they refused to give up the guidance of their god, Mantis, for the "District Commissioner."

In the very early days of analysis, just after the parting of the ways between Jung and Freud, Jung went through a period of which he says in *Memories:* "[It was] a period of inner uncertainty for me. It would be no exaggeration to call it a state of disorientation. I felt totally suspended in mid-air, for I had not yet found my own footing."[8] He felt that it was particularly necessary to find a completely new attitude to his patients, for he no longer felt that methods he had used while working in close connection with Freud were either valid or satisfactory. He said: "I resolved for the present not to bring any theoretical premises to bear on them [his patients], but to wait and see what they would tell me of their own accord. My aim became to leave things to chance." Later he saw that very little, if anything, happens "by chance"; what he had really done, as early as 1911, was to trust himself and his patients to the unconscious. By doing so, he made the discovery that by far the most fruitful way of interpreting dreams was to take their own facts as the basis of their interpretation, and that theory of any kind only distorts and obscures their meanings.

This method worked extraordinarily well with his patients, but Jung felt that he still had not yet found the firm ground that he needed under his feet, nor did he yet know and understand his own inner myth. He had to admit that he no longer lived by the Christian myth in which man has lived in the Western world for the past 2,000 years and that, although he had written a long book about myths,[9] he did not yet know his own.

He had several very illuminating dreams at that time, but he says that the dreams could not help him overcome his "feeling of disorien-

---

[7]Laurens van der Post, *A Mantis Carol* (London: Hogarth Press, 1975).
[8]Jung, *Memories, Dreams, Reflections,* p. 170.
[9]C. G. Jung, *The Psychology of the Unconscious,* revised as *Symbols of the Transformation,* vol. 5, 2d ed., *Collected Works* (Princeton: Princeton University Press, 1967).

tation." Since he did not understand them for many years, he was forced to search further for depth. The reader can read for himself, in the chapter on the "Confrontation with the Unconscious" in *Memories, Dreams, Reflections,* the steps—dark and dangerous as they often were—by which he found his own highly empirical path of active imagination. It took Jung many years, for he was not satisfied with learning to see the images of the unconscious or even with actively dealing with them in his fantasies. He did not feel at ease until he took the most important step of all: finding their "place and purpose" in his own outer life. This, he says, the most important step of all in active imagination, is what we usually neglect to do. Insight into the myth of our unconscious, he continues, "must be converted into an ethical obligation. Not to do so is to fall prey to the power principle, and this produces dangerous effects which are destructive not only to others, but even to the knower."

(This rather curious word, "knower," a literal translation of the more usual German word, *der Wissende,* means "the one who has experienced insight into the unconscious." A man who has had this most valuable insight and fails to draw conclusions from it regarding its place in his outer life becomes the victim of the power principle, which ultimately endangers him even more than his environment.)

Jung continues: "The images of the unconscious place a great responsibility upon a man. Failure to understand them, or a shirking of ethical responsibility, deprives him of his wholeness and imposes a painful fragmentariness on his life."[10]

I think I have said enough to make it very clear that active imagination is no lighthearted pastime. It is a very serious step which should never be undertaken lightly. It is true that it is not everyone's fate to face the unconscious as completely as Jung did; such an exploration of it is a vocation and should never be undertaken unless it is approached for this reason. But—and this is the reason I am beginning this book by giving some idea of the depths to which it may go and the changes in a person's whole life to which active imagination may lead—there is never any guarantee, if we once start on this path, as to where it may lead us. Above all, it should never be undertaken without a firm relationship to someone who will understand, or at least sympathize, for it sometimes leads into such cold and inhuman depths that *human*

---

[10]Jung, *Memories, Dreams, Reflections,* pp. 192f.

companionship is absolutely necessary to prevent us from becoming entirely frozen and lost. Although it is essential to have a human companion in whom one can confide, the actual active imagination is a very individual and even lonely undertaking. At all events, I could never do active imagination with anyone else in the room, however well I knew the person.

There is another warning note I should like to sound from the very beginning, because I have met several cases where, to my surprise, I found it was not generally known. That is: one should never take the figures of living people into one's fantasies. As soon as there is any temptation to do this, we should stop and *very carefully* inquire again into our motives for the whole undertaking, for it is only too likely that we are regressing into old, magical thinking; that is, trying to *use* the unconscious for *personal* ends, and not really using it in the only legitimate way: for exploring the unknown, in as scientific a way as possible, with the motive of finding our own wholeness. Here, we come to the great fundamental difference between using active imagination in the right or wrong way. The question is: Are we doing it *honestly* to try to reach and discover *our own wholeness,* or are we dishonestly using it as an attempt to get our own way? The latter use may apparently be very successful for a time, but sooner or later it always leads to disaster.

But if we honestly want to find our own wholeness, to live our individual fate as fully as possible; if we truly want to abolish illusion on principle and find the truth of our own being, however little we like to be the way we are, then there is nothing that can help us so much in our endeavor as active imagination. Ultimately, it can lead to far greater independence and free us from depending on analysis, or any other *outer* help, than anything else that I know—but I say *ultimately* because it is the most difficult work that I know.

Jung once said to me that, in cases where his patient should do active imagination, he even regarded it as the touchstone as to whether he or she wanted to become independent, or whether the patient wanted to remain dependent on him as a sort of parasite. When I asked if I might quote this, he replied, "Not only may you, but I ask you to do so whenever you can."

The analyst should interfere with active imagination as little as possible. When I was being analyzed by Jung, he always wanted to hear if I had done any active imagination, but after listening carefully to any that I had done, he never analyzed it or commented on it at all, except to point out if I had used it wrongly. Following that, he always asked for dreams and analyzed them with the greatest care. This was to avoid influencing the active imagination, which should always be allowed to develop in its own way. The patient often finds this very difficult, it is true; unfortunately, things are not so simple and direct as they were in the days of Rebecca. Most of us must laboriously clear away many layers of relying implicitly on the "District Commissioner" and the purely rational security that represents, before we can simply and trustfully "enquire of the Lord" to find our way to the absolute knowledge in our own unconscious.

A disciple asked a learned Rabbi, not so very long ago, why it is that God used to speak directly to his people so often, yet he never does so now. The Rabbi, who was evidently a very wise man, replied, "Man cannot bend low enough now to hear what God says." That is exactly it. We shall only hear what God or the unconscious says by bending very low.

Seeing and, at all events, accepting to some extent our own shadow is really a *conditio sine qua non* of experiencing the unconscious, for if we are still indulging ourselves with illusions about who and what we are, we have no chance whatsoever of being real enough to see the images of the unconscious or to hear its voice. Nature and the unconscious always go straight to the point, which is usually very different from what we expect. We need a very unbiased mind, which has learned to value the truth above everything, in order to register and value what we see and hear.

Therefore, I seldom encourage people who are working with me to do active imagination in their early analysis; rather, I do my best to focus their attention on the reality of the unconscious until I feel that they really know from experience that they are dealing with something which is just as real as the outside world. There are exceptions; a few people who are naturally gifted in this respect may find active imagination a great help, even in the earliest stages. Such people can use it legitimately from the very beginning of their analysis, but they are rare.

If active imagination seems to be a way that you can profitably follow, and if you are fairly sure that your true motive is to know more about yourself and more about the unknown part of man, the first thing to realize is that it follows the principle of the Chinese rainmaker of Kiau Tchou. This story has been told very often, but Jung, who gave us little direct advice, once said to me: "Never give a seminar (and not often a lecture) without telling the people this story.'' At one of the very last Christmases shortly before his death, when he attended the Club[11] dinner, he told it to us again. Now there was certainly no one in the room who did not know the story well, yet, after he had told it, the whole atmosphere of the party changed. I realized, as never before, why he had instructed me to repeat it so often.

> There was a terrible drought in that part of China where Richard Wilhelm was living.[12] After all the ways to bring rain that the people knew had been tried, they decided to send for a rainmaker. This interested Wilhelm very much, and he was careful to be there when the rainmaker arrived. The man came in a covered cart, a small, wizened, old man who sniffed the air with evident distaste as he got out of the cart, and asked to be left alone in a small cottage outside the village; even his meals were to be laid down outside the door.
>
> Nothing was heard from him for three days, then it not only rained, but there was also a big downfall of snow, unknown at that time of year. Very much impressed, Wilhelm sought the rainmaker out and asked him how it was that he could make rain, and even snow. The rainmaker replied, "I have not made the snow; I am not responsible for it." Wilhelm insisted that there was a terrible drought until he came, and then after three days they even had quantities of snow. The old man answered, "Oh, I can explain that. You see, I come from a place where the people are in order; they are in Tao; so the weather is also in order. But directly I got here, I saw the people were out of order and they also infected me. So I remained alone until I was once more in Tao and then, of course, it snowed."

The greatest use of active imagination is to put us, like the rainmaker, into harmony with the Tao, so that the right things may happen around us instead of the wrong. Although speaking of the Chinese Tao may perhaps impart a rather exotic flavor to what is really a simple matter of everyday experience, we find the same meaning in our most colloquial language: "He got out of bed on the wrong side this morning" (or, as the Swiss say, "with the left foot first"). This expression aptly describes a psychological condition in which we did not arise in harmony with our own unconscious. We are ill-tempered and disagreeable, and—it follows as the night follows the day—we

[11]Zürich Psychological Club.
[12]Richard Wilhelm, Sinologist, author and friend of C. G. Jung.

have a disintegrating effect on our environment, the exact opposite of the effect which evidently emanated from the rainmaker of Kiau Tchou.

One can see these effects very clearly in the two opposite activities of prayer and black magic. The mystics bent their whole endeavor to obtaining union with God or, as we would express it, in going into themselves until the ego was replaced by the Self to a great extent. There are a great many stories of effects—even described as miraculous —which the mystics are again and again asserted to have had on their environment. St. Gertrude, the Benedictine Abbess, for instance, was supposed to be able to influence the weather.[13] There are endless stories of her ability to avert hail by prayer, to bring about a cessation of a severe frost, to save the harvest at the last moment from storm, and so on. It is interesting that in her recorded prayers she emphasizes that she does not wish to impose her ego will on God, but would like to draw His attention to the facts! That is, she attempts to produce a complete harmony between herself and God, which will not be disturbed whether he answers her prayer or refuses it.

We are not concerned with whether these effects, natural or miraculous, actually took place, but with the fact that countless people have believed that they did. This in itself is psychological evidence pointing to a deep-rooted human conviction that harmony with God or the Self has an effect on the environment.

The same holds true of the widespread conviction that witches can provoke storms. They were always supposed to do this in connection with the devil or some demon; that is, with a disorderly power. Supposedly, they went out of themselves, created a disorder like the ill temper of which we have just spoken, and brought about the wrong weather, in exactly the reverse sense to the rainmaker of Kiau Tchou.

Whether the state of one man can actually influence the weather does not concern us, for it is impossible to prove it one way or the other.[14] I have only given these examples because they form extreme and visible cases, believed in all times and places by a *consensus gentium*, of the emanations which proceed from a harmonious or disordered relation of man to his own unconscious. It is evident that both the *unio mystica* of the saint and the witch's pact with the devil

[13]St. Gertrude, *Life and Revelations of St. Gertrude* (London: Burns and Yates, 1870).
[14]C. G. Jung, *Psychology and Religion: West and East,* vol. 11, 2d ed., *Collected Works* (Princeton: Princeton University Press, 1969), par. 4.

are too one-sided: the one believes in a completely righteous God and dismisses evil more or less as a *privatio boni,* and the other hopes that the devil, the lord of this world, is the more powerful of the two and therefore takes his side, hoping to get more out of him, so to speak. Our task in coming to terms with the unconscious, therefore, is much more difficult than the foregoing examples. We are obliged to deal with both sides at once, which is characteristic of the problem of our time.

Both the prayer and contemplation of the mystic and the witch's pact with the devil are closely related to active imagination. That is, both present an *active* attempt to come to terms with an invisible force, to explore the unknown country of the unconscious. The reason the effect of the mystic is more favorable than that of the witch can be explained psychologically by the fact that the mystic attempts to give up all ego demands, whereas the witch tries to use the forces of the unconscious for his or her ego purposes. In other words, the mystic tries to sacrifice the one-sided ego for the sake of the whole, whereas the witch attempts to use forces which belong to the totality for the sake of the part—the limited conscious ego.

As mentioned before, we have all experienced the fact that our conscious intentions are constantly crossed by unknown—or relatively unknown—opponents in the unconscious. Perhaps the simplest definition of active imagination is to say that it gives us the opportunity of opening negotiations, and in time, coming to terms, with these forces or figures in the unconscious. In this aspect, it differs from the dream, for we have no control over our own behavior in the latter. Of course, with the majority of cases in practical analysis, the dreams are sufficient to reestablish a balance between conscious and unconscious. It is only in certain cases (but we will consider this point in more detail later) that more is required. But, before we proceed, I will provide a short description of the actual techniques that can be used in active imagination.

The first thing is to be alone, and as free as possible from being disturbed. Then one must sit down and concentrate on seeing or hearing whatever comes up from the unconscious. When this is accomplished, and often it is far from easy, the image must be prevented from sinking back again into the unconscious, by drawing, painting or writing down whatever has been seen or heard. Sometimes it is possible to express it best by movement or dancing. Some people cannot get into touch with the unconscious directly. An indirect approach that often reveals the unconscious particularly well, is to write stories, apparently about other people. Such stories invariably reveal the parts of the storyteller's own psyche of which he or she is completely unconscious. We shall see an excellent example of this approach in "The Case of Sylvia" (Chapter 3).

In every case, the goal is to get into touch with the unconscious, and that entails giving it an *opportunity to express itself* in some way or other. (No one who is convinced that the unconscious has no life of its own should even attempt the method.) To give it this opportunity it is nearly always necessary to overcome a greater or lesser degree of "conscious cramp" and to allow the fantasies, which are always more or less present in the unconscious, to come to consciousness. (Jung once told me that he thought the dream was always going on in the unconscious, but that it usually needs sleep and the complete cessation of attention to outer things for it to register in consciousness at all.) As a rule, the first step in active imagination is to learn, so to speak, to see or hear the dream while awake.

Jung writes in his commentary on "The Secret of the Golden Flower":

> *Each time the fantasy material is to be produced, the activity of consciousness must be switched off again.*
>
> *In most cases the results of these efforts are not very encouraging at first. Usually they consist of tenuous webs of fantasy that give no clear indication of their origin or their goal. Also, the way of getting at the fantasies varies with individuals. For many people, it is easiest to write them down; others visualize them, and others again draw or paint them with or without visualization. If there is a high degree of conscious cramp, often only the hands are capable of fantasy; they model or draw figures that are sometimes quite foreign to the conscious mind.*
>
> *These exercises must be continued until the cramp in the conscious mind is relaxed, in other words, until one can let things happen, which is the next goal of the exercise. In this way a new attitude is created, an attitude that accepts the irrational and the incomprehensible simply because it is happening. This attitude would be poison for a person who is already overwhelmed by the things that happen to him, but it is of the greatest value for one who selects, from among the things that happen, only those that are acceptable to his conscious judgment, and is gradually drawn out of the stream of life into a stagnant backwater.*[15]

[15]C. G. Jung, *Alchemical Studies*, vol. 13, *Collected Works* (Princeton: Princeton University Press, 1968), pars. 21–23.

In other places, Jung includes movement and music among the ways through which it is possible to reach these fantasies. He points out that with movement—although sometimes of the greatest help in dissolving the cramp of consciousness—the difficulty lies in registering the movements themselves and, if there is no outer record, it is amazing how quickly things that come from the unconscious disappear again from the conscious mind.

Jung suggests the repetition of the releasing movements until they are really fixed in the memory and, even then, it is my experience that it is as well to draw the pattern made by the dance or movement, or to write a few words of description, to prevent it from disappearing altogether in a few days.

In the same commentary, Jung says of the types:

> One man will now take chiefly what comes to him from outside, and the other what comes from inside. Moreover, the law of life demands that what they take from outside and inside will be the very things that were always excluded before. This reversal of one's nature brings an enlargement, a heightening and enrichment of the personality, if the previous values are retained alongside the change—provided that these values are not mere illusions. If they are not held fast, the individual will swing too far to the other side, slipping from fitness into unfitness, from adaptedness into unadaptedness, and even from rationality into insanity. The way is not without danger. Everything good is costly, and the development of personality is one of the most costly of all things. It is a matter of saying yes to oneself, of taking oneself as the most serious of tasks, of being conscious of everything one does, and keeping it constantly before one's eyes in all its dubious aspects—truly a task that taxes us to the utmost.[16]

It takes, as a rule, a very long time—many years, usually—before the two sides of the personality, represented by conscious and unconscious, can be brought into Tao. Although, as mentioned before, this term may have an exotic sound in Western ears, it is really the most practical of words. Concerning it, Jung says:

> It is characteristic of the Western mind that it has no word for Tao. The Chinese character is made up of the sign for "head" and the sign for "going." Wilhelm translates Tao by Sinn (Meaning). Others translate it as "way," "providence," or even as "God," as the Jesuits do. This illustrates our difficulty. "Head" can be taken as consciousness,

[16]Ibid., par. 24.

and "going" as travelling a way, and the idea would then be: to go consciously, or the conscious way.[17]

There is another technique in dealing with the unconscious by means of active imagination which I have always found of the greatest possible help: conversations with contents of the unconscious *that appear personified*. Jung used to say that, as a rule, this was a later stage in active imagination, and I did not even realize the possibility until I worked with Jung himself. It is indeed recommended in the early "Two Essays,"[18] and those who have read the chapter on the "Confrontation with the Unconscious" in *Memories*[19] will recall that he took to it fairly early in, although not at the beginning of, his own experiments with the method. Those who have already read *Anna Marjula*[20] will remember that she eventually used this method almost exclusively, although she used the painting method—the visual in contradistinction to the auditory method—for many of her earlier years, and at times, combined the two methods very successfully.

It is, of course, very important to know *to whom* one is speaking, and not to take every voice as uttering the inspired words of the Holy Ghost! With visualization, this is comparatively easy, as one sees in the case of Edward (Chapter 2). He seems to have no difficulty in knowing who is speaking to him, for he always sees, and usually describes, the figure before he speaks to it, with the exception of the voice he calls "the Devil." But it is also possible when there is no visualization, for one can learn to identify the voices, or the way of speaking, so that one never need make a mistake. Anna Marjula often had no visualization at all, and yet she learned to be sure who was speaking. Moreover, these figures are very paradoxical: they have positive and negative sides, and one will often interrupt the other. In this case, you can judge best by what is said. And one should always remember that it is very unwise to cling to the positive and minimize the negative. Concerning this in his "Late Thoughts," Jung says:

We must beware of thinking of good and evil as absolute opposites. The criterion of ethical action can no longer consist in the simple view

[17]Ibid., par. 28.
[18]C. G. Jung, *Two Essays on Analytical Psychology*, vol. 7, *Collected Works*, 2d ed., (Princeton: Princeton University Press, 1966), par. 322f.
[19]Jung, *Memories, Dreams, Reflections*.
[20]*Anna Marjula: The Healing Influence of Active Imagination in a Specific Case of Neurosis*. Part 1 is reprinted in this volume (Chapter 7).

*that good has the force of a categorical imperative, while so-called evil
can resolutely be shunned. Recognition of the reality of evil necessarily
relativizes the good, and the evil likewise, converting both into halves
of a paradoxical whole.*

*In practical terms, this means that good and evil are no longer so
self-evident. We have to realize that each represents a judgment. In
view of the fallibility of all human judgment, we cannot believe that
we will always judge rightly. We might so easily be the victims of mis-
judgment. The ethical problem is affected by this principle only to the
extent that we become somewhat uncertain about moral evaluations.
Nevertheless we have to make ethical decisions. The relativity of
"good" and "evil" by no means signifies that these categories are
invalid, or do not exist. Moral judgment is always present and carries
with it certain characteristic psychological consequences.*[21]

It is never more necessary to remember these facts than in active
imagination, although they add considerably to the difficulties. However, I would like to point out that, especially for introverts, active
imagination is a golden opportunity to realize these truths, which can
be a very great help when we are forced to face them outside, as we
constantly are in the modern world.

There is one very important rule that should always be retained in
every technique of active imagination. In the places where we enter it
ourselves, we must give our full, conscious attention to what we say or
do, just as much—or even more—than we would in an important
outer situation. This will prevent it from remaining passive fantasy.
But when we have done or said all that we want, we should be able to
make our minds a blank, so that we can hear or see what the unconscious wants to say or do.

Jung quotes a passage in the "Psychology of Transference" which
describes this blank very well. The description is in a letter of the
English alchemist John Pordage, to his *soror mystica*, Jane Leade. He
writes:

*Therefore if the human will is given over and left, and becomes
patient and still as a dead nothing, the Tincture [we should say the
Self] will do and effect everything in us and for us, if we can keep our
thoughts, movements and imaginations still, or can leave off and rest.
But how difficult, hard, and bitter this work appears to the human
will, before it can be brought to this shape, so that it remains still and*

[21]Jung, *Memories, Dreams, Reflections*, p. 329.

—

calm even though all the fire be let loose in its sight, and all manner of
temptation assail it.[22]

Here, Pordage is in exact agreement with the writings of Meister
Eckhart, who also makes the human will responsible for not realizing
the will of God. If we examine ourselves carefully, we shall see that
wanting our own way is indeed responsible when we cannot see or hear
what the unconscious wants to reveal to us. To reach the enduring
condition that Pordage describes is indeed a lifetime's work. I have
only seen it achieved once: by Jung himself. And even he did not
achieve it until after his long illness in 1944, when he was nearly
seventy. He says of this:

Something else too, came to me from my illness. I might formulate it
as an affirmation of things as they are: an unconditional "yes" to that
which is, without subjective protests—acceptance of the conditions of
existence as I see them and understand them, acceptance of my own
nature, as I happen to be.[23]

To reach this condition, however, for long enough to see or hear the
unconscious point of view is fortunately much easier, and it is absolutely essential in every technique of active imagination.

The technique for both the visual and the auditory methods consists
first of all in being able to let things happen in the way Jung describes
in the passages quoted from the *Commentary on "The Secret of the*
Golden Flower". But images must not be allowed to change like a
kaleidoscope. If the first image is a bird, for instance, left to itself it
may turn with lightning rapidity into a lion, a ship on the sea, a scene
from a battle, or whatnot. The technique consists of keeping one's
attention on the first image and not letting the bird escape until it has
explained why it appeared to us, what message it brings us from the
unconscious, or what it wants to know from us. Already we see the
necessity of entering the scene or conversation ourselves. If this is
omitted after we have once learned to let things happen, the fantasy
will either change as just described, or—even if we hold onto the first
image—it will remain a sort of passive cinema, or we listen as if it were
the radio that speaks. To be able to let things happen is very necessary, but it soon becomes harmful if indulged in too long. The whole

[22]C. G. Jung, *The Practice of Psychotherapy*, vol. 16, 2d ed., *Collected Works*
(Princeton: Princeton University Press, 1966), par. 512.
[23]Jung, *Memories, Dreams, Reflections*, p. 297.

purpose of active imagination is to come to terms with the unconscious, and for that we must have it out with the unconscious (have an
Auseinandersetzung[24] with it), for which it is necessary to have one's
own firm viewpoint.

Reading the *Odyssey* again from the point of view of active imagination is enormously helpful in realizing the interplay between conscious and unconscious in our own active imagination.[25] The
standpoint of the unconscious in the *Odyssey* is wonderfully shown by
the behavior of the gods; its positive, helpful aspect is illustrated
particularly well by Pallas Athene, and its negative destructive side, by
Poseidon. The most powerful of all, Zeus, is sometimes on one side
and sometimes on the other.

The conscious standpoint is equally well illustrated by the main
figure, Odysseus, and also in the sections in which Odysseus is absent
by such figures as Telemachus (Odysseus's son) or Menelaus. Although
Menelaus only comes in the fourth book of the *Odyssey,* it is he who
teaches us a particularly valuable lesson in the technique of active
imagination: the importance of sticking to one image. In fact, space
allows me to deal in detail with only this example, although it would
be possible and very fascinating to use the entire poem as a prototype
of active imagination. It would naturally be necessary to take it, as
Marie-Louise von Franz always takes myths and fairy tales, as a prototype at the root of the later individual technique of active imagination. It would in no way fit a personal application such as we shall use
in the examples of modern active imagination in later chapters, in the
cases of Edward and Sylvia, for example, but focusing on the *Odyssey*
in this manner would be very insightful.

While he was a boy, Telemachus, the son of Odysseus and
Penelope, watched helplessly while the infamous suitors of his mother
wasted his inheritance, and even pessimistically and obstinately
believed that his father, Odysseus, was dead. The latter was indeed
the last of the surviving conquerors of Troy to reach his home, and the
son he had left as a baby was grown to manhood before anything
definite had been heard of Odysseus. His nineteen years of wandering
at last moved all the gods of Olympus to pity, except Poseidon, who

[24]This untranslatable German word means having it out with, discussing, analyzing,
all with a hint of an eventual coming to terms.
[25]Homer, *Odyssey* (Penguin edition).

pursued the heroic Odysseus right to the end with "relentless malice."

But when Poseidon was visiting the distant Ethiopians, Zeus decided it was time to intervene on Odysseus's behalf; he was sure Poseidon could be brought to relent, for he could not hold out alone against the united will of all the other gods. This was taken up enthusiastically by his daughter, the "bright-eyed Athena." Hermes, the messenger, was sent to the sorceress, Calypso, who was holding Odysseus on a distant island, to tell her that she must free her long-suffering guest, for it was now the will of the gods that he should at last return to his home. Athene herself undertook the task of "instilling a little more spirit" into Telemachus, so that he would finally call the suitors to order, and start off on a quest to gather knowledge of his father, undeterred by the counterplots of the suitors.

Thus inspired, Telemachus defied the suitors. Without his mother's knowledge, but with the reluctant help of his old nurse, he set off on the ship arranged by the goddess, manned by gallant and loyal youths of Ithaca, to seek knowledge of his father, or at least to hear how he had met his end.

First, Telemachus went to the court of Nestor, the horse tamer, but Nestor could give him no direct help, for he had been one of the first to reach home and had no news of the men left behind. Nestor sent Telemachus on to Sparta, to the court of Menelaus, who, he felt sure, would be able to tell him more. One of Nestor's sons drove Telemachus there in a chariot drawn by the two swiftest of Nestor's wonderful horses.

Hospitably received by Menelaus and his wife, Helen of Troy, on whose account the Trojan War had been fought, Telemachus was immediately recognized as Odysseus's son. Then Menelaus could not do enough for him, and though he, like Nestor, could not give him direct news of his father, he gave him some helpful information. Particularly, Menelaus told him how to deal with the immortals—in our language, representatives of the unconscious or archetypal figures—which can still be of the greatest help to us in active imagination today.

Menelaus told Telemachus how his anima had taught him to deal with the situation when he was delayed on an island called Pharos, off the mouth of the Nile, by contrary winds. He had reached the point of despair (as it sometimes seems we have to do before we will face active imagination in its inexorable reality), for he had used up all his supplies. His whole crew, as well as Helen and himself, were faced with starvation if the wind did not change.

One day, when he was walking on the shore in deep dejection, he was approached by the beautiful Eidothea, "daughter of the mighty Proteus, the Old Man of the Sea." First, she chided him severely for his lack of initiative in allowing himself to be cooped up on the island, where they were all growing weaker every day. Menelaus assured her that he longed to leave, but could only think he must somehow have offended the immortals who were now denying him any favorable wind. The friendly goddess told him that only her father, Proteus, could tell them how they could get home. Menelaus must set a trap for him and force him to explain the whole situation. Menelaus begged her to tell him how to "catch this mysterious old being," and she then enlightened him as to what he should do.

The next morning he met her, with the three best men of his crew, as arranged, at daybreak. They gathered at the mouth of the cave where Proteus always went for a midday nap which he only took after counting his seals, as a shepherd counts his sheep. The goddess then covered all four men with the skins of four freshly flayed seals and laid them in lairs that she had scooped out in the sand, filling all their nostrils with a sweet-smelling stuff so that they could endure the stench of the "monsters of the deep." She then left them to carry out her instructions by themselves. All morning, as she had foretold, the seals came up "thick and fast" from the sea, and lay down in companies all around them. At midday, the old man himself emerged, found all of his fat seals awaiting him and counted the four men, entirely unsuspiciously, among the rest. Then he went into the cave for his midday sleep.

This was their moment. He was hardly asleep before the four men jumped on him and held him fast. As Eidothea had warned Menelaus, Proteus's "skill and cunning" had not deserted him and he transformed himself "into a bearded lion and then into a snake and after that a panther and a giant boar. He changed into running water too and a great tree in leaf." But they set their teeth and held him like a vice. Then, as the goddess had foretold, at last he tired of his magic repertoire and took his own form again. Breaking into speech, he asked questions and allowed Menelaus to question him.

He then revealed that Menelaus had blundered in leaving Troy so quickly. He should have stayed "and offered rich sacrifices to Zeus and all the other gods" if he "wished to get home fast across the wine-dark sea." Now he could only return to Egypt in order to make "ceremonial offerings to the everlasting gods." When Menelaus heard he must take "the long and weary trip over the misty seas to Egypt," he was heartbroken but, knowing there was no escape, he promised Proteus to do exactly as he advised.

Then he asked more questions, this time referring to the safety of his countrymen, whom he and Nestor had left behind at Troy. After warning him that his tears would flow, Proteus gave him the information he wanted, of which I will mention two examples. Agamemnon, Menelaus's brother, had been murdered an hour or two after reaching his home by the treachery of his wife and her lover, Aegisthus (Clytemnestra was Helen's sister, for the two brothers had married two sisters). The second fate I will mention was the most important to Telemachus. His father, Odysseus, was unhappily imprisoned on a distant island by Calypso, the witch.

After staying some time in great luxury with Menelaus, Pallas Athene warned Telemachus that it was time he went home. She guided him home by a circuitous route to avoid the trap to kill him that had been set by the infamous suitors. Instead of letting him go home, she guided him to his loyal swineherd's cottage where he found his father (who had at last returned to Ithaca after nineteen years of wandering), disguised as a beggar.

My chief point in relating this material from the *Odyssey* is to show the importance of clinging fast to the first image that appears to us in an active imagination, not allowing it to escape us by quick transformations, as it still will do if it is left to itself. But I have used a little more of the *Odyssey* than that which I cited in another book,[26] so as to draw the reader's attention to the importance of a collaboration between the conscious and unconscious. If he had not been helped by what we call the unconscious, which Homer depicts as the immortals, what chance would either Menelaus or Telemachus have had of getting back to his home? Without the knowledge that Proteus gave him, would Menelaus ever have returned to Egypt, when he says it broke his heart to do so? Yet only in Egypt could he get rich-enough sacri-

[26]Barbara Hannah, *Jung: His Life and Work; A Biographical Memoir* (New York: G. P. Putnam's Sons, 1976), pp. 115f.

fices to appease the gods so that they would send him favorable winds. And Telemachus would undoubtedly have been killed in the suitors' trap if he had not had the guidance of Pallas Athene.

All this is even clearer in the main story of the *Odyssey*, that of Odysseus himself, but we have seen enough to be able to see how the same immortals will still guide us today, though we call them by different names in our modern material. I will try, in later chapters, to point out the parallels between the ancient *Odyssey* and our own efforts.

The only figure of the unconscious that we have mentioned so far is the shadow. This is indeed the figure nearest to consciousness and the only one, in its personal aspect, that can be made entirely conscious. Nevertheless, the dreams often make it necessary to deal with the animus or anima simultaneously with, or even before, the shadow. This is usually because the opinions of the animus would make it impossible to see the shadow as it really is; in the case of the anima, her tendency to make the man fall into moody discontent will prevent him from seeing any value in realizing his own shadow qualities. But the full *Auseinandersetzung* with the shadow must be undertaken before it is possible to have it out with either the animus or anima.

Once when I was having great difficulty in analysis in realizing the figures of my unconscious, Jung put the fingertips of both hands on the table before him. Then he told me to imagine myself as a two-dimensional being, a plane-being, so to speak, and to tell him how I should then experience his hand. Naturally I should only have been aware of the plane surface of his fingertips, and how should I have known that in the third dimension they were attached to each other by the hand? Obviously I could not have known it. I could only have observed the plane surfaces of the fingertips, and slowly learned from the way these appeared, the texture which belonged to each, and how widely they were separated. If one hand, for instance, was widely separated from the other hand by the extension of an arm, I would experience the fingertips of the one hand as being closer together than those of the other hand.

Jung then explained that we are exactly in the same position with regard to the unconscious. We are only conscious of three dimensions, whereas the figures of the unconscious approach us from an unknown fourth.

One must never push such parallels too far, but this example may serve to explain why it is necessary, in a real *Auseinandersetzung* with the unconscious, first to become conscious of the personal shadow. Everything we do not like is forgotten as quickly as possible, or in terms of our simile, it is pushed into the next dimension and lost from our sight. If the plane man, for instance, did not like the black in the design on his plane, he could push it into the third dimension and lose sight of it. However, any fingertips that approached him from that third dimension would touch his plane covered with that rejected black substance. It goes without saying how much that would disgust him with his attempted *Auseinandersetzung* with the unconscious, and shows us why it is wise to know the personal shadow as thoroughly as possible before we try to face the more distant figures in our psyche.

We have already seen that the shadow can represent the whole unconscious while there are personal factors unknown to us, which then become contaminated with the archetypal shadow. But the next nearest figure to us, the animus or anima, only has a personal aspect and is mainly a figure of the collective unconscious. This is the reason that we can interpret the gods and goddesses in the *Odyssey* as animus and anima figures. The conscious figures, such as Odysseus, Telemachus and Menelaus, had a much more ambivalent conception than we have of humanity, and indeed, of their gods, who were both positive and negative in about equal degrees. It was with the coming of Christianity that the white opposite alone was accepted, while the dark became more and more repressed and eventually was identified with the devil. It was a necessary development at the time, but it led to the repression of the personal shadow and to our present necessity of rediscovering it.

Active imagination can be of great use in getting to know the personal shadow and separating it from the collective shadow with which its unknown parts are contaminated. With the help of the dreams, it is usually quite possible to get to know the personal shadow because it is material that, although painful, is not difficult to realize. We all know both the positive and negative qualities of the human being which belong in the personal sphere. We can also recognize the opinions of the animus and the moods and other feminine traits which are produced by the anima without too much difficulty, though again it may be very disagreeable. But when it comes to an *Auseinandersetzung* with the animus or anima, we enter the unknown and then the real difficulty begins. Jung even said that anyone who had succeeded in the task could write ''master'' after his name.

It should be mentioned before continuing that, although the *work*

on the shadow must be done by the conscious ego, its successful conclusion, so that we can face the figure of animus or anima, depends on
the intervention of one of these figures, or the *Auseinandersetzung*
between shadow and ego will end in a deadlock instead of a union of
opposites. One can see this particularly well in the case of Robert Louis
Stevenson's *Dr. Jekyll and Mr. Hyde,* as I hope I showed convincingly
in my account of that book.[27] One sees exactly the reverse in Emily
Brontë's *Wuthering Heights,* where t is the intervention of Heath-
cliff's anima, the elder Catherine, that saves a deadlock between the
opposites in that story.[28]

In the *Auseinandersetzung* with the animus or anima, active imagination is of the greatest posible help in a majority of cases. We shall
see this particularly clearly in the case of Edward (Chapter 2), although
that case is, in one way, an exception, in that the *Auseinandersetzung*
with the anima precedes the work on the shadow. In the case of Anna
Marjula (Chapter 7), Anna shows a more usual development for, as
she works on the animus, the shadow intervenes wherever she has not
yet seen it in her own psychology. The development also shows very
clearly that the *Auseinandersetzung* between the woman and animus
will also end in a deadlock if the help of the Self is not sought and
found. All Anna's conversations with the Great Mother show the
helpful role played by this figure, although the main theme is the
Auseinandersetzung with a particularly destructive animus. In Anna's
case, her later conversations with the Great Spirit (printed here for the
first time) show an unusually thorough *Auseinandersetzung* with the
positive side of the animus (again assisted by the figure of the Great
Mother). This was rewarded with a singularly peaceful and happy old
age, although most people in her present circumstances could find a
great deal about which to complain. Nevertheless, she has written to
me more than once to say that she is happier than at any previous
period of her life. Although there is still a great deal more to say, I
think it will be better said in connection with the actual material,
where it will be more evident and therefore more convincing.

[27]Barbara Hannah, *Striving Toward Wholeness* (New York: G. P. Putnam's Sons,
1971), pp. 38ff.
[28]Ibid., pp. 190ff. especially pp. 247–250.

CHAPTER 2

A Modern Example of a Man's Active Imagination
The Case of Edward

Jung often said that the first half of life should be devoted to establishing one's roots in *outer* life. It is necessary to reach the place where one belongs and to establish the outer conditions (in profession and private life) that suit one, which generally include marriage and founding a family. But when one reaches middle life, the direction changes. One should begin to turn to the inner life, said Jung, for the second half of life is inevitably directed toward old age and death. To put it more simply, life is the goal of the first half of life; death, of the second.

The example which we will examine first is a long active imagination which took about a year and much hard work to accomplish. It was undertaken by an author, who was in his early forties. At the time, he thought he had a problem connected entirely with the first half of life. Edward, as we will call him, was suffering from a temporary attack of impotence; naturally, he was willing to undertake anything that could possibly cure it. He was, however, already over the threshold of the middle of life and was an unusually thoughtful man, with a strong spiritual destiny.

Edward, who was in analysis with one of Jung's assistants, also knew

29

Jung personally and had read many of his books. Therefore, when it was suggested to him that he might gain some enlightenment on his problem by means of active imagination, he was very willing to try. He was looking eagerly for some point at which to start when he remembered a recent dream, dealing directly with his problem. He reported his dream as follows:

> *I am wandering round in an unknown great city, where I suddenly find myself in a brothel. At first I am in a kind of entrance, a bar, where I am flirting with two pretty, young prostitutes. Then a woman of a very different kind comes towards me. She is exceedingly beautiful, with a serious, intelligent expression, her tall, well-made figure is entirely swathed in black silk. Her coal-black hair is combed back severely and her black eyes are flashing. She lowers her eyes till they meet mine, slowly raises her glass, as if to drink to my health, and says: "À bientôt."*

Edward started his active imagination by taking up the situation exactly as it ends in the dream. I will quote the first episode in full, so that the reader may gain an impression of how these conversations go, and of how other figures try to break in and interrupt the line of the conversation.

Jung says of such conversations: "Archetypes speak the language of high rhetoric, even of bombast. It is a style I find embarrassing; it grates on my nerves, as when someone draws his nails down a plaster wall, or scrapes his knife against a plate. But since I did not know what was going on, I had no choice but to write everything down in the style selected by the unconscious itself."[1] As the fantasy developed, this became more and more the style forced on Edward.

The first episode begins with Edward's reaction to the last incident in the dream. Highly astonished and impressed by the woman's appearance, he silently raises his glass and drinks to her health. Then he continues:

She:	*"What are you doing here?"*
I (embarrassed, stuttering):	*"I . . . well, really . . . I got here without meaning to."*
She (mockingly):	*"When one observes your desirous glances toward the young girls, one is not inclined wholly to believe you."*

[1]Jung, *Memories, Dreams, Reflections*, p. 178.

I:	*"Yes, I expect you are right; the devil probably led me here. But what are you doing here? You really do not look as if you belonged to this house!"*
She (very quietly and sadly):	*"I am bewitched, cursed, exiled in this hell! (Sighing) How many years have I suffered in this miserable prison. I must wait here till a man comes who can liberate me. (Quickly, with a trembling voice) I do not mean material liberation, marriage, or the like. No, no! Someone must come who is different to all the others who simply seek physical satisfaction. But is such a one likely to come to a brothel?"*
I (moved, ashamed):	*"That must really be terrible for you. And are you also obliged to take part here?"*
She:	*"Yes, to a certain extent."*
I (astonished):	*"And how could you remain so beautiful and refined in this mudhole?"*
She (mysteriously, almost in a whisper):	*"I have special qualities and possibilities, poisons and antidotes. It is not easy to get me down. (Looking at me with flashing eyes) But still: how I must fear and wait; how dependent I am on a man who will take my part! The more he would listen to me, the more I could give him. (Excited) But when the men only bring their primitive animal side, there is nothing right that I can do with them— and I myself must always remain in this prison!"*
I (somewhat incredulous):	*"Yes, and what would that be?"*
She (impressively):	*"To lead the man where he could see nothing, to lead him to things he has no idea of!"*

(The strange, new quality in what she says is difficult to follow. I feel tired for a moment and, as if to recover, I find myself glancing with desire at her beautiful body with its tight-fitting frock of black silk.)

The Devil (to me):	*"That would be sweet, and how? Her chatter is nice, but how much nicer to see her naked! Ask her to go to bed with you! After all, you are in a brothel, aren't you?"*
I:	*"Be quiet! You know I am impotent."*
Devil:	*"Have a try, perhaps it will work with her."*
I (furiously):	*"Hold your tongue, you beast."*
Devil (hisses):	*"You are an ass to let the best tid-bit escape you."*

I shake my head.

Devil (furious):	*"Never fear, I will teach you." (Exit)*
She (uneasy):	*"What is the matter with you, all of a sudden? Your expression is so rigid, and the glitter in your eyes does not please me at all." (She turns away with tears in her eyes.) "Oh! Oh! How tragic. The usual thing is happening. Lost again! Return to my prison! And I was so hopeful. I had a better opinion of you. . . ."*
I (upset, ashamed, I seize her arm and turn her back):	*"Please forgive me; it only overcame me for a moment. I will pull myself together!"*
She (freeing herself, sternly):	*"Really? You must keep a better hold on yourself and not let every impulse pull you away. If you are not able to tame your heart for a moment, you will never hear my message."*

(I lead her to a table that stands apart, and order something to drink.)

She (after a pause, urgently):	*"Now I must ask you again: What do you want here? What are you hoping to find in this dirt? Do you seriously believe you can find pleasure as a gift in this miserable place? You are not the man for that. Here in this brutality, in this want and sickness? You cannot deceive yourself about this! Have you no scruples? Have you illusions when you*

enter such a place? Does it not disgust you with yourself?''

I *(touched,
    stammering):*

''Yes—it is true . . . it is as you describe it . . . it is shameful.'' (After a pause) ''Perhaps you will judge me less severely when I tell you that, on one side, I am driven by an overpowering urge for sexual experience and, on the other, I am impotent. This is such torture, such a chastising tension which repeats again and again that one grasps at a straw in order to escape somehow, at least for a moment. So I half hoped to see or experience something here that might bring me a little satisfaction . . . or perhaps even that I might rediscover my potency!''

She *(very much
    moved):*

''Oh! You miserable creature! You think you can overcome your impotence in such a way? In that you let yourself go entirely? No, in this way you would only fall into complete misfortune, into a place or rather a trap, from which you would never escape. There is a reason for your impotence, a spiritual reason! You must search for this. Otherwise you are lost!''

Prostitute *(her ripe, sensuous body only covered by a short skirt, she approaches our table, presses against me and strokes my head in a maternal way):*

''What sermon is she preaching to you? Is she preparing you for confirmation? There is an atmosphere here like in church!''

(I try to escape her, but she sits on my knee and throws her bare arms round my neck.)

Devil:

''With your mother complex, you could hardly find anyone better. Just like Rubens's figures, isn't she? Have a try with her; she is certainly not diseased—she looks too appetizing! She could certainly teach you a thing or two!''

Prostitute (embracing and kissing me, whispers in my ear):
> *"Come upstairs to my warm, soft bed!*
> *Come, my dear boy."*

She (getting up in   "If that is how it is, I can go!" (Exits)
a fury):

I (tearing myself loose, pushing aside the struggling prostitute, I rush
out and can just catch her in the passage. I hold her fast.):
> *"Stop, stop! I have freed myself. Come with*
> *me, we will leave this infernal hole."*

(I pay quickly while she is putting on her coat; then we leave the
place.)

She does not go out into the street, however, but disappears through
a door in the passage. Edward, following her, finds himself on a dark
staircase that leads down into the depths.

It is the old motif of the Savior's coming from Nazareth, the most
despised place. The solution is right there, under her hated prison and
his most sensuous and lowest fantasies. Or rather, the inevitable starting
point is there—the only place that can eventually lead to the solution.
But the staircase, as it descends, is cut in the rock and dripping with
moisture, and Edward becomes more and more frightened as she hurries
down and he stumblingly follows. At last, he can bear it no longer and
calls to her to stop and tell him where they are going. She stops for a
moment, looks at him searchingly, but hurries on.

In the meantime, the temptation to turn back is almost irresistible,
and these doubts are supported by the devil. But the deep and favorable
impression she has made on him overcomes his doubts, and he decides
to follow her at all costs. At last, she stops for a moment and smiles at
him so encouragingly that he feels calmed and strengthened.

The devil evidently feels desperate and makes another determined
effort to turn him back. Indeed, he succeeds in making Edward feel he is
a fool to leave the warmth and comfort of the brothel to be caught in a
"nocturnal maze," and makes him regard it as "his punishment."
Still, he steadfastly refuses to turn back, and he hurries after her in spite
of the terrifying roar of water and the air that rapidly grows colder. As
the path becomes more and more difficult, however, she pauses and
helps him over the worst, until they come to a boat and a veiled male
boatman standing in it.

The devil makes a determined effort to stop him from embarking, saying that it will lead to his certain death and asking him to consider what will become of his family. (Edward is married and at the time had two young children at school.) While he is hesitating, she speaks to him for the first time on their descent and tells him he must now choose between the betrayal of his better Self and an adventure with her. Like Churchill, she promises him nothing but "blood, sweat and tears," for there is no safety where they are going; nevertheless, he must now choose. Silently, he follows her and climbs into the boat with considerable difficulty. The boatman pushes off and Edward is committed to an adventure into the unknown.

The whole descent and embarkation are so very vividly described that one realizes the experience was completely real to him and required a courage which Edward entirely lacked in outer life. Apparently, this was a turning point in his life. One feels that the Self, like Zeus, the chief of the gods of Olympus, has decided that at last it is time to intervene on behalf of a sorely tried human being. Exactly as in the *Odyssey,* this cause is taken up enthusiastically by the anima. In Homer's epic, the anima is the goddess, Pallas Athene; in our fantasy, it is the superior woman who so much impressed Edward in the brothel and who was afterwards called the "Guide." Just as Athene decided to instill "a little more spirit" into the discouraged youth, Telemachus, so Edward's anima decides to instill "a little more spirit" into Edward. She succeeds in getting him to "embark on an adventure" at last, and, for the time being at any rate, to give up his pessimistic despair. Just as Telemachus could never believe that his heroic father, Odysseus, was still alive, so Edward could not fully believe in life or in himself. In both cases, however, the anima is very successful at instilling "a little more spirit."

But Athene did not succeed in making Telemachus more optimistic about his father, and Edward, though more enterprising than ever before, still retained his easily discouraged and frightened nature throughout this active imagination. This is one of many signs that the whole experience is completely genuine. When someone shows a heroism that is quite foreign to him, the fantasy is open to suspicion: it is probably being unduly influenced by consciousness. But Edward has to be rescued from his discouragement by other figures in his psyche again and again, and one feels there is no wishful thinking at work. Moreover, the unconscious is left completely free. Edward has evidently mastered the first step in active imagination: the ability to let things happen.

The fantasy is characterized with the fact that Edward is an introvert. Such a fantasy would be useless to an extravert; in fact, he would never have had it, for the extravert is quite enterprising enough in the outer world and could respond to all the situations which frightened Edward to death, with sufficient adequacy. An introvert, however, is anything but enterprising in the outer world, and if one tries to improve him outwardly, one only drives him deeper and deeper into the mire.

To make this point clearer, I will mention the case of a very introverted general practitioner. Never stating exactly what his trouble was, he simply called it "insuperable difficulties in the medical practice." His analyst suggested that he take up the situation with a positive anima figure of which he had dreamed. He agreed to this, but started off by raping this figure! In response to his analyst's protest, he at last defined his difficulty: a terribly strong urge to rape all his younger female patients. It had grown worse and worse, until he had begun to doubt his ability to control it much longer. His analyst then withdrew his objections, for he knew that, as an introvert, the physician would be able to deal with the situation *inwardly*, bad as it turned out to be. *Outwardly*, it would have spelt ruin to his whole profession and developed into a situation entirely beyond his control.

Edward was equally incapable of outwardly dealing with his fear of life. Good advice on the subject would have been worse than useless; whereas inwardly—afraid though he was—he learned to cope with his fear and even to deal adequately with the most dangerous situations in many of his adventures. This also had an outward effect, for, after three months of working hard at this fantasy, he entirely and permanently overcame his impotence. But we must now accompany him on his adventures to see what it was that helped him so effectively. Anyone who has seriously tried to do active imagination will know what it cost Edward to get to the point we have reached, and those without experience should read the chapter on the "Confrontation with the Unconscious" in Jung's *Memories, Dreams, Reflections*[2] to get at least a secondhand impression of what such a venture entails.

Before we follow Edward out of sight of land and onto the stormy waters of the unconscious, I must explain his main problem. He had had a very difficult childhood, unsupported by his cold mother and very much disliking his coldly rational father. While he was still a young boy, his mother died of cancer. Since her husband refused to let her go to the

[2]Ibid., p. 170.

hospital, Edward was condemned to watching her die, inch by inch, in their own home. The result of this experience was a profound distrust of life. When he undertook this step into the unconscious at 42, he had not yet really lived at all. He had, it is true, married and supported his family by his efforts in his profession, but he had confined himself to "potboilers," colorless, dull efforts of his own, never letting his considerable creative powers loose in his writing. Therefore, he had a severe feeling of inferiority and felt no joy in life whatsoever. As a deep introvert, he had no doubt of the reality of the collective unconscious; his active imagination, with its adventures and hairbreadth escapes, required an enormous effort, and sometimes it took him several days or weeks before he could find enough courage to face the next step. He was, however, committed to going through with it when he made his choice and got into the boat.

Immediately, they pass out of sight of land, and are in the deepest darkness. The only light faintly glows from a torch in the bow of the boat, a torch which the boatman makes Edward renew with great difficulty from time to time. The beautiful woman—whom he subsequently calls "the Guide"—becomes more related to him, covering him with a rug, feeding him occasionally, and, whenever he is completely exhausted, even giving him an elixir which entirely renews him.

His first encounter is with a flock of vulture-like birds which are feasting on a corpse in the water. Edward exclaims in horror, but the Guide merely tells him calmly that "such things happen down here." She adds, with flashing eyes and speaking severely, "No more illusions! It's a matter of life and death now." One is reminded of the alchemists saying: "Many have perished in our work."

Barely escaping destruction in a narrow, rocky gorge, they sail into calmer water. Almost immediately, a beautiful golden butterfly lands on the hand of the Guide. After a bit, it flutters off, and the Guide tells the boatman to follow it. At first, the impenetrable darkness remains, then a faint light appears on the horizon. They come upon a "fairly-like picture"—an island with the most beautiful flowers imaginable. To Edward's horror, they pass this heavenly place, but his protests are brushed aside by the Guide, who tells him to be comforted and encouraged by the beauty he has seen, but that a very long journey and many tasks must be fulfilled before he will have earned landing in such beauty.

Completely exhausted, Edward is given bread, smoked meat and wine by the Guide, who allows him to fall into a deep sleep with his head on her lap. He is awakened by a violent thunderstorm and he is terrified as they steer straight toward it. The water turns reddish-yellow and suddenly, as though out of a volcano, an enormous sheet of flame shoots into the air and forms a wall in front of them. In the blinding, white-hot center of this flaming wall, two stars appear and turn out to be eyes. These blue eyes, which stare at Edward, belong to the Spirit of Fire, Water, Wind and Ice. Edward throws himself in panic to the bottom of the boat, shrieking, "We are burning! We are on fire!" But the wall of fire lifts just enough for the boat to pass under it, through a "wave of heat, light and steam."

One can compare this with the experience of Telemachus. Most of the time, Pallas Athene appears as a helpful human being to him, but when she appears as an Immortal, Telemachus is nearly as frightened as Edward. One sees this particularly well in the scene in which Telemachus meets his father in the swineherd's cottage. Athene changes Odysseus from his disguise as a dirty, old beggar, into such a heroic figure that Telemachus cannot believe it is truly his father. He is sure that Odysseus is an overpowering Immortal. It takes long persuasion to convince Telemachus of the man's identity. If you re-read the *Odyssey,* you will see that the same dread surfaces at times even with the heroic Odysseus. After all, the Scriptures tell us that "the fear of God is the beginning of wisdom." Therefore, we cannot be surprised that Edward is terrified when the Spirit of Fire appears to him.

Indeed, he feels as weak as though he had been through a long illness, but the Guide gives him a drink that pours through his tired limbs and gives him renewed strength. The Guide then rejoices in what they have been through, saying that here at last she can breathe; she is in her element and feels freed from "the deadly imprisonment of his brothel fantasy" at last. She is also delighted that the spirit looked at Edward as if he had a task in store for him. Edward finds this still more terrifying, for this figure is "so gigantic, so burning, he would be the death of me." The Guide admits he is dangerous, warns Edward that he should oppose him on no account, and assures him that, if he will adapt to him with all the devotion of which he is capable, he will be given strength that he could never find by himself. She then says that this great fire spirit seeks people in order to express himself in the outer world.

Although this active imagination was completed years before Jung wrote his *Memories,* we find exactly the same idea here that Jung expresses in analyzing his dream of the Yogi who had his own features and whom he felt was asleep, dreaming Jung's life on earth. Or, Jung says, "To put it another way: it assumes human shape in order to enter three-dimensional existence, as if someone were putting on a diver's suit in order to dive into the sea. . . . In earthly form it can pass through the experiences of the three-dimensional world, and by greater awareness take a further step towards realization."[3]

Edward felt that it would destroy him entirely to serve this gigantic, burning figure, whereas the Guide felt it was the greatest honor that could befall him. This fire spirit is evidently a first appearance of the Self, and Edward is faced with the task, so much praised by Meister Eckhart, of giving up his own will so that God's will, or in psychological language, the Self's will, can replace it.

In a long conversation between the Guide and Edward, we learn that she feels he has entirely failed in the tasks of the first half of life, and she reproaches him severely. He feels aggrieved, an attitude ably supported by the devil, and tries, very unsuccessfully, to turn the tables on the Guide. Edward now learns that he imprisoned her in the brothel because the only fantasies which he ever permitted himself were of a pornographic character. She had tried in every way to rouse him and make him live at last. Finally, as a desperate last effort, she had made him impotent. This horrifies Edward, but at last she persuades him that his only chance is to try to make the best of the second half of life; to accept all the dangers of the world to which she had brought him, and do the best he can with it.

Until now—except for changing the torches when necessary—Edward has taken no *active* part in the fantasy. Enduring the dangers has been all that was asked of him, but now, as he changes the torch, the veiled boatman hands him another torch and a high pair of boots. The Guide informs him that he must now undertake a task entirely by himself: he must free an imprisoned woman in a cave on the island which they have just reached. She frightens Edward still more by telling him that he must strike at the serpents immediately with the switch she gives him, and that the fire in the torch must be used to frighten away the other animals. Although afraid and feeling very inadequately armed, he again decides to obey and lands by himself on the island.

[3]Ibid., pp. 323f.

Edward describes this venture very vividly and at considerable length, so I have had to abbreviate it a great deal. First he has to face a snarling pack of dogs which must be frightened away and even burned by the torch. Then he meets a lot of poisonous snakes that he has to kill swiftly with the switch, as they strike at him. To his horror, he finds he is on the edge of a volcano's crater, which is evidently very near eruption. The path leads down into this fearful crater and then, to his relief, up again, where he reaches the comparatively cool temperature of a cave. There, he finds that he has stumbled on the cave where the woman is imprisoned.

She is anything but attractive, having been bound in the cave for a long time. She is skinny and looks like a bundle of rags; horrified, Edward sees that she has four eyes, all squinting horribly. She is bound with very thick and resistant ropes, and he has the greatest difficulty in cutting through them. The devil suggests that he save himself (for the sound of the volcano is growing steadily more menacing), but resisting, he at last frees the woman and carries her out of the cave. Freedom, however, soon revives her, and she indicates the way to safety. Edward has lost his switch and calls out to her to beware of the snakes. They, however, are afraid of her four eyes; as long as she keeps the snakes in sight, they only slither harmlessly away.

With the volcano erupting behind them and everything lit up by the glare, they reach the boat and are helped in, but even the boat is threatened by the eruption. Fortunately, the wind is with them and they escape into calmer waters. Once they are safe, the Guide congratulates Edward on his completion of a job which she had feared was beyond his strength, and revives both him and the four-eyed woman with a draught of her elixir. The woman's squints at once disappear and all four eyes glow in a "victorious and enchanting" fire: red, green, blue and yellow.

The Guide tells "Four Eyes" that they must now take care of Edward, who is at the end of his strength. She prepares a comfortable bed for him, where he can at last sleep soundly. "Safe, happy and indescribably tired," he sinks into unconsciousness, but still hears their conversation as though from far away. We learn some very interesting facts from this long conversation between these two aspects of his anima. Chief among these is that this whole land, and Edward himself, are in the power of an old witch, the terrible archetypal kernel of Edward's negative-mother complex. His mother had died too early for Edward to have a personal mother complex, but the place of this was filled, far more destructively, by the archetype of the negative mother. Edward begins to sense her image and later he sees, destroys and eventually transforms her. Often the gap left when the mother dies in a boy's childhood is partially filled by a loving father, but Edward's father was a cold, rational man, who gave the poor child no warmth or relatedness whatsoever, and thus left him vulnerable to archetypal influence.

The archetype of the negative mother had been able to imprison both these anima figures, but only because Edward was unable to resist it, and he himself has been bound and imprisoned quite as badly as the women. When he was still very young, the witch had weakened his enterprising spirit and bound him to her with poisonous sweetness, till she had him securely entangled in her net. He never turned on her until the torment of his impotence drove him to rebel at last. By rebelling, he has also freed these two anima figures to act, and they both promise themselves that the witch will be entirely destroyed.

In this witch figure we find another parallel with the *Odyssey*. The witch, Calypso, who holds Odysseus prisoner for so many years on a distant island, was the chief cause of all the trouble in the *Odyssey*. Such witch figures are always the result of a mother complex, either personal or archetypal, and imprison not only the man but, as we have already seen in Edward's case, also imprison the positive anima figures which could help him. It was exactly the witch's doing that robbed Telemachus of his positive father image until he was already an adult, and that plunged him and his mother, Penelope, into such endless difficulties with the infamous suitors. Edward's difficulty here, therefore, is based on an archetypal pattern, and he cannot be held personally responsible. But just as Odysseus had to build his own boat to escape from the witch's island, so now Edward as to find his own way to save himself from his destructive mother-witch. But both Odysseus and Edward get a great deal of help from their animas and ultimately from the highest God: in our language, the Self.

The Guide shows considerable feeling for Edward and is determined that he shall not be broken, for then they would all be lost. She thus reveals herself as Edward's own individual anima, whereas Four Eyes is a far more archetypal figure. Four, as the complete number, is an attribute of the Self; therefore, this figure of the archetypal anima is contaminated with the Self. Jung used to say that the overwhelming power of the anima or animus only came when she or he was able to stand between the Self and the human being. Edward had one glimpse of the Self, it is true, when he saw the Spirit of Fire in the midst of the storm. Since his only reaction was fear that approached panic, the anima was easily able to stand between him and the Self, which we shall see even more clearly in another aspect of the anima which appears at the end of the fantasy. Edward has succeeded in establishing a relationship with his individual anima, but the archetypal world of the collective unconscious is still an alarming fact and quite undifferentiated by him.

There are only faint hints of this differentiation between the individual and the archetypal figures of the anima in the story of Odysseus, for this differentiation developed very slowly in the course of history. Jung once pointed out, in a discussion on the story of Amor and Psyche in Apulieus's *Golden Ass,* that whereas Psyche became a goddess—that is, a purely archetypal aspect of the anima—she gave birth to a daughter, not a son. The daughter represented another anima figure in the birth of the individual aspect of the anima. This aspect is represented by the Guide in Edward's fantasy. We must remember that Apuleius lived about 1000 years after Homer and, though purely pagan himself, was born synchronistically into a world where a new symbol of the Self—Christ—already had many hidden followers. The individual aspect of the anima, the bridge between conscious and unconscious, has developed enormously during the Christian era. (One example is the figure of Beatrice in Dante's *Divine Comedy*). The work Jung did on the anima finally brought it right into man's consciousness.

Fortunately, the Guide succeeds in holding back the impatience of Four Eyes, who is thirsting for an immediate revenge on the witch who had imprisoned her so painfully for so many years, and Edward is allowed to sleep. When he wakes up, he is given a sustaining meal and only then does he realize the significance of a second boat which was tied to their own and had appeared mysteriously while he was away on his quest. He and Four Eyes are to set out together for the lair of the witch with the intention of destroying her.

This time, however, Edward is well-armed. He is given a pistol, with a great many rounds of ammunition, and a still more deadly rifle. He is also provided with very high rubber boots in which he can wade to a considerable depth. He has already been provided with new clothes, for his own had been burnt and torn to pieces during his adventure on the volcanic island. Four Eyes has also been given some of the Guide's elixir, so that she can revive Edward in an emergency, but he does not know this at the time.

The adventure which we have followed so far only represents eight parts and took about two months in time, whereas his journey with Four Eyes and all the dangers they meet consists of fourteen parts and occupied Edward for most of six months. He describes it very vividly and in detail, and one sees that he was completely involved in it, but that he often despaired of the outcome. Four Eyes remains much more impatient and demanding than the Guide, but she slowly realizes that, since the outcome depends on Edward's survival, she must at least keep him alive.

The witch has indeed established her lair in a well-defended place. To begin with, the island is exceedingly difficult to land on and demands endless patience in cutting away weeds to get their boat up the backwater. When they land, they are met by one deadly animal after another, such as poisonous toads the size of a calf, serpents of every kind and, worst of all, a praying mantis as large as a man. This especially frightens Edward because of a dream he had had, many years before, of such a creature. Usually, he shoots promptly and with perfect aim (like all men of his country, Edward was an excellent shot), but Four Eyes has to scold him before he takes aim at the praying mantis. He pulls himself together in time, however, and the body of the praying mantis hurtles down into the abyss.

In the course of these and many other adventures, they discover a dove chained by the leg, which Four Eyes says is a prisoner of the witch which must be freed. Edward, who has lost his knife on the volcanic island, says it is an impossible task, but Four Eyes tells him to search in the pockets of his new clothes. There he finds a knife, even better than his own. It includes a saw which will cut through metal. It is, however, a long and weary job; Edward would like to give up halfway through the task, but Four Eyes will not hear of such faintheartedness. At last, he frees the bird. After joyously circling over their heads, the dove sits on Edward's shoulder, gratefully rubbing its head against his face. Four Eyes remarks that before they have finished, they will have every reason to be grateful to the dove.

This immediately proves to be the case, for the next obstacle they come to is a high, wrought-iron gate. At first, this seems to be a fatal obstacle; as usual, Edward thinks they are beaten, and for once, Four Eyes is at a loss. But with a joyful cry, the bird flies over the gate. After some time, it comes back with the key, although it is almost too heavy. Thankfully, and after some difficulty, for the lock is very stiff and has evidently not been used for years, they open the gate and stand on the other side.

Apparently, however, they have gained nothing. The ledge upon which they have been walking comes to an end, and the only way to continue is on the other side of the abyss. Even Four Eyes is daunted at first, but the dove comes to their rescue once more. With a tremendous effort, it succeeds in bringing up the end of a rope. Hanging onto the gate, Edward pulls up a narrow plank which is attached by an iron ring to the rope; it just reaches across the abyss, and Four Eyes crosses by it at once, lighting the darkness with her torch. Edward is, however, more afraid than ever. The plank is not only narrow, but it also swings about dangerously; moreover, he cannot bear heights. Spurred on by the taunts of Four Eyes, he starts across, but his giddiness almost overcomes him in the middle of the precarious bridge. He says afterwards that he would certainly have crashed into the depths, but that the rays of her four eyes seemed to draw him over, and he thankfully collapses on the floor of a cave on the other side.

Four Eyes allows him no respite, however. They have to press on through a narrow crevice in the rock. Edward can hardly squeeze through, and just as it gets a little better, they hear a faint groaning. "Another prisoner of the witch," Four Eyes exclaims, and they see a face pressed against a window in the rock: a terrible face which looks as if the whole head had been split apart and had grown together again badly. It is so pale that Edward is uncertain if he is looking at a corpse or a very sick man. Another faint groan convinces him it is the latter. Their combined efforts fail to move the door, but at last Edward smashes the lock with the butt end of his gun. The cell is so small that the prisoner could only kneel or sit. Edward pulls him out. He is very light, and they see that he is a dwarfed hunchback with a clubfoot. He is hopelessly cramped and his clothes are in rags. Four Eyes tries to pour her elixir down his throat, but Edward stops her while the dwarf is completely unconscious. The moment he gains consciousness, he eagerly drinks the elixir, which has its usual revivifying effect.

The hunchback can hardly believe he is finally free, but he greets the dove as an old friend that visited him daily—his only consolation until it was imprisoned itself. When he hears that his liberators are on their way to kill the witch, he rejoices and tells them that he knows every inch of the way and will guide them safely to her. When they get back to the passage, he hurries ahead with the dove flying over him. Edward says that they are the most curious pair he can imagine: the beautiful, white, elegant dove and the hideous little hunchback, limping painfully after it.

The hunchback stops them, saying that if they continue on the way, the witch will see them coming, seize them in her octopus arms, and eat them. He then shows them how to swing open a rock, revealing a low tunnel. Edward must first crawl, then lie flat. Four Eyes takes his gun and pistol, but even so, Edward soon becomes stuck, hopelessly, he thinks, and he is terrified of the darkness and of suffocating. Four Eyes and the hunchback ahead of him shout that the passageway improves, but Edward cannot move. The hunchback comes back, however, and fishes Edward's torch out of his pocket. Between being able to see and the help of the hunchback, Edward at last emerges into a cave where he can stand upright.

Four Eyes, as usual, is very impatient with him and accuses him of never wanting anything but rest. Finally, she gives him her elixir, which has all its old magical effect. The hunchback tells them they are now near their goal and must creep noiselessly, for the witch will not expect them from that side. Giving the dwarf the pistol and keeping the rifle himself, Edward crawls after the hunchback, with Four Eyes behind him. The devil makes a last effort and taunts him with his fear, but this time, Edward knows it is too late to turn back and manages to repulse him. Still, Edward is very afraid; although the hunchback and Four Eyes attack every octopus arm, Edward is petrified by the Medusa-like stare of the witch's eyes and fails to shoot at her head as he should. But the dove attacks the eyes and, freed of this petrifying stare, Edward shoots her through the head and she sinks down, at last lifeless, to the bottom of the pool. The fearful noise of the battle is followed by a complete, awesome silence.

After a pause, something white appears at the other end of the pool. Edward is about to shoot when he realizes it is a very beautiful woman, naked, with four breasts: the witch transformed into a positive mother goddess! She thanks Edward for redeeming her and, as the ruler of that land, arranges a glorious banquet, waited on by many beautiful, naked girls. The Guide and the boatman, at last unveiled, come up from the boat and all the figures we have met in Edward's adventures take part in the feast.

This last scene is the only one in the whole fantasy that does not come quite so genuinely and undoubtedly from the unconscious. One wonders if Edward, feeling that nearly a year was long enough for any fantasy to last, rather contrived this happy end, and if, therefore—as indeed turned out to be the case—Edward still had a lot of work in front of him before he would reach the degree of individuation which was his own spiritual destiny, foreseen in the final banquet.

Nevertheless, the unconscious does break through very genuinely in some places. Chief among these is in the figure of the boatman, who was always veiled before the banquet, and who turns out to be a shadow figure of whom Edward has often dreamed and whom he always cordially disliked. The exact opposite of Edward, who is very good-mannered and gentlemanly, the boatman is a very primitive person with many animal qualities. He even eats at the banquet more like an animal than a man, which revolts Edward terribly. He has more trouble in making himself drink with the boatman than with any of the other figures, and one is not quite sure of his eventual acceptance.

We must, however, not overlook the fact that the Guide, when she brings the unveiled boatman to Edward, says that he is the counterpart of the hunchback. Who, then, is the dwarf hunchback? From the context of the Cabiri, those dwarf, creative gods, the hunchback clearly represents Edward's creativity. As I mentioned before, Edward had never been able to bring this creativity into his work. Therefore, he had only produced very colorless efforts when he worked for himself. We learn now why this was so: the witch had imprisoned his creativity in such a narrow cell that it could only sit and kneel. Through this great effort, Edward had freed his creativity; indeed, his work changed entirely after this point. It became full of life and color, and Edward thoroughly enjoyed it, instead of regarding it as a duty that must be performed.

Marie-Louise von Franz, in her new book on projection, has a chapter on demons entitled, "Exorcism of Devils or Integration of Complexes" in which she points out that integration is always the most crucial point.[4] We should certainly consider Edward's fantasy from that point of view. The only figure that can be wholly integrated is obviously that of the boatman, who is clearly Edward's own personal shadow. He is the exact opposite of his conscious personality, and the one which Edward is obviously going to have trouble integrating. But if he can accept his animal-like nature, it would make him a far more complete and efficient character. It is noticeable, for example, that whereas Edward himself was

[4]Marie-Louise von Franz, *Projection and Re-Collection in Jungian Psychology: Reflection of the Soul*, trans. William Kennedy (La Salle: Open Court Publishing Co., 1980), pp. 95ff.

continually afraid—even near to panic and despair—the boatman accepted every danger that confronted them and always managed to steer their boat, quietly and safely, through every peril, even aiming for the center of the storm and straight at the curtain of fire. He took every order of the Guide's and efficiently carried it out, whereas Edward himself was always protesting and really only succeeded in the end through the efficiency of the other figures. So it would clearly have been Edward's first and most urgent task, after the fantasy, to assimilate all the qualities of his personal shadow.

One can never completely integrate one's own creativity; rather, one must work with it and give it every chance to develop. Edward does this in the fantasy when he lets the hunchback lead and help him when he becomes stuck in the crevice of the rock; he is really already doing inwardly exactly what must be done in one's outer creative work. It is also very noticeable that once he gets used to his rather revolting appearance, Edward likes and trusts the hunchback and is very appreciative of his help. There is none of the revulsion that he shows toward the boatman. It is true that he notices the latter's great skill and courage in navigating their boat, but only while he is veiled and he can ignore his personality. As I pointed out in Chapter 1, Edward was rather unusual in that he met the anima problem *before* he had assimilated the personal shadow.

In contradistinction to the personal shadow and the creative daimon, we also have, on the masculine side, the figures of the devil and the Spirit of Fire. The devil is evidently the great Tempter, Satan himself, a purely archetypal figure, and Edward is quite right to repulse him. He could not assimilate this figure without the most terrible negative inflation. It is very significant that the devil is the only figure that we have met constantly who is not at the banquet.

The Spirit of Fire is also a very archetypal figure, who is also absent from the banquet. He is very constructive, however, and we learn from the Guide at the banquet that he has been helping Edward throughout the journey, or he could never have succeeded. (He is really the counterpart of the devil, who could also be called his shadow.) Naturally, at this stage of his development, Edward would be totally incapable of dealing with sheer evil. Edward, as we have seen, was also terribly afraid of the Spirit of Fire, which makes just one appearance. Afterwards, we only hear of him twice: the Guide gets more consideration for Edward from the impatient Four Eyes when she tells her that the Spirit of Fire is interested in this quest; the second time is when the Guide says that it is only through his help that Edward has succeeded.

We find the same split of positive and negative figures in the *Odyssey,* in the highest representatives of all, whom Homer calls the Immortals or gods. Poseidon played a negative role throughout the epic poem, a role which is parallel to the role played by the devil throughout Edward's fantasy. Just as the Guide tells Edward he could never have succeeded without the help of the Spirit of Fire, so Telemachus, or even Odysseus himself, could never have succeeded without the help of the positive gods. Zeus himself tells us at the beginning that Poseidon, who is pursuing Odysseus with relentless malice, cannot possibly hold out "against the united will of the immortal gods." He could, however, presumably have held out forever, had Odysseus not received help from the Immortals. Zeus intervenes in a very visible way, through Hermes and Pallas Athene, whereas the positive aspect of the Self works entirely behind the scenes, except for his one appearance to Edward in the storm, and we only learn of what he has done through the Guide at the final banquet.

This is a difference which makes it much more difficult for modern man to relate to the Self than it was for the ancient Greeks to relate to their gods. In fact, it is often only through the context found in the old myths that we can see how much the unconscious is helping us, for it certainly seems to work much more invisibly than it did in antiquity. This is because modern man no longer bases his life on the order in the unconscious, as the ancient Egyptians and Greeks did on the order of their gods—only to mention two examples among a multitude. We believe that we can consciously invent our own order, although the state of the world today should convince us that this is the most foolish illusion. Therefore a figure, like Edward's Spirit of Fire, is obliged to work invisibly, for, as we have seen, Edward only falls into a panic if such a figure shows himself openly.

The Self is such an infinitely greater figure than the ego that there is, of course, no question of integrating it. Jung used to say that the Self was both individual, even unique, and universal, the central and presiding archetype of the collective unconscious. We have to relate to the Self, doing our best to let it unfold its individual and unique pattern that is our destiny to live, but we must also know that we shall never comprehend it, for it stretches into infinity.

The reader may object that none of the figures in Edward's fantasy, except perhaps the devil, corresponds to the popular idea of what a demon is, but I used the word in the sense of "daimon." In the ancient view, every figure or image that was between God and man was considered a daimon. In this sense, the anima is a daimon, and we must consider her three aspects that appear in this fantasy in that light. Of these three, by far the most individual and related to Edward is the Guide. She can even be said to be the anima in her right place: the function or bridge between conscious and unconscious. She leads Edward out of his miserable outer life and into her own realm: the unconscious. She looks after him there and, although she is often very severe with him and critical of the way he has lived his life, she seems to realize that everything depends on his survival and is careful to help him to survive.

Four Eyes is also an anima figure and must have a connection to Edward, or he would not have had the task of liberating her and she would not have complained to the Guide that she was imprisoned because he spinelessly gave in to the witch. But she is far more archetypal in character than the Guide, and comes from such a deep level that she has characteristics that really belong to the Self: her *four* eyes which flash *four* colors, an attribute of wholeness. She is another aspect of the anima, more related to the Guide than to Edward himself. It is the Guide who knows where she is imprisoned and sends Edward to release her, and it is only through the Guide's intervention and her mention of the Spirit of Fire's regard towards Edward, who is an image of the Self, that her impatience does not destroy him on their journey to find the witch.

The transformed witch is also an aspect of Edward's anima, and even more archetypal in character, with *four* breasts, and thus contaminated with the Self. She is represented as the all-giving mother, the exact opposite of the witch who deprived Edward of everything that makes life worth living. Probably, as he gets more familiar with the unconscious, all these aspects of the anima will turn out to be one and the same.

The fourth aspect of the anima is represented by the dove. Besides the obvious relationship of the bird to the spirit, the Holy Ghost is often called the *vinculum amoris,* the bond of love, between Father and Son. Moreover, in an alchemical allegory by Philalethra, quoted at some length by Jung in "Mysterium Coniunctionis,"[5] it is the doves of Diana

[5]C. G. Jung, *Mysterium Coniuntionis,* vol. 14, 2d ed., *Collected Works* (Princeton: Princeton University Press, 1970), pars. 189ff.

that "temper the malignity of the air." It is noticeable that the devil only makes one rather weak effort to discourage Edward after they have liberated the dove and that, besides fetching the key and the end of the rope, it is the dove that makes it possible for Edward to shoot the witch by tempering her Medusa-like, petrifying stare. The dove is so related to Edward and Four Eyes—he sits on the shoulder of Edward or the hunchback whenever he is not engaged in an invaluable job—that he can be said to represent Eros, the feminine principle. Moreover, while he had his liberty, the dove was most related to the hunchback, visiting him each day.

Since Edward was deprived of all relationship by his cold mother, it is not surprising that the Eros principle should be the most unconscious part of his feminine side. Jung used to say that when we dreamed of a personified part of our psyche as an animal, it meant that this was still far away from us in consciousness. And indeed, the Eros principle was still very far away from Edward. This is shown by his idea, in the dream which began the fantasy, that he could find relationship in a brothel. That is a typical masculine mistake; a man often confuses sexuality with relationship. Jung even says in "Woman in Europe": "A man thinks he possesses a woman if he has her sexually. He never possesses her less, for to a woman the Eros-relationship is the real and decisive one."[6]

Although Edward's reaction to life itself, to the food and drink and to all joy, changes completely in the banquet scene, his reaction to sex remains the same. During the banquet, Edward sees the unrebuked boatman fondling the naked waitresses. He neglects his food and tries to do the same. This immediately draws a rebuke from the Guide, who tells Edward to leave the girls alone and to confine himself to the women on earth. Evidently, the boatman is not yet enough of a part of Edward's consciousness for him to be under the laws for mortal man. Both the Guide and Four Eyes had complained earlier that it was Edward's sexual fantasies that had imprisoned them, so one understands the horror of the Guide when she realizes that Edward is still unchanged in this respect. He casts the same glances at the waitresses as he did at the prostitutes in the beginning of the fantasy. He has been deeply wounded in this area, it seems, and still has a lot of work ahead of him before this part of him can change. It is, however, very noticeable that the whole land is changed after the witch is transformed.

[6]C. G. Jung, *Civilization in Transition*, vol. 10, 2d ed., *Collected Works* (Princeton: Princeton University Press, 1970), par. 255.

The country which has always been described as a rocky wilderness abounding in poisonous animals, becomes green and fertile and overflowing with food and wine of every kind. This is a clear reference to Edward's environment, as well as to himself, being changed by this fantasy.

The East has long been convinced that the inner efforts of the individual have an effect on his whole environment, but this idea seems very difficult for the West to grasp. I remind the reader of Wilhelm's story of the Rainmaker, told in Chapter 1 of this book. I also remind the reader of what Jung said when asked if he thought there would be an atomic war. He thought it depended on how many *individuals* could stand the tension of the opposites in themselves. Nothing helps us more to stand this tension than active imagination, and I am sure that a total effort, such as Edward made in this fantasy, had a beneficial effect on much more than himself.

CHAPTER 3

One Beginning Approach to Active Imagination
The Case of Sylvia

In order to provide a contrast to Edward's case, the next example is that of a woman, Sylvia, who is a painter. Like Edward, she was just past the middle of life when she decided to make this considerable effort to reach the unconscious. Sylvia's effort, however, comes from an earlier stage in active imagination than Edward's. Although it was by no means her first attempt, it was the first time she managed to break through to the depths of her central problem.

Sylvia had not been at all fortunate in her parents. Her father was a classic example of a negative father; her mother, though good-natured enough in herself, had never had the strength to stand up to her husband, so she was no protection for the children. Jung says of the father's effect on the daughter in the *Mysterium Coniunctionis:*

> *The father is the first carrier of the animus-image. He endows this virtual image with substance and form, for on account of his Logos he is the source of "spirit" for the daughter. Unfortunately this source is often sullied just where we would expect clear water. For the spirit that benefits a woman is not mere intellect, it is far more: it is an attitude, the spirit by which a man lives. . . . Hence every father is given the opportunity to corrupt, in one way or another, his daughter's nature.*[1]

[1]Jung, *Collected Works*, vol. 14, par. 232.

Sylvia's father had taken full advantage of this opportunity. He criticized his daughter constantly, and she grew up with the poorest opinion of herself in every way, strongly supported in this devaluation by her animus. She was unusually pretty, and had married when she was in her late twenties. She had two sons whom she adored. Except for one shortcoming, her marriage might have fully made up for her unsatisfactory childhood and youth. Although a very nice man in most ways, her husband had a very negative relationship with his own mother. This unfortunate circumstance caused him to have fits of being as critical of her as her own father, instead of giving her his steady support and the confidence in herself which she so much needed. Therefore her low self-image remained unchanged.

In her own eyes, nothing having to do with herself could be positive, including her own unconscious. Therefore, she had great difficulty in trusting, or even approaching, the unconscious. It was really a triumph that she succeeded in carrying through this fantasy, but she was still a considerable distance from the unconscious, as we shall see in the form which this active imagination takes.

Sylvia relates the fantasy as someone else's story, taking place in the time of her grandparents, because her father had faith neither in himself nor in life. She therefore had to go back to her ancestors' time and, as we shall see, she had to go still further back, to so-called pagan times, in order to find the solution to her problem. Just as she could not find it in the father, neither could she find it in Christianity.

The fantasy is about a godmother who, although a rich woman, had died a few years before leaving the goddaughter only one, apparently insignificant, object: an old key. The goddaughter had kept it on her writing table ever since, and somehow could not get it out of her mind. To do so, she decided to write down the story which her godmother had told her about the key when she gave it to her, shortly before her death.

The godmother had not been an attractive girl; very early she had decided to put all thoughts of love and marriage aside and to devote herself to excelling in her profession. She succeeded so well in this endeavor that she found herself in one of the highest positions of a large firm while she was still very young. She earned enough to afford anything she wanted, and she never allowed herself to think of things that would have been beyond her means.

The godmother lacked all zest for life and never really longed for anything, but buried herself more deeply in her work. The only time she noticed any deficiency in her lifestyle was during weekends. This led her into her first indiscretion during one Saturday lunch at her usual restaurant, which, in its turn, led to the whole adventure. Herr Schulze, a strange man, who was not even congenial to her, invited her to drive to Lucerne with him. Since it was a lovely day, she accepted. He possessed a car of his own, which was a rarity in those days.

The drive itself was an enchanting event for the godmother; she often felt as if they were actually flying, and the large old house in the old quarter of Lucerne, to which he took her, was also very beautiful. She did not wake up from her enchantment until Herr Schulze shut and locked the door of the room they were in and began to make love to her. When she rejected him, he became angry and tried to beat her. In a wild panic, she seized an unusually sharp paper knife and stabbed him in the back. To her horror, she found that she had killed him.

She subsequently discovered that he was using the beautiful old house as a brothel, and that many young girls were his prisoners there. Although she immediately gave herself up to the police and had to stand trial for murder, she was entirely acquitted, for she had only acted in self-defense. Since her would-be seducer had left no will and had no family nor heirs, all of his money and the old house, named, suitably enough, ''The House of the Golden Pig,'' were inherited by the girls by whom he had earned his fortune. There were fifteen of them, mainly still in their teens, so she found herself, with the help of a lawyer, responsible for their futures.

To study this closer, we must remember that the fantasy is related by a godmother who acts as a pseudonym for Sylvia. This first episode in her adventures is very typical of a woman with such a negative father complex, whose destructive effect has not been mitigated by the mother. The fantasy showed that all the father could give Sylvia in forming her spirit was business capacity and efficiency. Although the godmother shows us that Sylvia could have excelled in this capacity, she never tried to do so. Therefore, these elements worked in her as a tendency to maneuver her life by rational calculation and to repress all spontaneous feeling. The father figure also remained active in Sylvia as an animus figure, which treated her just like the man who picked her godmother up at that Saturday lunch. What little spiritual interest Sylvia's father had possessed and passed on to her showed itself in conventional Christianity which, although she thought she believed in it, was not really genuine. It was, at all events, not sufficient to fill the godmother's free weekends. The mother had not given Sylvia any genuine idea of relationship that would have warned her not to even imagine going off with an uncongenial man, so the animus literally caught her and flew away with her in fantasy. The animus had already gained possession of the young girls, who symbolize her feminine nature, and prostituted them.

Prostitution is often the result of such a father as Sylvia's. I have known more than one case of such girls becoming prostitutes, to the horror of their highly respectable, hypocritical fathers. This was a fate that might easily have overtaken Sylvia, but evidently, she had the strength of mind to kill the temptation. It is clear from the fact that she attributes the whole adventure to her *godmother,* that this situation is fortunately being lived by the Self, who is able, in the old house which is the Self's own symbol,[2] to put an end to the danger of Sylvia's ego becoming a prostitute.

As for the rest of the fantasy, everything happens to the Self, and the ego is only the observer, until toward the ending's enantiodromia. The ego is a somewhat distant observer, as is shown by the fact that Sylvia herself never enters or plays a role in the fantasy, as Edward, for example, did from start to finish.

Her godmother is quite willing to take charge of the girls (the Self naturally had always had a very different relationship to the feminine principle, Eros, than Sylvia did herself) and asks them all to a meal in the most beautiful room in the house. She tells them about their inheritance, which breaks through their previous apathy, and they can hardly express their joy. They find it impossible to go back to their families or to their previous lives, and they are all unanimous in not wanting to continue as prostitutes. None of them wants to continue in the "House of the Golden Pig," so they decide to sell it profitably and invest the money in buying a ruined castle in the woods near Lucerne.

They buy the old ruined castle and, except for the architect and the necessary builders, they allow no man to come near them. The feminine principle is segregated and kept from the animus. To prevent any man from entering, they build an unscalably high wall around all the land which they have bought. As far as possible, the girls help with the

2*Author's note:* My own godmother lived in a beautiful old Elizabethan house; I frequently dreamed of this house and Jung always took it as the house of the Self.

construction; when it is finished, they manage it entirely by themselves. Some of them find employment in the kitchen and house. Several devote themselves to surrounding it with a most beautiful garden, where they find delight in growing rare plants. Four are very musical and form a quartet, practicing indefatigably and delighting them all with a concert every night. A few devote themselves to Sylvia's own pursuit, painting, and several beautiful carpets are woven.

One of the girls, who is called Erica (heather), finds a block of stone in the garden and spends a long time sculpting it into a statue of a beautiful youth. This piece of work arouses the interest of all the other girls and, as the statue approaches completion, Erica finds herself constantly surrounded by a group of enthusiastic onlookers.

It is rather interesting that Erica is the only one of the girls who is ever mentioned by name. Erica, which means heather (*Heiderkraut*), is a plant that, according to the lexicon of German superstition, is sacred to the mother goddess. It is said that it should therefore bloom at every women's festival.[3] White heather is known to be very discouraging to the devil, and a wreath of it placed round a mirror is said to keep the house from all misfortune. As we shall see, it is just this statue, sculpted by Erica, that inspires the household to its first festival. Therefore, it is significant that the creator's name should be the same as the name of the plant of the mother goddess and credited with the power to banish the devil.

It is very interesting, but not surprising, that all the girls, whom the animus had imprisoned for so long, should find interest in fields where the father cannot follow them, as indeed Sylvia herself had done when she took up painting. Evidently, the feminine nature has been preserved intact and is now in the hands of the Self. All the arts, the garden, and the household are far from the interests of the father, and all these fields of endeavor are shown as possibilities for Sylvia. It is also very significant that it is the statue, which reveals itself later as clearly being the god Eros, which is the one place that draws all their interest. Eros, relationship, is the principle of women, so this is really the most favorable circumstance in the whole fantasy. Jung used to say that women who had found their own principle, could do everything for love of a man, whereas women who could do much for love of a thing are rare. In fact, one could say that the unconscious produced this fantasy for the purpose

[3]*Handwörterbuch des deutschen Aberglaubens*, s.v. "Heiderkraut."

of showing Sylvia her own principle, which had been barred to her by her unsatisfactory parents.

The musical quartet—which delights them every evening—is also quite related. Music symbolizes feeling, a function which has been the most difficult one for Sylvia, due to the constant rational calculation of her animus: he always managed to repress her spontaneous feeling, as we have already seen. Sylvia is actually very fond of music, which has evidently been some compensation to her for her stifled feelings.

Here, Sylvia's consciousness already fails to note that the one thing which attracts the interest of all the fifteen girls is the statue of a youth of unearthly beauty. Her godmother lends herself to the organization of a wonderful celebration for the baptism of this figure, which the girls carry to an island in the center of a small lake in the garden. For days, the kitchen is full of preparation for the feast, and the garden is lighted by innumerable Chinese lanterns. The statue itself is decorated with flowers. When the moon is full, all the rejoicing girls dance and sing around the statue and, calling out that his name is Ulysses, they sprinkle him with water. When the apparently happy girls fall into melancholy, each retires alone into silence.

For the first time, Sylvia's consciousness has received a clear warning. Although these fantasies will sometimes roll on for a considerable length of time, with consciousness only watching as an observer, it is then a matter of passive, not active, imagination. It is more like watching a cinema than like an attempt to bring about a reconciliation between conscious and unconscious. The fact that the girls call the statue Ulysses should have penetrated to Sylvia's consciousness and warned her that a long and painful journey had to be undertaken, right into antiquity and the time of the Greek gods, in order to find the treasure of her missing Eros. But she fails to register the warning; therefore, the next event in the fantasy takes her entirely by surprise.

The god-like statue comes to life and, singing most beautifully, passes out of a previously unseen door in the wall, followed in single file by all fifteen rejoicing girls.

Even now, Sylvia's consciousness fails to wake up in time. It just watches the inexplicable event in a benumbed state, from which it arouses itself only too late.

The last girl disappears through the door into a beautiful light, which is shining in the wood beyond. By the time she gets to the door to call the girls back to her, it has become an old iron door covered with ivy, shut in her face, with only a large keyhole visible. The restored castle has also disappeared; only the old ruin it had been when they bought it, remains.

We have already met with Ulysses (or Odysseus, in the Greek form) as an archetypal image or foundation for the journey that Edward undertook. Indeed, Edward's whole active imagination could be called an odyssey. Naturally, since Sylvia is a woman, Ulysses appears very differently here: as a magnet that draws all the girls who represent her feminine nature. Most unfortunately, however, he draws them away from Sylvia herself, which the animus will always do if it is not sufficiently recognized by the woman. As we have seen, there have been several indications that something of the kind might happen.

This part of the fantasy shows very vividly what eventually happens to fantasies if the conscious ego is only a spectator and takes no active part. It is an interesting contrast to Edward's active imagination. Because his conscious ego always took an *active* part, the fantasy developed for nearly a year and never showed any signs of disappearing. Sylvia's, on the other hand, was passive imagination; she only watched it as if she were in the auditorium of a cinema and wrote it as if it were a story. Therefore, the girls, who symbolize her feminine nature, disappear again into the unconscious, leaving her only a keyhole for which she must find the key.

The beautiful statue of the god-like figure is clearly the god Eros, the treasure she needs above all, but, as mentioned previously, the name given him by the girls shows her that a long and arduous journey, with many more adventures, must be undertaken before she can reach her goal. This goal lies in antiquity, for the feminine principle has been too much neglected in the Christian era for her to be able to find it there.

With Edward, we saw how much clearer the interaction of conscious and unconscious is in the stories of the antique gods, such as Homer's *Iliad* or *Odyssey,* than we find it now. Christianity has not only repressed the eros principle by its purely masculine God, but it has also repressed the dark side, while trying only to differentiate the light. This was necessary at the time, but it is sad that we now, after 2000 years, have to return to so-called pagan times to find both the dark and the light in equal measure. During the Christian era, the light opposite was differentiated for a long time, but the modern world shows us daily how dangerous it is to repress evil for too long. Like the gods in the Far East, the Greek gods were both positive and negative, so it is only logical that both our fantasies have turned our thoughts back to the ancient gods.

Although the fantasy disappears, Sylvia's effort has not been in vain. She has accomplished the first stage in active imagination, and she has allowed things to happen in her unconscious. Indeed, her fantasy does not end with the disappearance of the god and the girls.

Jung often mentioned the legend of the treasure that rises to the surface during nine years, nine months and nine days. If a conscious person is there to take it, well and good; if not, it will sink down again and take another nine years, nine months and nine days before it appears again. Sylvia missed that moment when she did not follow the treasure out of the door in time. Such fantasies will never stay very long if the conscious ego does not take part—if it does not realize that they must be brought up into consciousness, into actual life.

The godmother, symbolically the Self, has shown Sylvia the very heart of her problem and what she will have to do to attain its solution. Though the fantasy continues, Sylvia still lets it happen to her godmother, who has now clearly become an image of the limited conscious ego that has no idea of what has happened to it.

When the godmother discovers that all that has been done to the ruin and its environment has disappeared, she sadly leaves Lucerne and returns to the town she calls X, where she works. To her great astonishment, no one at the office has noticed her absence; in other words, the fantasy, though it seemed to cover many months or even years, has all taken place during the weekend, and she has returned to work as usual on Monday morning. Although at first the godmother could work as was customary, the fantasy had left its mark upon her. This secret, which she could share with no one, made her feel as if she were isolated and rejected by everyone.

Jung speaks of the effect of such fantasies early in the second part of "Psychology and Alchemy." He says:

> Such invasions have something uncanny about them because they are irrational and incomprehensible to the person concerned. They bring about a momentous alteration of his personality since they immediately constitute a painful personal secret which alienates and isolates him from his surroundings. It is something that we "cannot tell anybody." We are afraid of being accused of mental abnormality—not without reason, for

*much the same thing happens to lunatics. Even so, it is a far cry from the
intuitive perception of such an invasion to being inundated by it patho-
logically, though the layman does not realize this. Isolation by a secret
results as a rule in an animation of the psychic atmosphere as a substitute
for loss of contact with other people.*[4]

This is exactly what happens to the godmother, as Sylvia continues
the story. The godmother does not understand the experience in the
least, so it manifests itself in her body, as such things often do. She is
frequently unwell, although previously she had always been healthy,
and finds herself unable to work. Finally, she becomes really ill. She
runs a very high temperature for many weeks, after which the doctor
orders her a holiday in the mountains. This at last gives her time to
consider what has happened to her. She undertakes several long walks
alone and decides to take the last few days of her sick leave in Lucerne to
try to discover what has really happened.

As mentioned before, Sylvia still sees all this as happening not to
herself, but to her godmother, and it becomes increasingly clear that
this figure is no longer the Self, but Sylvia's ego, which is blindly
groping after the truth.

The godmother goes into the old quarter of Lucerne and easily finds
the old house, "The Golden Pig." It has been renamed "The Golden
Boar," however, and the ground floor has become a first-class restaurant. It is early afternoon and she is almost alone in the restaurant, but,
after ordering a simple meal, she manages to make some inquiries of the
manageress. She learns, to her amazement, that the restaurant has been
there for many years and that the whole house belongs to a Fräulein
Altweg, who lives in the top story.

After her meal, the godmother climbs the stairs to Fräulein Altweg's
apartment, for she longs to know more of the house's history. She is
received most hospitably and, though hesitantly, she begins to pour out
her story. The godmother begins by saying that she had known the
house before, when it was the property of a Herr Schickelgräber, the
lawyer to whom her girls had sold the house. Fräulein Altweg is obviously utterly amazed and says that Schickelgräber is the name of her
grandfather, who was one of the most famous lawyers of Lucerne, and
from whom, through her mother, his only child, she had inherited the

[4]Jung, *Collected Works,* vol. 12, par. 57.

house. But she says, "It is impossible that you knew him; he died sixty years ago and you are much younger than I am." Fräulein Altweg notices the godmother's inner distress and begs her to tell her the whole story. "I know you will be telling the truth," she adds. To her unutterable relief, at last she is able to break her isolation and share everything with Fräulein Altweg.

After she has finished, Fräulein Altweg eagerly searches through all her old documents, and they find that quite a lot of what the godmother had experienced is founded on fact. Herr Schickelgräber had actually bought the house from Herr Schulze's heirs, and letters reveal that the latter had been murdered. At this point, both the women have the feeling that Sylvia had experienced a vision of a time long past.

Early in the twentieth century, a book containing the account of such an experience was very widely read in England, for its authors were two women whose veracity could not be doubted and, although they published under noms de plume, their real identities were known from the beginning. The first was Miss Ann Moberly, daughter of the Bishop of Salisbury, who became the first principal of St. Hugh's College for women in Oxford and built it up so successfully that by about 1907, it had become one of the four leading women's colleges in Oxford. Her co-author and friend was Miss Eleanor Jourdain, who had been vice-principal of St. Hugh's for some years. At the time of their experience, she was head of a large school for girls in England, with an affiliate branch for her elder girls in Paris. Both, therefore, were very well-known women.

In 1901, they visited Versailles and found Trianon exactly as it was in the time of Marie Antoinette. Not only were the people they met dressed in the costumes of 1789, but the grounds were also as they had been then, which, in many respects, differed from the way they really were in 1901. They spent the next ten years in research to verify the accuracy of what they had seen, and in investigating every possibility that there had been any cinematographic photography, or anything of the sort going on at that time, to account for what they had seen. Only when they were fully satisfied that their experience had been completely genuine did they publish their book.[5]

[5]It was published in 1911, under the title, *An Adventure*, by the pseudonyms of Miss Morison and Miss Lamont, and became famous at once. I vividly remember reading it as a girl of twenty, and how it was being discussed everywhere. It was reprinted many times and went into several editions. As far as I know, it was reprinted for the last time about 1947 by Faber & Faber, Ltd., London. This edition is long since sold out, but it is still possible to obtain a secondhand copy. I found it extremely interesting.

Jung describes a somewhat similar experience which he and Toni Wolff had at Ravenna in his *Memories, Dreams, Reflections*.[6] I have heard both Jung and Wolff speak of it as one of the most mysterious events that had ever happened to them. In fact, I had the impression that Toni Wolff was never really convinced that she had not actually seen those frescoes in everyday reality, although it was fully proved that they had not been in existence for centuries.

I had a similar experience myself in Paris in the spring of 1913. I was dining at a restaurant with my father, sister and uncle, when the scene abruptly changed and, although the restaurant remained the same, the whole atmosphere of it and the people in it were transformed. They all became extremely anxious and turned eagerly to everyone who came in, as if asking for the latest news. After a few minutes, it changed back to the original scene. Everything was normal and extremely cheerful, but it left me profoundly disturbed.

The next morning, we went down by train to spend a few days in the forest of Fontainebleau. The King of Spain was to arrive there later in the same day. As our train passed through a cutting, several soldiers came over the top to see that nothing suspicious had been thrown from our train. (It was the time when many successful and unsuccessful attempts were made to assassinate royalty.) The conviction shot through my mind: "What I experienced last night was a state of war, and it is very close." Although I tried not to believe it, I was, in some small corner of myself, certain during all the sixteen intervening months that we should have a war and, though horrified, was not really surprised when it broke out in August of 1914. With few exceptions, everyone at that time was convinced that we had become much too civilized for such a barbarity to befall us!

The godmother, however, was not to find matters so relatively simple. For one thing, it was very strange that Herr Schulze should have had a motorcar, for surely they did not exist over sixty years before the year 1930, in which she claims to be living. And how could she have killed Herr Schulze, as she clearly remembered doing, so many years before she was born? However, the worst of her isolation is over, now that she has found such a sympathetic companion as Fräulein Altweg, and the two sit up most of the night puzzling over all these questions.

[6]Jung, *Memories, Dreams, Reflections*, p. 284.

The next day, they decide to go to the woods where the old ruin is located. It is a very hot July day and the godmother says that, on account of the heat, they both are transported into a state between outer reality and dream. Everything is just as it was before the girls rebuilt the ruin, and in the trance-like condition they are in, they are hardly surprised to see a hairy, satyr-like being, half human and half goat, waving frantically to them and trying to draw their attention to an object he is holding in his hands. At last, he throws this object over the rushing water of the stream. When they pick it up, they discover the old key, the object that the goddaughter in the fantasy had received later from her godmother. When they attempt to wave and announce the safe arrival of the key, they find that the old Pan has disappeared. The ruin also seems to recede to a great distance; all that they can see is a rainbow, forming a bridge over the rushing stream. They find the rainbow bridge very reassuring.

Sylvia now had to realize that, through the fantasy, she had been deep into the unconscious where, as Jung often used to say, there is no time, or a totally different time from our own. In her fantasy she had experienced the present day, the last century and antiquity long before the time of Christ, all in a bewildering mixture.

As Marie-Louise von Franz pointed out to me, the name Schickel-gräber reminds one of the original name of Hitler (Schückelgruber), which shows us what happens if we contact these depths in the unconscious with no understanding of what we are doing. Just behind the antique—Eros, Ulysses, Pan and so on—lies primitivity. As Jung has noted, it was only Nietzsche's classical education which made him speak of Dionysius, when he touched these depths in his writing. Jung said that Nietzsche really meant Wotan and his wild horde, which were only asleep in the German unconscious. And when Hitler and his Nazi followers took over the idea of the superman from Nietzsche, they were at once possessed by Wotan and all the primitive forces which were never very far from the surface in Germany. Jung used to say that the veneer of Christianity was much thinner in Germany and the other Nordic lands; the Germans had not been converted as other nationalities had been, but were forced to accept Christianity. This is probably the underlying cause of all the wild and primitive things that happened in a civilized country like Germany during Hitler's time.

Therefore, when Sylvia is confronted with Ulysses, the god Eros and

old Pan in her fantasy, she is projecting her own longing for paganism
and wild primitivity into classical antiquity. This is the real reason the
problem of love is so difficult in these so-called "civilized" days, for it
leads us far beyond the realm of Christian values, and even beyond
classical times, into a dangerous, primitive wildness which we fear and
which we have no idea how to touch. Nevertheless, the truth is that
women must face these wild, primitive forces in themselves (and the fact
that human nature is really capable of all the atrocities that happened in
Germany during the Nazi regime, and are still happening on a worldwide scale today) before they can find the missing Eros and the feminine
principle in themselves.

Sylvia finishes the fantasy by saying that unfortunately Fräulein
Altweg died not long afterwards, so the godmother was once more
alone. But the godmother's experience did not leave her in peace; for
some time, she spent all her spare moments in those woods, without
ever seeing another trace of the old iron door where the key must have
belonged, of Pan, of the old ruin, or of anything else that she had seen
in her vision and with Fräulein Altweg. She bequeathed the key to her
goddaughter, Sylvia, in the hope that she would one day find the
mysterious door which she now had the means to unlock.

A rather ominous note is struck in the last sentence of the fantasy.
The writer claims to be a much occupied business*man* who has no time
for such things. Now, the whole story has been told from the feminine
point of view, and it is concerned from start to finish with Eros and the
feminine principle; in other words, with the heart of Sylvia's problem as
a woman. Therefore this sudden change to the masculine sex—whose
principle is Logos and action—points to the danger of once more falling
a victim to the animus image imprinted on her by her father, and thus
of losing the impetus to find the right use for the key.

Apart from this danger, however, one feels that Sylvia has gained a
great deal from this fantasy. Above all, it has set her a task: to rediscover
the god Eros and all the girls who made up her totality, her process of
individuation. It has shown her the most worthwhile goal for her entire
life.

Marie-Louise von Franz pointed out to me the extraordinary similarity
in the motif of the key in Sylvia's fantasy and an important scene in the
second part of *Faust,* where Faust is engaged in the search for "the

Mothers."[7] Mephistopheles gives him a key which he disdainfully calls "this little thing." Mephistopheles tells him not to despise it, for it will scent out the way and lead him to "the Mothers." To Faust's amazement, the key grows in his hand, becomes luminous and flashes forth light. Mephistopheles tells him to follow it down, then adds, "I could just as well say up." This sentence, often quoted by Jung, shows a complete harmony between the opposites—a vital factor in the process of individuation.

As we have seen in her fantasy, Sylvia also despised her key. She complained that her godmother, a rich woman, had only left her an "insignificant object"—the old key. Yet in reality, her godmother had left her the most valuable possession that exists for women: the key which can lead her to the god Eros and to her totality. If she, like Faust, can hold it in her hand, light will come out of the darkness left her by her father, and, in the second half of life, she will be able to find the confidence and security in the Self that she was denied during the first part by her apparently unsatisfactory parents. I say "apparently," for people with satisfactory parents and a happy first-half of life seldom have the incentive to look deeper, and often lose their way in futilities.

As Jung says in *Memories*, "The decisive question for man is: Is he related to something infinite or not? That is the telling question of his life. Only if we know that the thing which truly matters is the infinite can we avoid fixing our interest upon futilities and upon all kinds of goals which are not of real importance."[8] Sylvia's key has given her a unique chance to answer "the telling question" of her life in the affirmative, for it is just the infinite to which her key will lead her if she can cease despising it and trust herself to its guidance.

[7]Goethe, *Faust*, part 2, act 1.
[8]Jung, *Memories, Dreams, Reflections*, p. 325.

CHAPTER 4

The Unconscious Prepares for Death
The Case of Beatrice

The case of Beatrice is a more advanced instance of active imagination than either of the foregoing examples. It shows that this form of active meditation can prepare those who use it correctly for the most unexpected crises—even for death itself. The following material comes from the last seven months before Beatrice's death, and shows how she was drawn gradually toward the center, and how she left the standpoint of the ego and learned to adopt the standpoint of the Self.

Beatrice had been in analysis for many years and was already analyzing very successfully herself. She was not destined to have a long life. Dr. Jung had warned her analyst that he thought an early death was most probable, and indeed, she only reached her middle fifties.

Beatrice had already done a great deal of active imagination by the time our material begins; she found it more and more of a refuge when things went wrong. Discretion prevents me from describing these difficulties more explicitly, so I will only say that they were typical of a married woman of her age. Her children were growing up and leaving home, which of course left her with more difficulties with her husband than had hitherto been the case. She was exceedingly fond of him, but inclined to be more anxious about him than was necessary. She was also a good deal tortured by unfounded jealousy, though she had the redeeming virtue of being conscious of this fact. She was what Jung, in his article on "Marriage as a Psychological Relationship," calls the "container"[1] in a marriage. Jung further defined the container as the partner in a marriage who had the most facets, whose feeling was not contained totally within the marriage, or the partner who "looks out of the window." In her own practice, she was also inclined to develop countertransferences to her men analysands, and one of these was distressing her when our material begins.

Beatrice had a very positive animus who guided her in her active imagination; in addition, the image of a flower in a deep wood was becoming more and more important to her. This was roughly the starting point of our material.

She addresses this flower:

You, marvelous gold and silver flower, are like a shining center in me, out of which I am learning to live. I can no longer live out of myself, but must live from this other center where my divine spirit man also lives. The mystery of the flower unites me with timelessness, even with eternity.

It is clear that this flower is Beatrice's symbol for the Self. It is the center that is drawing her to it. This material shows us how aptly Jung described this center in *Psychology and Alchemy:*

We can hardly escape the feeling that the unconscious process moves spiral-wise round a centre, gradually getting closer, while the characteristics of the centre grow more and more distinct. Or perhaps we could put it the other way round and say that the centre—itself virtually unknowable—acts like a magnet on the disparate materials and processes of the unconscious and gradually captures them as in a crystal lattice. . . .

Indeed, it seems as if all the personal entanglements and dramatic changes of fortune that make up the intensity of life were nothing but hesitations, timid shrinkings, almost like petty complications and meticulous excuses for not facing the finality of this strange and uncanny process of crystallization. Often one has the impression that the personal psyche is running round this central point like a shy animal, at once fascinated and frightened, always in flight, and yet steadily drawing nearer.[2]

[1]C. G. Jung, *The Development of Personality*, vol. 17, *Collected Works* (Princeton: Princeton University Press, 1954) pars. 331c ff.
[2]Jung, *Collected Works*, vol. 12, par. 325.

Beatrice is doing her best to approach this center of which Jung speaks. Indeed, she even hopes to live from it instead of from the conscious ego. Yet, like all of us, she is shyer of it than she realizes, and she still runs away from it from time to time, as we shall see.

Beatrice continues:

The flower is the house that I have built for myself in eternity. I have already moved into this house in order to have a place for my soul to live when my body decays. It is a piece of the heavenly garden of paradise.

Here, Beatrice was probably influenced by an article of Richard Wilhelm's on "Death and Renewal in China,"[3] in which he explains that the Chinese do not prize life as we do. Some of the oldest Chinese documents point out that the greatest good fortune which a man can meet is to find a death that crowns his life, and the greatest misfortune is to find an untimely death, rather than his own specific death. The Confucians believe that one should prepare for that event; in the course of life, one should try to build a body, a kind of subtle body of a spiritual nature, made of thoughts and works—a body that gives consciousness a support when it must leave its former assistant, the physical body. Beatrice is evidently hoping that this flower will develop into a subtle, spiritual body that will support her consciousness when she dies. I do not know if Jung had told her of his premonition that she would die young; nevertheless, she must have felt it herself, for she was unusually interested in building this support at a relatively young age. She was very right to do so, as we shall see.

From the material that follows, one feels that Beatrice was overly optimistic, or rather that she was anticipating the future, when she says she has already moved into the house. She has realized its objective existence, however, and it is obviously her goal to move into it.

Like many of us, Beatrice was very anxious about world events. She decided to talk to her positive animus, to her spirit man, about this. She says:

Great Spirit Man: Help mankind that we do not destroy each other and that we do not founder. Help us against the dark demons that are threatening us. Help us against the evil god that would destroy us and that thinks out more evil than we are up to.

___

[3]Richard Wilhelm, *Spring: A Magazine of Jungian Thought*, Analytical Psychology Club of New York (1962).

He replies:

Think of the flower, for everything is one in it.

Then she sees a white bird. It flies into the flower, bathes in its light, and then flies out, into the world.

Her spirit man is right to draw her attention to the united opposites in the flower, for the only hope for our torn world is that the warring opposites would unite. This was the main endeavor of alchemy. The alchemists were always trying to marry the opposites to each other, for it is only when opposites are united that true peace is to be found. When we examine the state of the world, as Beatrice was doing here, we find that everywhere, one opposite is trying to gain power over the other. Collectively we cannot do anything, for, as Jung constantly said, the only place one can do anything is in the individual, in ourselves. It follows the principle of the rainmaker (see Chapter 1): if the individual is in Tao—a place where the opposites are united—he has an inexplicable effect on his surroundings.

Whether Beatrice realized it or not, she was doing all she could for the state of the world when she obeyed her spirit man and went to the flower. The bird which she watched fly into it and fly out again into the world gives us the key: we cannot hope to be freed permanently of the warring opposites in this world, but we can realize that there is a place *in us* where they are united, and we can learn to visit it, thereby enabling its light to fly out into the world. If enough people realize the importance of this and go to this inner place, they will be able to stand the tension of the opposites outside, as Jung said was essential for the avoidance of atomic war (see Chapter 1). The bird shows us how to do this.

Beatrice left a record of her visits to this flower, which occurred at least twice a month. She probably had it in mind most of the time, and indeed, her visits become progressively more frequent.

In her next record of visiting her flower, she has realized the united opposites in it more clearly than ever before. She says:

I go to the miraculous flower and contemplate it. In it, something has become one that was two opposites. That is the miracle. Perhaps the spirit of this flower could heal the world and protect it from war. I pray it to do so.

And a fortnight later:

I go to the place where two have become one, where gold and silver, sun

*and moon, have united, and where man also can become one with
himself and with each other.*

In alchemy, the sun and moon represent the extreme opposites. Jung
goes into this in considerable detail in the *Mysterium Coniunctionis*.[4]
The sun, of course, represents the masculine opposite, and the moon,
the feminine. To marry these two was to unite the two most extreme
opposites. From this fantasy, Beatrice can realize that the Self in her is
standing the tension of the most extreme opposites, which the ego by
itself would be quite unable to do. Gold and silver are also a generally
used pair of opposites in alchemy: gold is always attributed to the sun,
and silver, to the moon.

Next, Beatrice complains that her countertransference is disturbing
her profoundly. She is unable to understand its meaning, so she goes to
the wood and tells her spirit man how sad this is making her. She accuses
him of appearing in the man and asks him not to be so cruel.

More and more, we see that she is taking her outer troubles to the
flower or to the spirit man; a fortnight later she is walking in what she
has named her "fairy-tale wood," calling him repeatedly. At last he
comes, walks beside her and takes her to the flower. They stand silently,
before it, hand in hand, and "contemplate the great miracle of unity."
She asks him if there is a fire that burns without consuming itself and
destroying everything it reaches. He tells her to look at the flower and
witness how brightly and warmly it burns without consuming itself or
destroying anything else. He tells her that the flower is the symbol and
the child of their love and of all the love she has ever given to anyone.
Then he chides her for being sad and tells her to suffer her countertransference gladly, because it belongs to her psychology and is right.

This infuriates Beatrice, and she angrily claims the right to weep and
to be sad. She accuses him of cruelty, telling him that her love for him
has changed to hate, that he is a monster and she wants nothing more to
do with him.

Such sudden revulsions are not uncommon in deep plunges into the
unconscious. In a difficult outer situation, one suddenly loses the belief
in one's whole fantasy, or believes one has made it all up. I have found
that the best way to combat this problem is to think of how objectively
active imagination has helped me in the past, until slowly I trust it
again.

[4]Jung, *Collected Works*, vol. 14, pars. 110–133 and 154–233.

But sometimes the unconscious itself does something to bring one to one's senses, and this is what happens to Beatrice here. She cannot shake off the fantasy, however much she tries; she is still in the wood, but it has become pitch dark. Both the flower and her spirit man have disappeared; she is afraid that she will fall into an abyss if she takes a step in any direction.

She sinks down in despair, but it is too cold to remain lying on the ground. She decides to walk slowly on, even if she should fall into the abyss, for she thinks it could not be worse than her present fear. She thinks of her husband and home, and decides that she has lost everything through her love of her spirit man—a love which has now turned to hate. Touching the bottom of despair, she even accuses her beautiful flower of deceiving her, for it has claimed to be eternal and yet it has now disappeared.

Beatrice, "like a shy animal," is indeed in flight from her center. But such darkness as she is experiencing is what St. John of the Cross called "the dark night of the soul." What Beatrice seems to have entirely forgotten is that she has brought it on herself by blaming her spirit man for all her troubles, and that she still blames him. One wonders whether the old mystics also brought their dark nights of the soul on themselves and forgot what they themselves had done. As I tried to make very clear in my book on the life of Jung, as long as a person forgets his own original trespass, every kind of misfortune can come upon him until he remembers and suffers its guilt.[5] But Beatrice is still projecting all blame; therefore, the pitch darkness persists.

At this point, something very important happens: she realizes that, dark though it is, her slow walk is going well and she asks in surprise, "Perhaps the darkness itself is nourishing me?"

This is exactly what she has failed to realize in the outer world. She has rebelled against the suffering and obscurity of her countertransference; she can see no good in her suffering. Her love of her spirit man has turned to hate because she suspects him of having been the cruel cause of it all and then of not even allowing her to weep. As an introvert, it is naturally not easy for her to see value in outer suffering. The unconscious quite often does what it has done to Beatrice: it creates the rejected obscurity and darkness *inwardly*, where it is much easier for an introvert to see its value and to realize that it actually nourishes her.

[5]Hannah, *Jung: His Life and Work,* pp. 42ff, 82f.

But she is still very lonely and afraid the situation will never change. She wonders if repentance would change the relationship, making it as good as it was before. She continues:

> But I cannot repent; he has hurt me too much. Why should I repent? I cannot love him again, yet I have lost everything I had with him. I know he was my god, my light and my warmth, but he was also my torture and despair. Therefore I can no longer love him. I prefer this darkness.

Then she bumps her foot against something hard and, reaching out with her arms, she finds a curious wall of books. She throws the books away, one by one, and stumbles through them.

Evidently, Beatrice has come to the place described by the alchemists: "Tear up the books that your hearts be not broken." Reading books— "one book opens another"—is recommended again and again in alchemy as the way par excellence to understand "our art," but suddenly, everything Beatrice has learned secondhand has become a hindrance. Only one's own experience is vital, for one's own way is always unique, although up to a late stage in the individuation process, books containing other people's experience can show one the way to go. At this point, Beatrice can only stick to the fact that she has *experienced* the darkness as nourishing her, and that she must therefore accept her whole suffering as a necessary part of life. "Suffering is the fastest horse that leads to perfection," as Meister Eckhart tells us.

Throwing away the books has an immediate effect on Beatrice. She sees something like a distant light—a dim glow, less dark than its surroundings. She stumbles in its diretion. To her surprise, she sees someone walking beside her. When she asks who he is, he answers, "Your friend." Although she is glad to be no longer alone, she defiantly replies, "I have no friend." They go on in the darkness, side by side. At first they are silent, then he tells her that she only thought she was alone. He is always there, he says, for he is her fate; it is useless to fight against him, for the two of them are one. Without reproach, he shows her that sometimes he comes to her from outside, as he has now in this countertransference which she hates to accept. She objects that the man is so strange to her that he is surely not part of herself. He asks her, "Do you then know who you are?" She admits that she has never known her identity, and that sometimes she thinks she is an incomprehensible person, with an incomprehensible fate. Even as a child, she sometimes wondered about this and said to herself, "There is that peculiar woman,

Beatrice, as she is called. Who is she really?'' She asks if she must go through much more suffering with him. He replies, "But now you know we belong together; surely that diminishes the suffering and makes it bearable.'' Then the man quickly quotes John Gower: ''A warring peace, a sweet wound, an agreeable evil.'' Jung quotes this same passage at the beginning of his introduction to ''Psychology of the Transference.''[6]

Beatrice has now accepted the fact that she brought the darkness on herself by refusing her outer suffering and by blaming her spirit man for everything that has happened to her. Jung used to say that whereas men overcome by action—by killing the dragon—women overcome by keeping still and accepting their suffering. This is the last time Beatrice fights her fate; from now on, she accepts her suffering in a far more feminine way.

This new state of acceptance makes the dim light become a little brighter, and a geometric form begins to appear. She asks her spirit man if it is the eight-petalled flower seen from above, the child of their love, the fruit of much torture and pain. He assents and she says, ''Everything has become one in it, you and I, within and without.''

It is a great improvement when Beatrice sees her flower as a mandala —the foundation which man has always used to express the inexpressible, whether he has called it God or, as we do, the Self. She also realizes her whole fate as *one*, whether within or without.

Again, she is very impressed by the warmth of the fire which her mandala radiates, without consuming itself or hurting anything. When the spirit man says that she must pass through this fire or she cannot become fireproof—able to endure everything—she consents at once. He gives her his hand and leads her into the fire. When they feel its heat, she is afraid, but she also feels an incomprehensible determination to go through with it, no mater how much it hurts her, because she cannot go on as before. They walk on the glowing embers and are surrounded by flames, but they do not wound her; on the contrary, she feels bathed and penetrated by the fire, as if it were burning away all her futilities.[7] When she is in the center of the fire, she faints; she does not sink to the ground, however, for she has been holding the spirit man's hand all the time. She realizes slowly that doing so has left her very strong and no

[6]Jung, *Collected Works*, vol. 16, p. 167.
[7]Jung, *Memories, Dreams, Reflections*, p. 325.

longer subject to decay. She is reminded of the diamond body. But she
is no longer quite in it, although she is nowhere else, and she objectively
watches her spirit man embracing and kissing another woman in the
center. As they both leave the fire slowly and with bent heads, she goes
with them.

Here the fantasy takes an unexpected, but very right, turn. The ego
cannot identify with the Self without getting disastrously inflated.
Beatrice sees the royal pair objectively and herself only as the observer,
just as Jung watched them in the visions which he had during his 1944
illness. He says of this: "I do not know what part I played in them. At
bottom it was I myself. I was myself the marriage. And my beatitude
was that of a blissful wedding."[8] It is a complete paradox: they are
oneself and they are not, and one cannot identify with either opposite.

To walk through the fire is a condition of many, if not all, rites of
initiation, and it always occurs for the purpose of shedding superfluities.
Beatrice is slowly establishing her relation to the infinite and having her
attachments to futilities burnt away.

In actual life, the fire consists of going through equally intense suffering. Beatrice had already seen the value of this suffering when she
realized that the darkness was nourishing her. But naturally, she must
experience it in many different forms, for the mystery of eternity is so far
beyond our comprehension that we can only get a feeling of rapport
with it through the most diverse experiences. As we saw when Beatrice
had to throw away the books, intellectual realization no longer suffices.

She speaks again of the mystery of love and of the pain it gives her.
But she is greatly helped by what he tells her about always following the
numinous, whether it appears to her from within or without. She
always felt disturbed by her excessive anxiety about her husband and at
the apparent senselessness of her countertransference and the strangeness of the man in whom it appeared. As an introvert, it is meaningful
to her to learn that it had always been her spirit man, whether it was
walking through the fire inwardly with him, or appearing to her in an
outward projection. He also tells her that when one is in the fire,
inwardly or outwardly, one naturally does not see its basic pattern. For
that, the observer needs distance, such as they had when they
approached the flower from the dark and she saw it for the first time as a
mandala.

8Ibid., p. 294.

The next time she takes up the fantasy, her spirit man has become a bear man. Jung speaks in a letter of a vision in which the Swiss saint, Niklaus von Flüe, saw the figure of a pilgrim clothed in a bear skin that contained a golden luster.[9] Jung says that, on the one side, he saw this pilgrim as Christ and, on the other, as a bear, and that this is as it should be: the superhuman needs the subhuman to balance it. This is probably the same reason that Beatrice's spirit man became a bear. She had gotten too high up and, as we shall see later, was repressing too many emotions that she thought she ought not to have. For example, it is very difficult for any mother when the children grow up and leave the home. But Beatrice was so determined *not* to be a devouring mother and to leave her children quite free, that she did not allow herself to realize how miserable it had made her. These emotions were therefore repressed and, as Niklaus needed the brutal coldness of the subhuman animal's cold feeling to leave his wife and family in order to become a hermit, so Beatrice needs something of the same kind to enable her to concentrate all her energy and interest on her inner life, as the unconscious seems to increasingly demand of her.

She evidently feels that this coldness is demanded of her, for in the next part of her vision the fire is replaced by snow. Welcoming the strength and warmth of the bear, she says to him:

> *"My spirit man, my God, my great, strong bear, take me in your arms and carry me through the cold snow. I have become tired and weak and I cannot walk any longer. With your help and protection, I was not burnt in the fire. Now carry me through the snow that I do not freeze."*
>
> *He bends down and lifts me carefully, without scratching me with his claws. He is enormously strong and I feel all the strength of a wild animal in him. Also, he warms me with his bodily warmth and his thick, soft fur. I am happy with him; my fear has left me.*
>
> *"Oh, do not put me down on the cold ground again. Carry me to our home where the miraculous flower blooms. I see it from afar, glimmering through the cold night. It is my goal and my indestructible order. My spirit man, I know that under your skin you are a king, a god. But your animal warmth protects me, and I also need your strength and knowledge."*
>
> *He replies, "I need you also, you poor little human being."*

[9]C. G. Jung, *C. G. Jung: Letters,* 2 vols., eds. Gerhard Adler and Aniela Jaffé (Princeton: Princeton University Press, 1973), vol. 1, pp. 364ff. Cf. also Marie-Louise von Franz, *Die Visionen des Niklaus von Flüe* (Zürich: Rascher Verlag, 1959), pp. 83ff.

Like Niklaus von Flüe, Beatrice sees her spirit man as a god, so that it is appropriate that she also sees him as a bear, for we must go as low as we go high, and vice versa, in order to keep the opposites balanced. She needs her animal instinct, for the bear is an excellent mother while her cubs are small, but ruthlessly kicks them away from her as soon as they are able to fend for themselves. Then she devotes herself to her own concerns, as the unconscious is demanding that Beatrice should do. Beatrice realizes that she needs the bear's warmth and strength to help her in perhaps the most difficult journey in life: the journey from ego to Self. It is sometimes a very cold journey, as it is here, and sometimes leads through the fire of suffering, as it did previously. But the unconscious is giving her its full support by providing her with the right companion for each trial. If one can trust it and meet its demands, the unconscious always plays fair; as her spirit man told her, however, when you are in the fire (or in the snow), you cannot see the basic pattern.

Later, she continues:

I am always searching for the center as a protection from my emotions. But, on the other hand, it is just emotion, jealousy and my counter-transference that lead me to the center. Without them I should never go there, for I should not be forced to go.

That she realizes the value of her emotions is certainly the effect of the bear. Before he had appeared, she was continually trying to rise above them. To do so is also necessary, for we cannot be constantly swayed, this way and that, by our emotions. But they should not be repressed, as Beatrice was evidently trying to do; rather, they should be accepted. And we must learn to stand the pain and fear that they cause.

Trying to understand the center, she admits that, like all of us, she does not understand it at all, but realizes more and more that it is a complete paradox. She says she lives near the fire and the Self protects her from the Self. And she realizes that when she is farthest from God, she is also nearest to him: she is farthest from him in emotion, but that is when she needs him most and searches most earnestly for him. He is the wild, terrible fire of her passion and he is redemption from it.

As Jung writes in *Psychology and Alchemy:*

Has it not yet been observed that all religious statements contain logical contradictions and assertions that are impossible in principle, that this is in fact the very essence of religious assertion? As witness to this we have Tertullian's avowal: "And the Son of God is dead, which is worthy of belief because it is absurd. And when buried He rose again, which is certain because it is impossible." . . . *Hence a religion becomes inwardly impoverished when it loses or reduces its paradoxes; but their multiplication enriches because only the paradox comes anywhere near to comprehending the fulness of life. Non-ambiguity and non-contradiction are one-sided and thus unsuited to express the incomprehensible.*[10]

Beatrice never seems to have fully realized this principle until her spirit man became a bear, at which time the full necessity of the paradox dawned on her and filled her.

The next time she goes to the flower through active imagination, Beatrice finds it surrounded by high walls; it is in a *temenos*. It has four doors on all sides, facing east, south, west and north. The bear man has the golden keys. He opens one of the doors and they pass through it. Immediately she feels happy and protected and asks her bear man: "Why?" He replies, "Because the walls keep out all demons." She tells him repeatedly how happy she is there, for the flower shines with a wonderful, healing light. She emphasizes that she is not *in* the flower, but stands beside it, in its protection and its mild warmth.

She asks the bear man, "Who built the wall?" He replies that God built it as a protection against himself, but that it is also he who makes the flower grow. Overcome once more by the paradox, she cries, "Terrible, good, helpful God!"

Here she realizes that good and evil also must be united and are united in God. Good and evil are the most burning pair of opposites that exist for us, at all events for all of us who were brought up in Christian morality. Christian morality had the great disadvantage of repressing evil, with the result that evil has now broken its bonds and is blindly possessing more and more people to live evil with no sense of what they are doing. Moreover, they are repressing good, the light opposite, quite as badly as Christianity repressed evil, the dark opposite. We can no longer afford to repress either opposite; we must see them both and live them consciously and responsibly, as Beatrice was genuinely trying to do. Unfortunately, very few people are conscious of this fact.

At this point of her life, Beatrice is doing active imagination much more frequently and goes to her *temenos* as often as possible. Once there, she sees a star shining in the black night. She asks herself who she

[10]Jung, *Collected Works*, vol. 12, par. 18.

is. Is she the star? She thinks it is a curious fate, if so; still, all her interest and passion are in the star. "If there is a man, then only for the sake of the star," she says.

In the seventh of his "Seven Sermons to the Dead," Jung writes:

> *When night was come the dead again approached with lamentable mien and said: There is yet one matter we forgot to mention. Teach us about man.*
>
> *Man is a gateway, through which from the outer world of gods, daemons, and souls ye pass into the inner world; out of the greater into the smaller world. Small and transitory is man. Already he is behind you and once again ye find yourselves in endless space in the smaller or inner-most infinity. At immeasurable distance standeth one single Star in the zenith.*
>
> *This is the one god of this one man. This is his world, his pleroma, his divinity.*
>
> *In this world is man Abraxas, the creator and destroyer of his own world.*
>
> *This Star is the god and the goal of man.*
>
> *This is his one guiding god. In him goeth man to his rest. Toward him goeth the long journey of the soul after death. In him shineth forth as light all that man bringeth back from the greater world. To this one god man shall pray.*
>
> *Prayer increaseth the light of the Star. It casteth a bridge over death. It prepareth life for the smaller world and assuageth the hopeless desires of the greater.*
>
> *When the greater world waxeth cold, burneth the Star.*
>
> *Between man and his one god there standeth nothing, so long as man can turn his eyes from the flaming spectacle of Abraxas.*
>
> *Man here, god there . . .*
>
> *Here nothing but darkness and chilling moisture.*
>
> *There wholly sun.*[11]

This makes it very clear why all of Beatrice's interest and passion has suddenly been transferred to this star, for she is rapidly approaching her death. It is clear that her impending death was known in the unconscious, and that the Self was preparing Beatrice by showing her the star, the one god and goal of each of us, to which the soul takes its long journey after death.

[11]Jung, *Memories, Dreams, Reflections*, "Septem Sermones ad Mortuos, Sermo VII" (1916), p. 389.

The star makes an immense impression on her. But evidently, she identifies with it a little too soon, deciding that she can leave her earthly emotions entirely and can immediately become sober and objective. This goads the bear man to fury, a real berserker rage, and he throws himself on her as if to tear her to pieces. She has no time to escape from him, so she falls to the ground before him and submits entirely "as if I were praying to a god." That appeases him and he does not attack. She asks him, "What had I done to you that you were suddenly so angry and wanted to kill me?" He replies, "I cannot stand such an abstemious attitude." She then promises him that she will no longer repress emotions "for the sake of being reasonable." Then they go together to the center: the flower.

Evidently, our instincts forbid us to ignore them while we are in our bodies, and indeed Beatrice was still often torn by her emotions because of her outer difficulties, jealousy and a wish to rebel against the outer, incomprehensible strangeness of her countertransference. I once told Jung of a man who had come back to life only after the doctors had thought he was dead. He reported that during that time he had been in a place more familiar to him than his own house and garden. He was immeasurably surprised that this familiar place was death. Jung said that was how he himself expected death to be. But, he added, "The ego won't like it. One must expect a protest from that side."

The bear man seems to be drawing Beatrice's attention to this protest, and she duly attends to what he says. But she is increasingly drawn to her *temenos;* at the end, she goes to it each day. One feels that when Beatrice passes over, it will indeed be more familiar to her than her own home, a blessing which she certainly owes to devoting more and more time and energy to active imagination.

Very shortly before her death, she is in the center and says:

> *I must now always stay in the center or the problem can never be solved on both sides. Perhaps I am the center. The mystery of the flower is in me; I am it and it is me. It has entered me and become a human being. I am two: ordinary human being and the mystery of the flower. I have grown from the center. My roots are in the black, forest earth, deep in the earth. Here I grew up. My petals have unfolded and then the miraculous flower is in the center, four golden petals and four silver petals. I am this shining flower from which a spring also bursts out. I flower brightly in the middle of the dark wood. Am I indeed the flower?*

This is the first time Beatrice has entered the flower, but by no means the first time she had wanted to do so. She repeatedly expressed this wish to her spirit man in whatever form he was presenting. But he always forbade her entrance, telling her it was dangerous, for it was often impossible to get back. This time, however, he makes no protest; the right time has come for her own specific death—she will no longer be able to find her way back to her earthly body, but may enter the subtle body which she has taken such pains to build.

Although the imagery is totally different, Beatrice is really describing the same experience that Jung met, after his illness in 1944, when he had the dream of the Yogi. He says:

In that . . . . dream I was on a hiking trip. I was walking along a little road through a hilly landscape; the sun was shining and I had a wide view in all directions. Then I came to a small wayside chapel. The door was ajar, and I went in. To my surprise there was no image of the Virgin on the altar, and no crucifix either, but only a wonderful flower arrangement. But then I saw that on the floor in front of the altar, facing me, sat a yogi—in lotus posture, in deep meditation. When I looked at him more closely, I realized that he had my face. I started in profound fright, and awoke with the thought: "Aha, so he is the one who is meditating me. He has a dream, and I am it." I knew that when he awakened, I would no longer be.[12]

He then comments that evidently at his birth, Jung's Self retired into deep meditation and meditates his earthly form. He continues:

To put it another way: it assumes human shape in order to enter three-dimensional existence, as if someone were putting on a diver's suit in order to dive into the sea. When it renounces existence in the hereafter, the Self assumes a religious posture, as the chapel in the dream shows. In earthly form it can pass through the experiences of the three-dimensional world, and by greater awareness take a further step toward realization.[13]

Beatrice regards the flower as the Self; here, she puts her experience into words: "I am an ordinary human being but also the mystery of the flower"; just as the yogi in Jung's dream had Jung's features, so he himself was the mystery of the yogi in meditation, and also an ordinary human being on a hiking trip. He is simultaneously only an observer of the beautiful flower arrangement on the altar, and the meditating yogi as well.

[12]Ibid., p. 323.
[13]Ibid., pp. 323–324.

But Beatrice has entered the flower and even feels herself putting down her roots into the dark earth. Since there is no protest from her spirit man, who usually looks after her so carefully, we may expect that a great change is coming. She was, however, allowed to return to her earthly body for a very short time.

The next day she writes:

> I go to the wall. The bear, my great, powerful companion, opens one of the four doors. We go in and he locks the door behind us. As soon as we are within the walls, he takes human shape. It is my royal spirit man with a golden, white mantle. I contemplate the flower. As I meditate upon it, I become, as I did yesterday, the flower itself, rooted, growing, radiant, timeless.
>
> Thus I take on the form of immortality. Then I feel quite well, and protected from all attacks from outside. It also protects me from my own emotion. When I am in the center, nobody and nothing can attack me. They can still attack and hurt me in my human form and I know that I must spend most of my time there. But I shall always have the opportunity now and then to become the flower. I am very happy about that, for I have only just realized that this is possible. I have long known the flower as an object, but now I know that I can also be it.

Beatrice was right that she still had her human form, but mistaken in thinking that she had to continue spending most of her time there. She died of a sudden and unexpected thrombosis the day after this last entry in her book of active imagination. As her spirit man had always warned her, if one enters the flower in one's lifetime, it may become impossible to return to one's human form. Therefore, Beatrice was only allowed to enter it on the last two days of her life. It is, however, very clear that the *temenos* is already "more familiar to her than her own house and garden" on earth. Moreover, she has reached the goal of our next example, the Egyptian World-Weary Man. She has a common home with her spirit man.[14]

In this final excerpt, her spirit man has become the Self, royally adorned with a golden mantle. He has shed his bear form, for it is no longer necessary to Beatrice. She may at last leave behind all the things that attack her from outside, as well as her own wild emotions. She may enter her haven of peace and become "the flower itself, rooted, growing, radiant and timeless"—her image of immortality.

[14]See below, p. 105.

Consciously, she does not yet know that she is at the end of her life, for she still fears she will have to pass most of her time in her human body, tormented by her emotions and by attacks from other people. It is clear that she is now much happier as the flower. Active imagination has led to complete independence and she no longer relies on any outer support. Therefore, one feels that the Chinese would call her happy; she has built her subtle body, and the right moment has come for her to die her own specific death. Sudden though her death was, from the conscious point of view, one cannot doubt that death found her fully prepared. Naturally, her husband, children and friends felt the sudden shock most terribly, but although she died apparently prematurely, one feels she must have been spared all the resentment that Jung used to say people who died young usually seem to feel. This is usually clear in the dreams of their family and friends, and I, at all events, have heard of nothing of the kind in the case of Beatrice. As far as one dare suggest anything about the Beyond, one feels that Beatrice had reached all the fulfillment that the unconscious had asked of her on earth, and could therefore find full support in the subtle body that had become even more real to her in her active imagination during the days before her death.

I think we are very privileged to have been able to study such a document, and I must end by thanking her husband most deeply for allowing me to include Beatrice's experiences in this book.

CHAPTER 5

An Ancient Example of Active Imagination
The World-Weary Man and His Ba

The best two examples of the so-called auditory method of active imagination[1] that I know come from long ago. The first is over 4000 years old, circa 2200 B.C. A figure of the unconscious breaks in on a man in such an unusual way at that time that at first he is completely shattered. Eventually, however, he proves himself capable of dealing with the situation in a manner that few, if any, of us could attain today.

The second example (Chapter 6) comes from the first half of the twelfth century A.D. and forms a complete contrast to the first. The conversation is begun by the man himself, who has evidently been much hampered in his conscious program by the interference of his anima. All we know of the "World-Weary Man" comes from the text itself and from the comments on the text by the Egyptologist Helmuth Jacobsohn;[2] the second example, however, is written by a very famous man, Hugh de St. Victor, of whom we know much more.

I have already contrasted these two texts in my first seminar on active imagination (1951), but, at that time, in spite of its excellence, I had to overcome considerable feelings of inferiority about using the first

[1]Conversation with a figure or figures of the unconscious.
[2]Helmuth Jacobsohn, *Timeless Documents of the Soul* (Evanston: Northwestern University Press, 1968).

example because of my ignorance of Egyptology and of the Egyptian language. It was only the fact that it was Jung himself who had handed me the text which Jacobsohn had just sent him in manuscript, and the good fortune that Jacobsohn was himself in Zurich during the time that I was giving the course, that enabled me to overcome my scruples. I must express my gratitude to them both for the generous help they gave me, without handing either of them any responsibility for what I say.

I have used the English translation I made myself at that time from the German original because I am more accustomed to it. I have compared it with an excellent newer translation by Richard Pope,[3] and there are no major differences.

The text had been translated many times before, but no one came anywhere near understanding it until Jacobsohn took it in hand. Those who know Legge's translation of the I Ching[4] and have compared it with Cary Baynes's more recent, excellent translation of Wilhelm's text[5] will know just what I mean. A comparison of the earlier translations of our Egyptian text with Jacobsohn's yields exactly the same result. It is impossible to translate such texts without some psychological knowledge, and Dr. Jacobsohn has a natural understanding of the psychology of the old Egyptians which it is difficult to praise too highly. I regret that space will not allow me to quote many more of his comments, but they can all be found in *Timeless Documents of the Soul*.[6]

It was ignorance of both the empirical existence of the unconscious and the fact that it appears in personified forms which hampered the earlier translators, who thought the two speakers were simply a conscious device for the author to express two tendencies of the time. Dr. Jacobsohn comments that if we give up all such preconceived opinions in considering the text:

> *We are confronted above all with a human tragedy of far greater dimensions than anyone has yet admitted. It is not only the man who cannot find his bearings in the time in which he lives and is therefore driven to the verge of suicide: that is just the theme, the starting point. But it is also the man who lives far removed from God and who has lost every support and who now discovers something which—according to the*

[3]Ibid., pp. 1–54.
[4]*I Ching,* trans. James Legge, 2d ed. (New York: Dover Press, Inc., 1899).
[5]*The I Ching, or Book of Changes,* trans. Richard Wilhelm, Cary F. Baynes, 3rd ed. (Princeton: Princeton University Press, 1967).
[6]Jacobsohn, *Timeless Documents of the Soul.*

existing evidence—had never yet been discovered by any Egyptian. He discovered that the Ba—man's own "soul"—represents a power already in man's lifetime, a power which, on the one hand, man cannot escape by means of his conscious will and which, on the other hand, he cannot yet understand with his conscious mind, so that at first he must try again and again to resist this power within himself. It is the tragedy of helplessness, not only in regard to the world but also in regard to oneself. This tragedy can only be experienced by someone who does not live as "a pious man" among godless people, but who has suffered himself from the terror and despair of being far removed from God. What happened to the World-Weary Man at the hands of his Ba in this hopeless situation must not be anticipated here: it is the real theme of the following research.[7]

We must remember that what we call the individual, only came into existence *after* death for the religious Egyptian of those days. The reader who is familiar with *The Book of the Dead*[8] already knows that every element of the individual was projected into the Beyond and that overwhelming importance was attached to the funeral and subsequent rites for the dead.

Although the text is separated from us by over 4000 years, it is curiously close to us in many ways. This is probably because it arose in a time when Egypt was in a state that was very similar to the predicament in which we find ourselves today. It was the time of the disintegration of the old kingdom, of the first revolution in history, a prototype which ranks with our modern revolutions: the priests were attacked and even murdered; the pyramid graves and temples were thrown down; the poor robbed the rich and tried to exterminate them; every little prince intrigued to become the Pharaoh. Suicide was so common that the crocodiles in the Nile could no longer cope with the corpses.

For a religious Egyptian, such as our World-Weary Man, this was an overwhelming psychological shock. Everything material and spiritual was crumbling around him, very similar to what is happening to us today.

The title of the text is "The World-Weary Man and His Ba." The "Ba" is always translated "Soul." Dr. Jacobsohn tells us in his introduction to the text that we do not know much of what the Ba meant to a man of that time, but the Pyramid Texts teach us that he repre-

[7]Ibid.
[8]E. A. Wallis Budge, *The Book of the Dead* (New York: Barnes & Noble, Inc., 1953).

sented a psychic being, divine in nature,[9] connected with the appearance of the individual and incarnated form of a god. The reader of *The Book of the Dead*[10] already knows that after death, all Egyptians who passed the tests became Osiris. The Ba of a human being also has something to do with the individual, manifested form of a particular human being and therefore—in contrast to the Ka—it could settle down on the mummy in a man's tomb. In other words, the Ka is a double, the vitality of a person; the Ba is the kernel, the divine spark of a person. The Ba is represented in Egyptian art as a human-headed bird and is often depicted as hovering over the mummy in the tomb. It is important for us not to forget that the Ba was entirely connected with the post-mortal state in the dogma of that time. The facts that he is connected with the incarnated form of a god and that he is male, not female, already point more to the Self than to the soul or the anima. This is confirmed at the end of the text. The Ba really represents the whole unconscious to the man.

Unfortunately, the beginning of the text is lost, but an incomprehensible fragment and the subsequent reply of the World-Weary Man make it quite clear that the Ba had frightened him nearly out of his wits by a most unexpected speech. We must keep in mind what a shock it must have been to a man of that time that the Ba should play any role at all while he was still alive. The Egyptians of that time saw themselves only as a fragment of a collective state and religion, and any individuality was projected into the Beyond.

In the first preserved speech, the man says:

Then I opened my mouth to my Ba, in order to answer what he had said!

The fact that the Ba has a different opinion from his own shocks the World-Weary Man beyond what exaggeration could represent. Has his Ba become indifferent? He should always be there, attached to the man's body by bond and rope. But now the Ba is attacking him because the man wants to die before his time. Then the man begs the Ba to desist and make the West, i.e., the land of death, agreeable to him, and to overlook his sins during the short time he will still live. He ends with an unconfident appeal to several of the gods to help him.

Translated into modern terms, the World-Weary Man has made a

[9]Pyramid Texts are a collection of Egyptian mortuary prayers, hymns and spells intended to protect a dead king or queen and insure life and substance.
[10]Budge, *Book of the Dead*.

discovery that we still make with horror today: that he is not the master in his own house, but that there is something in his own unconscious that crosses his conscious intention. This discovery confronts us in many ways, but often in active imagination, just as the World-Weary Man encountered it all those years ago.

Jung once analyzed a German doctor who was anxious to discover the method of active imagination for his patients, but who had never practiced it himself. Jung explained to him that it was unwise to recommend it without some personal experience, so the physician consented to try. After a bit, he saw a rocky cliff in the mountains and an ibex standing on it. Jung encouraged him to keep this image in mind. Two or three days later, the man arrived with a white face and reported that the ibex had moved its head! After that experience he flatly refused to do any more active imagination. Something had happened in his psyche without his conscious intention and this was a shock which he could not take. It is noteworthy that this doctor was the only one of Jung's patients to become a Nazi later!

Jung also had a case of a girl, in the very early days of his practice, who was engaged to a man stationed in the Far East. She convinced Jung that only outer difficulties were holding her back from joining him there, so Jung helped her to remove them. But instead of going to her fiancé, the girl became insane! The outer difficulties had only been projections of an immense inner resistance to the marriage. Jung always said that this case taught him a great deal.

The idea that the Ba should be attached to him by bond and rope is fundamentally an image of the way man tries to prevent these disturbing invasions of something autonomous from the unconscious. He tries to talk down the Ba with dogmatic opinions. We can see the same tendency in modern psychology: the Freudians already have a highly finished dogma and very little of the water of life, and although Jung himself remained open to correction from the unconscious until the end of his life, the same tendency is very visible in many of his followers. To a certain degree, it is inevitable; one must have breakwaters to prevent inundation, but it must never go too far or the living water of life will be excluded. As in the Odyssey, it is a matter of steering between Scylla and Charybdis.

In active imagination, we can constantly catch ourselves at the same game. We find it very difficult to regard it as a "Just-So Story"—to watch it objectively and then enter the game ourselves with the same

naive simplicity. We constantly try to correct the paradoxical unconscious with our one-sided, conscious understanding and to keep animus
or anima bound with rope and bond, just as the World-Weary Man
tried to do.

In regard to the man's idea of suicide, which apparently has been
opposed by the Ba, we must not forget that suicide was common in his
day. The era was a turning point in history, for there was no individual
conscience at that time. The so-called negative confession—which had
to be recited by man's spirit when he first reached the Beyond—is a long
declaration of all possible sins, but the deceased must declare that he has
not committed any of them.[11] The ancient Egyptian identified with
Maat, the goddess of justice, and left it at that. The idea was that it
would be a sacrilege to think that the human being had the power to
commit sin; such an assumption would be a hubris and an insult to the
gods.

This reveals a very primitive state of consciousness, but we can still
find many traces of it today. We all know people who simply cannot
admit that they are wrong. They are fearfully annoying, but it is always
possible that they really cannot afford it.

Jung once had a patient who evidently had relations with several
women. Jung counted them silently; they amounted to five. Then he
mentioned the word "polygamy." The man immediately retorted that
that was something of which he had a horror—he was strictly monoga-
mous! Jung reminded him of his secretary. He replied, "Oh, but that is
quite different. It is simply that the work goes so much better if I take
her out to dinner sometimes!" And afterwards? "Oh, yes, something
sometimes just happens."

Since this did not enlighten him at all, Jung further mentioned a Mrs.
Green. "Oh, that is just a matter of exercise. We play golf together and,
as her house is close to the links, I go back to talk with her, and, oh yes,
something sometimes happens afterwards." At about the third, the
penny at last dropped and he cried in horror, "Yes, you are right, I am
polygamous!" The shock made him impotent for many months and
Jung had a very difficult job to set him right. He had kept all his affairs
in separate compartments, such as "work," and "exercise." When the
compartments at last fused, he was absolutely horrified. Jung learned
about compartmental psychology from that case and about the dangers
of fusing such compartments with each other too suddenly.

[11]Ibid., vol. 3, pp. 355–377.

Similarly, all the old Egyptians had transgressed the laws of Maat, but at that time, they simply could not afford to know it. As we shall see, the Ba made our man face individual guilt, but he must have been one of the first men in history to do so, and we must never forget what an unusual experience it was for him.

Suicide is not mentioned in the negative confession, which is probably why our man hoped to get away with it. But he is evidently uneasy and very busy with an *intellectual* justification of his purpose. This was not difficult in those days, when the Beyond was regarded as a perfect life, exactly like a completely happy human life. Why not go there a bit ahead of time? It was really a rational idea in those days, but it is difficult to put ourselves in his position.

The Ba then replies:

> *Are you not then the man? Are you alive at all? What then is your goal that you look after the good[12] like a steward of treasures (i.e., one who cares for his treasures)?*

The Ba goes straight to the point. "Are you alive at all? What is your goal?" The Ba attempts to tear away the man's illusions, his excuses, his unreality, at one stroke. Nothing is more direct than the unconscious.

This speech reveals a stage in active imagination when the man had really seen *nothing* of what the Ba was; he was just projecting his own dogmatic ideas onto him. The Ba is evidently annoyed at the way the man is childishly trying to throw responsibility for the suicide onto him. As Jung has often pointed out, the unconscious is not in our space and time, and therefore takes relatively little notice of death. But what does interest it is whether or not we live our lives fully, enabling the Self to manifest on earth.

The question, "What is then your goal?" is asked to make the man think. It is like the dream of Monica, St. Augustine's mother, in which an angel asked her why she was so unhappy about her son. St. Augustine comments that of course the angel knew, but that it had asked her in order to make her think.

In "Woman in Europe," Jung says: "Masculinity means knowing what one wants and doing what is necessary to achieve it."[13] The Ba is evidently disgusted with the man's feminine attitude. He wants to "drift toward death," as he expresses it, in a completely passive way.

[12]Erman (an early translator) understood correctly here: "the good" is certainly meant in a moral sense.
[13]Jung, *Collected Works*, vol. 10, par. 260.

The Ba accuses him of looking after the "good" like a steward—one feels he means like a miser—after his treasures. After all, good and evil are only human abstractions, and the man is projecting human standards onto the Ba, who understandably enough refuses this appeal to overlook what the man regards as his sins, or rather he dismisses it as unimportant. As we shall see, the World-Weary Man's *only* idea of sin is failing to observe the rites prescribed by dogma, and the Ba's interests lie elsewhere, which becomes increasingly clear as the text continues.

The man, who does not yet understand the Ba, seems only to hear this reference to the "good" and he answers, "Yes, that is exactly what I am interested in: the good." He sees this as equivalent to the correct funeral rites and an ordered existence in the Beyond. He declares that he has not yet entered the Beyond precisely because this question is not settled. The man emphasizes that he is no robber, there is nothing brutal about him, and goes on with an attempt to bribe the Ba to consent to the suicide by promising him the most punctilious fulfillment of the funeral rites, so that his Ba will be envied by all the other Bas. He threatens the Ba with having no home in the Beyond if he lets the man be driven to death without helping him.

The modern equivalent to this speech would be one of us telling her animus or his anima that if he or she would only consent to do something just our way, he would at once be in such a lovely position that the animus of Mrs. Smith or the anima of Mr. Jones would be green with envy!

The World-Weary Man is again trying to control his Ba with dogmatic opinions about the Beyond. Since the Ba belongs to the unseen reality, it is obvious that the man is teaching his grandmother to suck eggs. He is hopelessly mixed up: he wants the Ba to settle the question of suicide, which is a question of this world where he must take the responsibility himself, and he wants to dictate to the Ba about the next world, which is a reality entirely beyond his comprehension.

On the other hand, and I want to emphasize this, the man is exceedingly right to defend his conscious point of view to the last ditch and *not* to give in to the Ba until he is really convinced. He went too far, but we can only learn by trial and error. The main reason that this text is so valuable, from the standpoint of modern active imagination, is that it represents a real *Auseinandersetzung* between conscious and unconscious.[14] Both defend their own standpoint with the greatest energy.

[14]"Having it out with and beginning to come to terms."

The Ba answers:

When you think of the funeral—that is sentimentality; it is producing tears in making people unhappy; basically it is fetching man out of the house in order to throw him on the hill . . . then you can no longer rise upward in order to see the light of the sun.

The Ba goes on to tell the man that the dead who had every rite fulfilled and beautiful granite pyramids built are not necessarily one bit better off than the weary ones; that is, those who die on the bank of the river and decay there without survivors or any funeral rites.

The Ba ends:

Now listen to me! Behold, it is good when men listen. Follow the beautiful day and forget your sorrow!

Evidently, the Egyptian religion was becoming stereotyped; the water of life was no longer contained in it, for the Ba definitely states here that the funeral rites alone are useless. He is not against them; he simply tells the man that putting his whole faith in them is useless and ridiculous.

Dr. Jacobsohn points out that the Ba is voicing a doubt that was just surfacing in the unconscious at that time: whether or not the traditional ceremonies were still an absolute value.[15] Probably it was this doubt that was behind the whole upheaval of the time, just as a doubt whether the Christian attitude to evil is still valid might be said to be behind most of our own modern disturbances. Fundamentally, the Ba spoke of the danger of depending on things outside ourselves.

I wish to remind you that active imagination represents a sort of give-and-take between conscious and unconscious. In our text, it is definitely the Ba who wishes to teach the man something he does not know. In the next text, this is reversed: it is the man who wishes to teach the anima. The World-Weary Man, as we have seen, tries to teach his Ba, but his efforts are to a great extent a failure, for it is the Ba who has the greater truth.

The sting of the Ba's sarcasm in his comments about the sentimentality of the man's attitude must have been a considerable shock to the World-Weary Man. The Ba is telling the man that he is practicing the wrong kind of active imagination; he is indulging in sentimentality and self-pity. This gives us a valuable hint as to the danger of this kind of indulgence, for the Ba says outright that if he goes on like this, he is already dead in this life and will never be able to come up again into the

[15]Jacobsohn, *Timeless Documents of the Soul.*

"light of the sun." The point is that you bewitch yourself by such indulgence in the wrong kind of fantasy; you lose touch with reality and you have a bad effect on yourself and other people. If the man had not eventually listened to the Ba, he would have spun himself into these unreal fantasies and inevitably, he would have perished. Moreover, we must not forget that the man emphasized that he declares that he is not brutal, yet he planned to kill himself. The opposite of brutality is always sentimentality.

Rauschning tells us in his book *Hitler Speaks* that Hitler—who could sign orders for the entire population of villages to be shot—cried for a whole afternoon over the death of his favorite canary.[16] And the pictures of him kissing babies, which were sometimes published in the Swiss papers, were absolutely sickening.

The final sentences of the Ba's speech are particularly impressive: "Now listen to me! Behold it is good when men listen. Follow the beautiful day and forget your sorrow."

This insistence on listening is very positive and useful to us today. We still find it difficult to listen to the real voice of the unconscious. We always deceive ourselves, thinking that it does not want to talk to us, but far more often we do not want to listen. We have our pet fictions about ourselves, which we do not want to give up, and basically we simply lose our nerve, for it requires real heroism to face the inexorable reality of the unconscious.

When the Ba says, "Follow the beautiful day and forget your sorrow," he is drawing attention to the vital importance of the here-and-now. There is a wonderful description of this "here-and-now" in Jung's seminar on *Thus Spake Zarathustra*.[17] I can only mention briefly what Jung said—that when we are *really* in the here-and-now, we are complete, and that is the most difficult and the most terrifying thing to be, but also the most worthwhile. The World-Weary Man evidently has no idea of the importance of the here-and-now or he could not even think of throwing his life away. The Ba challenges him first to become a man and then to become whole.

Either the Ba gave the man no time to reply to this speech or he did not react to it, for the Ba goes on to tell him two parables. These are very interesting and meaningful, so I will quote them in full.

16Hermann Rauschning, *Hitler Speaks* (London: Thornton Butterworth, Ltd., 1939).
17C. G. Jung, "Psychological Analysis of Nietzche's *Thus Spake Zarathustra*" (Private seminar given in Zürich during the 1930's).

The First Parable of the Ba

A man cultivates his plot of land. Then he ships his harvest and begins his voyage. His festival approaches after he has seen a storm come up one night (and after he) has kept watch on the ship at the time of sunset and (after he) has escaped with his wife, while his child has perished on the water that was treacherous in the night of the crocodiles. For at the end (of this experience) he sat there, recovered his speech and said: "I have not wept on account of the girl. She cannot return again from the West to the earth. But I mourn for her children who were (already) broken in the egg and who have seen the face of the crocodile god even before they have lived." [18]

In this case, the Ba uses symbolical language to help the man see what he could not directly understand. These parables are like the cinema flashes which suddenly break in on our own active imagination—too suddenly for us to play a part—or a dream which comes to correct or elucidate our active imagination.

Because there are no associations, such as there would be with a living dreamer, we must take up the context of the themes; space, however, forbids me to do this as thoroughly as I should. I will only mention that since Egypt was an agricultural land, the harvest is an especially important symbol there. As is well known, the god Osiris was very much connected with the crops. Africa is the land of storms, so when an African speaks of a storm, he means something terrific. The ship represents something built by human skill—a human way of getting about. One still speaks of the ship of the Church, for example.

The crocodile god plays a great role in the Egyptian religion. It is a most paradoxical god, highly positive in the days of our World-Weary Man, though afterwards it was identified with both Osiris and Set, his destroyer. One meaning of Sobek, the crocodile god, which is particularly important for us is that he gathers up the scattered pieces of the dead Osiris and united them again into a whole. The crocodile itself, on the other hand, was a great danger to the Egyptian of every age.

Evidently, the man in the parable is meant as an image of the World-Weary Man himself. Presumably, he is represented as a merchant because he has a one-sided attitude: he looks after the good as a steward after his treasures. The man is shown as having loaded all his harvest onto one boat; i.e., put all his eggs in one basket. Since the symbol of

[18]Jacobsohn, *Timeless Documents of the Soul.*

grain is so closely connected with Osiris—and the deceased were said to be reborn as Osiris in the Beyond—the Ba is evidently showing the World-Weary Man that he is risking the other world as well as this one by his attitude.

The storm is evidently an allusion to the tremendous emotional upheaval that the man is undergoing. The wind is the cause, and, as a symbol of mind and spirit, a brainstorm is probably a correct interpretation of its meaning. The man thinks he is making a calm and stoic decision to leave this life, but the real state of affairs in his unconscious is shown in the parable. The same idea is reinforced later in his grief, which even bereaves him of speech.

He is escaping with his wife, whom Dr. Jacobsohn takes as the Ba. This hypothesis is confirmed in the second parable. Since the Ba is a masculine figure in Egypt, he must have a reason for representing himself as a woman. As previously mentioned, the Ba is always translated as the "soul," and though, as we shall see, he turns out to be much more than the man's anima, he is perhaps introducing the World-Weary Man to the idea that the human soul is feminine. In fact, as Marie-Louise von Franz first pointed out to me, we can go further and say that the Ba is introducing the man to the whole principle of relationship and that he appears as a woman to show the man how he could relate to the Ba. Moreover, our man is blind to the feeling values; he is, for example, quite blind to the value of life which the Ba understands so well. And he is showing the man that not only can the Ba have a totally different opinion, but that he is as different from a human being as a woman is from a man.

We cannot consider the wife in the parable without the daughter, who perished in the shipwreck. This daughter seems to represent a more individual aspect of the anima; she is the man's daughter as well as the Ba's. The Ba was a recognized figure in the Egyptian religion and therefore, to some extent a collective figure, whereas the daughter is more representative of the man's own anima. She symbolizes the possibility of a truly individual realization and is in the greatest danger from the man's unrealized emotions. This is the moment of possible renewal, so it is terribly dangerous for him to be unaware of what is happening. The man does not think of suicide as death, but as moving on to a certain and better life; the Ba, however, is saying: "No more illusions; this is real, for heaven's sake; look out!"

The night of the crocodiles could be compared to Jacob meeting the dark side of God at the ford. Jacob held on until the light side appeared and blessed him.[19] It is a common idea with primitives that a dark and evil god rules the night and a light and benevolent god, the day.

We find the same idea in a magic papyrus translated by Preisendanz: the sun god rises as a scarab, flies upward as a hawk, and turns every hour into a new symbol, ending, as the sun sets, with the crocodile.[20]

But it is not the loss of the harvest, nor even of the daughter, which drives the man in the parable to despair, but the loss of the unborn children "already broken in the egg."

We should undoubtedly interpret these children as a yet-unborn possibility, as Jacobsohn himself does, which is in the greatest danger. The Ba, as the wife in this parable, represents the eternal, universal Self, which can never be destroyed. The girl is the individual field between man and Ba, produced by their contact. The Self can be born in the individual, and the children represent the seed of the whole process of individuation. This symbol contains the essence of the parable: the Ba has been constellated in this life and that is a great deal to accomplish, but not enough. This parable shows us very beautifully that everything will be lost if this unknown product of man and Ba cannot come into existence.

The Ba tears the veils away from the World-Weary Man's eyes: while he is chattering about funeral rites and about other Bas being jealous of his, the result of his whole life is in danger and will certainly be lost unless he can come to his senses before it is too late.

But all the same, the parable does not end on a wholly pessimistic note. We must remember that the crocodile god was an exceedingly positive deity in the time of the World-Weary Man, with the attribute of being able to gather the scattered pieces and join them into a whole again. Egyptologist Brugsch tells us that its figurative meaning is that of pulling oneself together, becoming quiet and relaxed, gathering up one's courage.[21]

When Jung arrived in East Africa, an old settler approached him at a railway station and, after asking if Jung were new to Africa, offered to

[19]*Genesis* 32:22–28.
[20]Karl Preisendanz, ed., *Papyri Graecae magicae*, 2 vols. (Stuttgart, 1973).
[21]H. Brugsch, *Geographische Inschriften Altägyptische Denkmaler* (Ger.) 1860 text ed.

give him a piece of advice. When Jung accepted gratefully, he said, "This is God's country, not man's country, and if things go wrong, just sit down and don't worry."

If the man can see his own wild emotions, understand the parable and, above all, give up the wrong way and learn the right way of doing active imagination, there is still a good chance that he may be able to rescue the situation, if, in the words of the old settler in Africa, he can sit down and not worry.

The Second Parable of the Ba

A man asks his wife for an evening snack, but his wife says to him: "Come first to supper." Upon which he goes out in order to sulk(?) for a time and then returns home in that he is like another while his wife is experienced for him: namely, that he is not capable of hearing her, but just sulked, with a heart empty for messages.[22]

This parable seems simple, but I found it exceedingly difficult to understand. It begins at the end of the first parable, where only the man and his wife were saved.

I must anticipate here and tell you that in the concluding speech of the Ba, it becomes clear that the Ba's goal is to teach the man to establish a common home for them both. This parable is the first appearance of this home, depicted in simple, domestic language. Evidently, it represents the limits of the man's individual existence; the frame in which man and Ba, ego and Self, can meet. A house, particularly an old house, is a very common symbol of the Self in dreams. It is the intimate realm, the introverted side, yet it also reaches into the outer world.

The bone of contention is surprising: the man wants a tidbit, while his wife insists on a whole supper. He behaves like a child who insists on the dessert at the beginning of the meal. It is possible that the Ba is referring to his idea of suicide, of wanting the joys of the Beyond ahead of time. This impatience in the matter of waiting until things have had time to ripen in our unconscious is often very evident in our own active imagination. As the *Rosarium* says: "All haste is of the devil"[23]—words which Jung frequently quoted. Moreover, the man would eat the snack alone, whereas he would eat the supper with his wife, which brings in the idea of communion, of relationship, of eros.

This parable shows the situation between conscious and unconscious

---

[22]Jacobsohn, *Timeless Documents of the Soul.*
[23]*Rosarium philosophorum, Artis auriferae,* vol. 2 (Basel, 1593), pp. 204–384.

in a very meaningful way. The unconscious prepares the supper, the *cibus immortalis,* the whole and eternal food, whereas the conscious always looks at this food in a one-sided way and wants silly snacks instead of eating the whole supper of a meaningful life. We are inclined to covet reasonable, rational things, whereas the roots of the Self are usually highly irrational.

The "going out to sulk" is a wonderful picture of what we always do when the unconscious serves us a supper which we do not like. We go out of ourselves; we leave our home, our mandala. We get emotional and are "beside ourselves."

Jung often said that basically, we are always deceiving ourselves when we say we do not know what to do about this or that. Somewhere we know quite well, but *we do not want to do it.* It took me years to see that this is the truth, for the idea that we do not know is deeply rooted. As the Chinese say: "There is a sage in every one of us (the one who does know what to do) but men will never steadfastly believe it, so the whole thing has remained buried." The supper is there for us, as it was for the World-Weary Man, but we still do not want to eat it.

The phrase, "while his wife is experienced for him," is, as Dr. Jacobsohn says, quite true in outer life.[24] Just where a man is weak, his wife is usually strong. This may be even truer of the unconscious: where we are weak, it is strong. It is in finding the compensating truth in the unconscious that active imagination is of the greatest use. But the man's difficulty is seeing the wife's point of view, just as we have the greatest difficulty in seeing the completely different point of view of the unconscious.

The parable ends by pointing out that the man was not capable of hearing his wife, having a heart empty for messages. The reader will remember that the Ba had previously drawn his attention to this theme: "Behold, it is good when men *listen.*" Fundamentally, the parable ends with a direct appeal to the man to continue his active imagination, but with a different attitude: to practice true active imagination, to make a tremendous effort to *listen* to the voice of the unconscious. He is told that his indulgence is merely sentimental and unreal, and this is having a terrible result: he cannot hear the truth and he has a heart empty for messages.

The World-Weary Man replies:

[24]Jacobsohn, *Timeless Documents of the Soul.*

Then I opened my mouth to my Ba in order to answer what he had said:
Behold, stinking is my name for your sake (more literally: because of your
existence), more than the stink of guano (bird manure) (?) on summer
days when the sky glows.

The beginning of his reply is then repeated in order to express his
horror at himself. The parables have at last opened his eyes and—in a
typical enantiodromia—he takes the opposite viewpoint. At first, he
thought that the Ba was doing something more horrible than exaggeration could represent; now he sees himself as entirely in the wrong. This
is a very common reaction when we first see our shortcomings and
mistakes; we are in danger of throwing the baby out with the bath
water.

The interesting point, however, is that the man gets away with it. He
is able to see himself with his name defiled without breaking down
because of the existence of the Ba. The name meant even more to the
ancient Egyptians than it does to us, as Dr. Jacobsohn points out, for
when the name was destroyed on a monument, it was believed that the
very substance of the deceased was wiped out.[25] The World-Weary Man
was evidently a man who could see his dark side without collapsing. It is
very interesting that he always says "for your sake," which could also—
as Dr. Jacobsohn says—be translated as "on your behalf" or "because
of your existence."[26] It is absolutely amazing that this man—brought
up in the traditional Egyptian religion, over 4000 years ago—should
realize the essence of Jungian morality today; namely, that we are
responsible for knowing of the Self's existence within us. Not knowing
this is really the arch sin. As the reader will remember, the Ba was not
interested in the man's ordinary sins—that turns out to be a projection
of the individual, dogmatic conscience onto the Ba—but the Ba is vitally
interested in being recognized and understood. He wants the World-
Weary Man to listen to him. And throughout this speech, it is clear that
the World-Weary Man has at last gotten the point.

The first five analogies, which the man uses to show that he realizes
he has defiled his name, have all to do with fishing or manure. This is
psychologically of the greatest interest, for it is in manure, in the
products which we have not been able to assimilate, that the seed of the

25Ibid.
26Ibid.

Self can grow. Moreover, it is often said in alchemy that the philosophical gold, the lapis, the precious thing, is to be found on the dunghill. As you know, dreams of feces and lavatories are very common and often refer to creative material that has not been properly realized. These sentences, therefore, anticipate things which are appearing again today, thousands of years later.

The similes which concern fishing are also highly psychological, for when we see and accept our shortcomings and mistakes, as the World-Weary Man does, and above all when we realize the empirical existence of the unconscious, we are at last in a position to fish up contents of the unconscious which we did not know existed before.

The following similes are also highly interesting. The World-Weary Man compares the bad smell of his name to lies that are being circulated about a woman. The Ba has represented himself as a woman, even as the man's wife; therefore this simile presumably refers to the Ba. We must remember that, in the days of the World-Weary Man, the dogma declared that the Ba played no role at all in a man's life until *after* his death. Therefore, our man is in a most vulnerable position, such as that which a woman often meets in her most precious relationship: she may find lies being circulated about her at any moment. It would be said of him, for example, that he is crazy, because he thinks he can talk to his Ba during his lifetime, and even claims to have an intimate relationship with him, such as a man has with a woman. Therefore it is very necessary for him to keep the whole relationship secret, just as Jung says we are still forced to do when we experience the unconscious at a deep level.[27]

The World-Weary Man then compares himself to a defiant child who is forced to belong to someone he hates, a comparison that exactly describes his first attitude toward finding that he already belonged to the Ba in this world.

In his last simile he speaks of a treacherous and rebellious city seeing itself from *outside,* which is fundamentally a comparison of the man's own attitude to the Ba. So far, he has been an unconscious inhabitant of this rebellious city, but at last he begins to see himself objectively. Yet paradoxically enough—for the city is also a symbol of the Self—he is still outside the home, like the man in the second parable.

Regarded as a piece of active imagination, this speech, with all its

[27]Jung, *Collected Works,* vol. 12, par. 57.

similes, shows an enormous advancement when one compares it with the previous speeches of the man. These former utterances showed complete ignorance of the Ba's point of view, or even that he had one at all, and were in no sense active imagination; the man simply instructed the Ba and projected his own dogmatic opinions onto him. The chief merit in the first part of the text—and this is an enormous merit—is that the man succeeded in objectifying his Ba and in recording what he had said. This corresponds to the first part of the work necessary in active imagination: collecting material from the unconscious and learning to let things happen.

But in the speech which we have just been considering, the matter is entirely different. Not only has he obviously allowed the astonishing material in the parables to work on him and *transform* him, for his whole attitude is fundamentally changed, but he is also allowing the unconscious to penetrate his own statements, as we can see in the extraordinary meaningfulness of the similes which he employs, similes which took thousands of years to mature and which are still relatively unknown today. If this speech were a part of our own active imagination, it would take us a long time to digest it, for it comes from both the conscious and the unconscious. It is a classic example of active imagination as it should be done.

In this advanced stage of active imagination, the conscious attitude keeps its line; he wishes to tell the Ba that he has realized his sins *toward him,* not toward collectivity, and that he is completely ashamed of himself. This attitude is actively and undeviatingly retained. Every sentence begins with it. But when he searches in his mind for new comparisons to explain his horror, it is clear that he allows the unconscious to pour in, for the conscious could never find such meaningful parallels that had taken thousands of years to mature.

If this were an active imagination produced by one of us, we would have to think very carefully about it before we could begin to understand it. It is excellent material with which to lay the foundation of the transcendent function, for it comes from both conscious and unconscious.

The World-Weary Man has assimilated something of the Ba here, for his style has become more like the latter's; he lets meaningful analogies pour out in a sort of parable form. Moreover, he has gained something of the objective spirit of the Ba, and the transcendent function is clearly forming between the two.

Dr. Jacobsohn ends his comment on the first reply by emphasizing that the World-Weary Man has gained confidence in his Ba, as well as a new sense of responsibility toward him, and that he goes on in the next speech to explain why he does not yet see a possibility of renouncing his wish to commit suicide.

The man begins this speech by saying:

To whom shall I still speak today? The brethren are evil, the friends of today are without love.

Each subsequent section also begins with the words: "To whom shall I still speak today?" and goes on to complain that everyone is avaricious, insolent, evil, a robber, unjust and so on. He can find no one who is mild and good, so he has no confidant and is lonely beyond measure.

No doubt there is still a certain amount of inflation and projection in this speech, but we must remember the days in which he lived and not judge him by modern standards.

The loneliness presumably comes from the invasion of the Ba, for as Jung points out in *Psychology and Alchemy*, "Such invasions are uncanny . . . They bring about a serious alteration in the personality because they immediately form a painful personal secret which alienates the human being from his environment and isolates him."[28]

The Ba has put an end to greed and power as goals worth living for, but the man is not yet sufficiently liberated from them to prevent him from resenting the same things in other people. Even 2000 years later, Christianity preached *leaving* the world, so we would be seeking an impossibility of our man if we expected him to stand the impact of the world with impunity.

But the fact that he explains his outer conditions to the Ba is very important to us, for we still find ourselves obliged to tell the unconscious about our outer conditions, and in extremity, to explain that we have reached the limit of our endurance. If we say this too soon, woe betide us, but if we are *really* at the limit of our endurance, the unconscious will hear us and often change its course. We must never forget that active imagination is a give-and-take; we must both listen to our unconscious—"Behold, it is good when men listen"—and give it the necessary information from our conscious side.

That this is absolutely necessary was once demonstrated to me during

---

[28]Ibid., cf. R. F. C. Hull translation.

a conversation with my animus. He suddenly said, to my great surprise: "We are in a very awkward position, linked together like Siamese twins, yet in totally different realities." He then explained to me that our reality is as invisible to him as his is to us. Therefore, in our efforts to see the reality of the unconscious, we must never forget to help it to see ours. Just as the man could not see the Ba's point of view at first, so the Ba also was unable to see why outer life had become so intolerable to our man, until it was explained to him in the next two replies. Jung also sometimes had to call a halt when the creative urge pushed him too far —to a point that was more than his health could stand.

In his third reply to the Ba, the World-Weary Man explains that death is standing today before his eyes like returning health to a sick man, like the scent of the lotus, like the end of bad weather, like a return from war, like a liberation from prison, and so on.

He then makes several profound statements as to the condition of the deceased in the Beyond, of which I will only quote the first:

> *Whoever is there, he will surely be a living god, and ward off the sacrilege of those who commit it.*

This is a most profound psychological statement, although we should no longer entirely project it into the Beyond, for it can be realized to some extent in this world. In psychological language, it would depict a condition of exchanging the ego for the Self, or, in the language of Jung, submitting our lives to our Number Two personality, instead of shortsightedly always wanting the way of the ego (the snacks) preferred by Number One.[29] The Self has divine qualities in which we can participate, but with which we must never identify.

The fact that the man speaks of actually becoming a living god belongs to the Egyptian dogma, which taught that everyone whose heart passed the test of being weighed became an Osiris in the Beyond. The danger of inflation was much less in those days, when ego personality was less developed, and the fact that it was entirely projected into the Beyond was a safeguard in this respect. In modern times, however, it is necessary for man to remember that "he is only the stable in which the god is born," as Jung put it.

Although the World-Weary Man uses such strong images to depict how he feels about death, basically he remembers the Ba's earlier

---

[29]Jung, *Memories, Dreams, Reflections,* passim.

advice: he follows the beautiful day and forgets his sorrow. However, he still projects it all into the Beyond. He has burst the bonds of his narrow consciousness, but whether he can sacrifice his idea of suicide is another matter, to which we shall return later.

I will quote the whole of the Ba's short concluding speech, for it is vitally important:

> *Now leave the complaint to itself, you, who belong to me, my brother! You may weigh down (further) the basin of fire*[30] *or you may embrace (more literally, snuggle up to) life again, whichever you would now say: Wish that I may remain here when you have refused the West, or wish also that you reach the West and your body goes to the earth, and that I may settle down after you have died: in any case, we shall have a home together.*

Here the Ba reveals himself beyond all doubt as the individual essence of this particular man; as the Self. It seems to me that the World-Weary Man's terrific effort to explain himself to his Ba in his last three replies have had an effect on the Ba. In one point, indeed, the Ba remains adamant: "Leave the complaint to itself." If the man regressed into a sentimental, self-pitying indulgence in the wrong kind of fantasy, he could still lose all he had gained, which applies to us today. Self-pity is in itself an involuntary and erroneous kind of imagination; fundamentally everything that we meet on our way through life belongs to our totality, to the whole of our supper, and must be accepted as such.

Undoubtedly, the Ba has also been affected by the man; for the first time, he accepts the possibility that it may be impossible for the man to continue his life. As Dr. Jacobsohn points out, it is true that one feels the Ba would greatly prefer the man to go on living; in fact, there is no alternative unless it is *really* impossible. But, at all events, the one vitally important point is that the Ba and the man should be together, whether in this world or the next.[31]

The development of the Ba in the Pyramid Texts, and which is also clearly visible in our text, reminds one of the development which is often to be seen in the psychic material of a present-day individual. When we first confront the unconscious, everything is contaminated with everything else; "all cats are grey in the dark," as Jung used to say.

[30]That is: "die of your sorrow." Just the "weighing down the basin of fire" shows clearly that it is a matter of a figurative expression.
[31]Jacobsohn, *Timeless Documents of the Soul.*

Then, as we grow accustomed to the dark, we begin to discern one figure from another. In our text, the figure of the Ba was at first anima, soul and Self. But at the end, he is clearly the Self, the Number Two personality.

When we face the unconscious for the first time, one of the most bewildering things is the contamination between shadow, animus or anima, and the Self. In fact, the animus or anima really owes its autonomous power entirely to the fact that it is able to stand between our consciousness and the Self.

In this early text, however, there is really no sign of the anima as a possessing daemon. Our man's horrified reaction to his first two speeches, however, shows that his initial feelings about the Ba were like those we have when the animus or anima interferes and brings our conscious plans to naught. In the Pyramid Texts, moreover, the Ba only reveals his true nature as the Self after his union with the universal knowledge.

In his "Commentary On 'The Secret of the Golden Flower,' " Jung points out that his experience in analyzing had taught him that the problems of his patients were seldom solved on their own terms, but that he had seen many patients who simply outgrew their problems.[32] The problems just faded out in contrast to a new, higher and wider interest. They appeared in a different light and now seemed like viewing a storm in a valley from a mountain top. But since, in respect to the psyche, we are both mountain and valley, it would be a vain illusion to feel ourselves above human emotions. We are still tormented by them, although we are no longer identical with them, for we have become aware of a higher consciousness which can look at the situation objectively and say: "I *know* that I suffer."

It seems to me that the net result of this old Egyptian piece of active imagination is just this: the man grew above his problem. It is not solved on its own terms, for he is still suffering from the conflict in his last speech. But he has become aware of a higher consciousness within him.

The Ba emphasizes the far more urgent need to wish for a common home, whether it be here or in the Beyond. He evidently feels that he will no longer go out to sulk, as in the second parable. The daughter and the unborn children in the first parable are not mentioned again, for they were an anticipation of a remote future of mankind. I feel that the

[32]Jung, *Collected Works*, vol. 13, pars. 1–82.

man would have done the most he could do if he had succeeded in establishing the common home for himself and his Ba. Moreover, the fact that he recorded this piece of active imagination was a notable achievement at that time—or, in fact, at any time—which can hardly be exaggerated.

A very instructive contrast to our text can be found in a little-known book by James Hogg, the Ettrick Shepherd, entitled *The Memoirs and Confessions of a Justified Sinner*.[33] Like our text, it is the story of a man who is confronted by a superhuman figure. In Hogg's book, the figure is called Gil Martin, who first appears in the exact likeness of himself. But Robert, the representative of the ego in the story, has a most despicable character from the beginning; he is mean, a liar and intolerably inflated, in contrast to the World-Weary Man who, although he did not understand the Ba at first, was obviously a most honorable man of complete integrity. Therefore Gil Martin, unlike the Ba, becomes more and more negative, even infernal, as the story progresses. He ends by possessing Robert entirely, persuading him to commit several murders, culminating in that of his brother and later of his mother. But Robert— and this is the point that I want to emphasize—makes no attempt to take a stand even against the suggestion of murder. He cannot say, as he is most certainly obliged to do, that as a human being he cannot possibly put an end to another human life. Apparently, Gil Martin gets it his own way, but that this is not at all what he really wants is shown in the most interesting sentence in the book. When Robert's sins catch up with him and he sees no possible solution but suicide, Gil Martin says to him: ''I have attached myself to your wayward fortune, and it has been my ruin as well as thine.''

Jung called Hogg's book ''the British *Faust*''!

[33]James Hogg, *The Memoirs and Confessions of a Justified Sinner* (London: The Cresset Press, 1947).

CHAPTER 6

An Early-Twelfth Century Example of
Active Imagination
Hugh de St. Victor's Conversation with His Anima

Before we begin with our material, I would like to make it clear that I will be concerned with this text only from the standpoint of active imagination. I will not touch upon its theological aspects, for that would not only lead me out of my own depths but also away from that which I feel is the main psychological interest of the material.

As I mentioned before, I originally worked on this text for my first seminar on active imagination in 1951, at which time I compared it with the conversation between the World-Weary Man and his Ba (see Chapter 5). The two texts form a most interesting contrast: the one shows how a man can hold his ground when something overwhelming breaks in on him from the unconscious, the other, how it is possible to influence the unconscious when one is wholly convinced—as Hugh de St. Victor evidently was—that this is necessary.

In the Egyptian case, consciousness was still extremely weak. The ego was just emerging from a complete *participation mystique* with the collective pattern. In our medieval text, the ego is infinitely stronger; in fact, it would be possible to contend that the ego is too strong and wins too complete a victory over the soul. We suffer today from both tendencies; therefore, I regard both these texts as enormously valuable parallels in considering active imagination. On the one hand, when we touch archetypal material directly, we are always in danger of being drowned in it, thereby losing our hard-won consciousness; on the other, our ego is inclined to be far too stiff and unbending in our attitude toward the unconscious.

Our text comes from the early twelfth century and is a conversation between a monk, Hugh de St. Victor, and his soul. I must mention his background very briefly. In 1108, William de Champeaux, a well-known Parisian theologian, wearied by his quarrels with his pupil, the famous Abelard, retired from his professorship in Paris and restored a ruined monastery on the Seine which was dedicated to St. Victor of Marseilles. Champeaux originally intended to devote himself and his monks entirely to the love of God and to have nothing more to do with scholastic science. But he was soon persuaded that science was also one of the highest services of God, and St. Victor's flourished as a center of science and religion.

Three monks who were particularly famous were Richard de St. Victor, Adam de St. Victor, and Hugh de St. Victor. Richard de St. Victor, a Scotsman, was the subject of a lecture by Jung in 1940.[1] In Richard's interesting *Benjamin Minor,* he compares knowledge of oneself to the Mountain of Transfiguration, for he, like all the Victorines, regarded knowing oneself as the "summit of knowledge."[2] Adam de St. Victor, a Frenchman from Brittany, wrote some very beautiful spiritual poems. Hugh de St. Victor, a German from Saxony and the most famous of all, left a great many writings, including our text of his conversation with his soul.

Very little is known of Hugh de St. Victor's early life. Until the eighteenth century, his origin had been forgotten and legend had attributed him a French, Flemish and even a Roman ancestry. In 1745, his real background was rediscovered in the Halberstadt manuscripts. (His uncle was Bishop of Halberstadt.) Hugh belonged to the German aristocracy, being the son, or possibly the nephew, of the Saxon Count of Blankenburg. When he was still under 20 years of age, Hugh left a Germany that had been torn by the dissentions between Emperor and Pope, and went to France, where he remained for the rest of his life. He

[1]Eidgenössische Technische Hochschule (E.T.H.) Lectures (1933–1941), 6 vols. Privately printed. Vol. 5, pp. 23–28; 1st ed., pp. 18–23.
[2]Richard de St. Victor, *Benjamin Minor.*

studied first in Paris, then went to St. Victor's at Marseilles. The exact year that he moved to St. Victor on the Seine is unknown, but he was given a professorship in 1125, and in 1133, the whole of the studies at the monastery was placed under his care. He died in February 1141, at the age of 44.

He was not only an exceptionally learned man, but he was also very good at getting along with his fellow men. His friends said with pride that religion and life were wonderfully united in him, but we also hear that he was exceedingly critical. Evidently, he found St. Paul's admonition to "suffer fools gladly" by no means congenial! Although he knew so much, we are told that he regarded knowledge as the "vestibule of the mystic life."[3] But Paul Wolff tells us that in the case of the Victorines, it is really not possible to separate the mystic from the theologian and philosopher, for the Victorine idea of the term *mystic* was very much wider than was the case with the mystics of the fourteenth and fifteenth centuries.[4] Everything that was symbolic or hidden in a symbol was called mystical at St. Victor. They regarded the whole world and everything that was in it as a symbol of God. Hugh used to exhort his students to learn everything they could, assuring them that in later life, they would find that nothing was superfluous.

Hugh began contemplation with the world because, as he says, the eternal word is revealed by contemplation of creation. The word itself is invisible, but it has become visible and can be seen in the works of the creator. The world is a book written by the finger of God, and each creature is a letter of God, so to speak. Therefore, mortal man, when he looks at the world, is like an illiterate man who looks at a printed page, for it conveys no sense to him. He only sees the outer forms, but has no eyes for the eternal idea expressed in it. It is, therefore, man's duty to learn to read the book of the world.

According to Hugh, nature and grace are the two ways by which man can reach God: the sign of nature is the visible world; the sign of grace is the incarnation of the eternal word. Man stands between angel and animal; the former sees only the spiritual side of reality, and the latter, only the outer reality. Man alone can see both. Soul and body are attached to each other by sense perception; the soul participates in the spiritual life of God through the idea.

The Victorines were both mystical and scientific. Hugh in particular

---

[3]*Encyclopedia Britannica*, 11th ed., s.v. "St. Victor."
[4]Paul Wolff, *Die Viktoriner: Mystische Schriften* (Vienna: Thomas Verlag Jakob Hegner, 1936), p. 16.

was always anxious to keep philological exactness and mystical interpretation together, for the latter would become altogether too speculative if the exact text were ever overlooked.

I have only related a bare minimum from the life and teaching of Hugh de St. Victor—just enough to give some idea of the soil from which our text arose, for it is the active imagination itself which is the most important thing for us.

In medieval times, the existence of the soul as an autonomous, independent being is no longer a shock, as it was to the World-Weary Man, for the soul has emerged from the unconscious and was an established fact for the twelfth century monk. The Self—or at all events, the light side of the Self—appears separated from the soul, as her bridegroom, Christ. The soul is regarded as entirely feminine, so it can be said to be identical with the psychological anima.

Such conversations are a form which is by no means rare in the Middle Ages. But, as far as my limited knowledge goes, they are usually an uninteresting, conscious device. It is quite possible that part of the answers of the soul in our conversation also arises from theological assumptions concerning the *anima naturalis,* and are therefore not wholly genuine. But the conversation takes so many unexpected turns that it seems impossible to doubt that the anima often slips in spontaneous material from the unconscious.

In the Egyptian text, it was the Ba, representing both the soul and the Self, who played the leading role and who changed the man, whereas in this text, it is the man who plays the leading role and who changes the soul. The man places himself on the side of the Self, of Christ, and is thus able to convince his soul to a great extent. She is allowed, however, and this is very unusual in such texts, to talk quite freely. She expresses her doubts as to the truth of his statements, as well as her extreme dislike to them. Hugh has a very definite program—the program of the Victorines—to disentangle his soul from the world and to make her one-pointed toward God. That the text strives only upward toward the light belongs to the time; it was the age when Norman architecture, with its comparatively low, rough arch, was giving way to the high, pointed arch of the Gothic style.

The text gives us a very graphic picture of how man can influence the unconscious. Jung once pointed out that the practice of any kind of magical influence or suggestion is only in its right place *when used on our own unconscious.* The people of Hugh's age were much more conscious of magical effects than we are—they did not doubt that words and thoughts had an effect both on themselves and on their environment. Therefore, Hugh attempted to use the magical effect which necessarily emanates from thought and word, *in the service of God* to prevent it from becoming daemonic, as it will when it is used consciously or unconsciously in the service of the ego. Psychologically, this is obviously exceedingly sound; it is using the forces of our psyche for the sake of the whole, instead of making the part—the ego—the enemy of the whole psyche by its personal greed.

Naturally, from our point of view, the dark is too repressed, although it is by no means wholly lacking. Medieval man was much nearer to the instincts than we are, and the way to greater consciousness therefore naturally led *upward*. Hugh of St. Victor's great insistence on philological accuracy gives us a hint of how there could have been no science, for instance, if man had not learned to be accurate and undeviatingly honest.

Every movement becomes one-sided if it is persisted in too long, but we must not let the fact that the cause of wholeness in the modern world demands an attitude which includes much more of the dark side of man, prejudice us in considering this text—a text which follows the Christian program of differentiation of the white in accordance with the age to which it belongs. Incidentally, we can also get a startling idea from it of how much we all still think in medieval terms. What was natural for Hugh in the twelfth century has, to a great extent, become a lazy habit with many of us today.

Summary of Text and Commentary

The title of the text is:

DE ARRHA ANIMAE
Conversation Concerning
the Betrothal Gift (or Dowry) of the Soul
Dialogue Between a Man and His Soul[5]

The man opens the conversation; it is undertaken at his initiative. He tells his soul that their conversation will be entirely confidential, so that

[5]Only the main points in the text are given, translated from the German in *Die Viktoriner: Mystische Schriften*. An English translation by Sherwood Taylor also exists, but there are no striking differences between the German and English translations.

he will not be afraid to ask the most secret things and she will not be ashamed to answer quite honestly.

Hugh goes on to ask her what it is that she loves most. He knows that she cannot live without love, but what has she chosen as the most worthy object of love? He goes through a long list of all the beautiful things of the world, such as gold, jewels, colors, and so on. Does she love any one thing above everything else? Or has she put such things behind her, in which case she must love something else, and if so, what?

This opening speech seems to show that Hugh is on much firmer ground than most of us would be when we speak to our anima or animus, for he has not only realized his soul as a vis-à-vis, but also that her field is eros, relationship and love, and that his own is logos, discrimination and knowledge. He speaks as a man would speak to a woman. He knows that she must attach herself to something, that she must love, and that she will remain in a complete *participation mystique* with the outer world unless he does something about it.

It would be rare, I think, to find a man today who had objectified his eros side and personified her to this extent, and who could set out to use his mind to differentiate his feeling by beginning such a conversation with his anima! It would be rare to find such a man, and almost impossible to find a woman who could achieve this differentiation between her own field and that of her animus. The fact that our civilization is patriarchal obviously makes it more difficult for women. We speak a masculine language and are so accustomed to saying, "I think," that it is very difficult to objectify the animus and to realize that often we should be much nearer the mark if we said, "He thinks in me." It is not difficult to know this theoretically, but it is very hard to put it into practice. If we can do so, however, we are for the first time in a position to consider whether we really say "Yes" or "No" to our own thoughts and words.

Jung recommended this as an actual technique for women who were trying to know their animus. He told me to think over any important conversation at a later time, trying to remember exactly what I had said, and then to consider if I would say the same again. If not, I should determine what had made me give an opinion, or say this or that, which was not what I really had thought. Further, I should try to catch the thoughts that passed through my mind and apply the same procedure to them.

I do not know whether he recommended the same technique to men with regard to their feeling. Men probably say, "I feel," much less often than women say, "I think," but they certainly also identify with their feeling exactly as women do with their thought.

Therefore it is striking that Hugh marks such a clear line between the realm of his thought and the realm of his anima, and sticks to this firm piece of ground throughout the text. We can learn a great deal from him which could be of the greatest use in our own active imagination.

The soul replies that she cannot love what she does not see; she has never been able to exclude anything which she can see from her love, but she has not yet found anything to love above everything else. Then she complains that she has already learned that the love of this world is disappointing; either she loses what she loves through its decay, or something she likes better comes in between and she feels bound to change. Thus, her desire still vacillates—she can neither live without love nor find the true love.

It was clear from Hugh's first question that his mind had already learned to see the eternal ideas behind the visible object. Remember, he taught that the world was God's book and that the human being is illiterate when he cannot read this book. It is clear from her answer that his own soul belongs to the illiterate and that she is caught in the *concupiscentia*—she has, as yet, no individual qualities, constancy or discrimination. Naturally, Hugh's feeling life would lack the differentiation of his mind.

This reply reveals a man whose anima would project herself indiscriminately, from one woman to the next. If he had not been a monk with a fixed program and, above all, if he had not made this amazing effort to objectify his anima, Hugh would obviously have been possessed by her and would have followed her peregrinations in a completely unconscious way. Presumably, this tendency was one of the reasons that drove him into this conversation. She is, however, not quite identical with this condition; she is rather an old soul, so to speak, and has already learned something from disillusionment.

Jung always said that there was not enough scientific proof of reincarnation for us to be sure there was any such thing. It was certainly a fact, however, that people's souls were of very different ages. Many people had to spend their whole lives learning things that were self-evident to others. Hugh's soul already knows that the love of temporal things is disappointing, which is something that many souls do not seem to know at all. In these materialistic days, I am afraid one could say that it is something the vast majority does not know, either in the conscious mind, where Hugh had evidently known it for years, or in the unconscious soul.

Hugh seizes on this point and tells her in his next speech that he is glad she is not entirely imprisoned in the love of worldly things. It would be worse if she had made her home in them, for now she is only a homeless wanderer and can still be recalled onto the right path. But she will never find eternal love while she yields to the attraction of the visible.

Hugh makes his philosophy very clear, calling forth an indignant protest from the soul: how can anything invisible be loved? If there is no true, eternal love in tangible and visible things, then every lover is doomed to eternal misery. How could anyone be called a man who, forgetting his human nature and disdaining the bond of community, only loved himself in a lonely and deplorable manner? Therefore, she says, Hugh must either consent to her love of the visible or produce something better.

This seems to be a strikingly clear description—given by the soul herself—of the way the anima is entangled in the external world: the Indian Maya, the dancer. It agrees with Jung's latest description of the anima in *Aion*.[6] The anima is an autonomous figure in Hugh and does not scruple to attack him in a way that reminds one of the Ba's remark: "Are you alive at all?" There is, of course, a lot to be said for her point of view; to a great extent, monastic life is a denial of the outer realization of the anima. We know nothing of Hugh's mother, but the mothers of his two great contemporaries, Norbert and Bernard of Clairvaux, certainly played a role in their sons becoming monks. During her pregnancy, Norbert's mother dreamed that she gave birth to a great archbishop, and Bernard's mother, that she gave birth to a dog that filled the world with its barking. A Churchman interpreted this dream to her at the time, saying that her son would be a great preacher. Since Hugh became a monk before he left Germany, when he was still under 20, we may be sure that he also had a significant mother complex.

Comparing the Ba's and the soul's attacks on the two men, we find that the Ba protests in a wholly constructive manner against the man throwing away his individual life, whereas the soul speaks from a more collective standpoint, saying "Don't do anything about yourself; it is

[6]C. G. Jung, *Aion: Researches Into the Phenomenology of the Self*, vol. 9, part i, *Collected Works* (Princeton: Princeton University Press, 1968), pars. 20–26.

morbid." It is therefore a more destructive nuance, for the general idea is that looking inwardly at yourself is morbid.

But at the end, she challenges him, as we read in *Aion* that the anima always challenges a man with her dangerous quality, in an effort to bring out his greatness.[7] He must produce something better if he wants her to give up the world.

Very intelligently, Hugh meets this danger by turning the tables and telling her that her own beauty transcends by far that of the world; if she could only see herself, she would see how foolish it is to love anything outside; and he sings a hymn of praise to her beauty.

This clever, if somewhat unscrupulous, appeal to feminine vanity is evidently partly designed to take the wind out of her sails by suggesting that he is autoerotic—that he only loves himself with a lonely and deplorable love. (One should remark in passing that it is possible, since he is so impressed by her beauty, that this active imagination was visual as well as auditory; i.e., that Hugh may have seen his soul—with the eyes of his mind, as Dorn expresses it[8]—while he was talking to her.)

If Hugh had been talking to an exterior woman, this speech would certainly have been unscrupulous, because of the dangerous magical effect which emanates from flattery. But, as Jung has pointed out, magic—which certainly includes flattery—is only in its right place when used on our own unconscious, and Hugh was talking to his anima.

But he evidently spreads the butter too thickly, for she is in no way impressed (in German, *er redet an ihr vorbei*). She replies coldly that one can see everything except oneself and that she is justified in calling anyone foolish who wishes to enjoy his love by looking in the mirror. He must give her a different kind of mirror if he wants anything of that kind. Love cannot endure in loneliness and is not love at all if it is not poured on a suitable companion.

It is becoming very clear that the soul is as extraverted as he is introverted, as is indeed only to be expected. It is useless to talk in the way Hugh is talking to an extravert, for at first all looking within strikes them as purely morbid and autoerotic. Moreover, from her point of view she is quite right; relationship to other people is indispensable. They might have argued this point forever, like the Gnostic text translated by

[7]Ibid.
[8]Gerhard Dorn, "Speculativa philosophia," *Theatrum Chemicum*, I, p. 275.

Mead in which Christ and John the Baptist can never reach a decision as to whether the mysteries should be given to the world or not.[9]

The important point in this speech seems to be that the soul asks him for *a different kind of mirror,* for this amounts to a confession that she requires the light of his consciousness; if he does not give it to her, she will remain stuck fast in the world. This point is of the greatest importance to the theme of active imagination, for it shows us that passive watching and listening are wholly insufficient. Only if we give the utmost from the conscious as well, can anything significant be achieved.

We find the same realization of the anima needing human consciousness in the Devatas (anima figures) of Buddha. I will quote two short examples:[10]

Sutra Three: Standing at the side, the Devata repeated the following lines to the Blessed One (Buddha):

> *Existence passes, short are life's days,*
> *No further protection has he who approaches old age.*
> *So keeping the danger of death before one's eyes,*
> *Surely one should work for merit and happiness to arise.*

The Blessed One replies:

> *Existence passes, short are life's days,*
> *No further protection has he who approaches old age.*
> *So keeping the dangers of death before one's eyes,*
> *One should surely look on eternal peace and avoid the lures of the world which entice!*

[9]George Robert Stow Mead, ed. and trans., *Thrice Greatest Hermes,* 3 vols. (London: 1949).

George Robert Stow Mead, *A Mithraic Ritual,* (Echoes of the Gnosis Series), (London: 1907).

[10]Jung, E. T. H. Lectures, vol. 3, pp. 86ff; 1st ed., pp. 98ff.

Note the difference in the last lines. Buddha is saying much the same to his Devata as Hugh does to his soul.

In Sutra Two we find:

One Devata says to   *Dost thou not know, fool, the word of the*
another (who has   *Perfect One?*
spoken ignorantly):   *Transient verily are all forms,*
                                            They are subject to the laws of appearance
                                                and disappearance;
                                            They arise and vanish again;
                                            To bring them to an end is blessed.

It is interesting that Buddha, some 1600 years before, should have to teach his anima very much as Hugh does in our text, and as any man who held such a conversation today with his anima would still have to do.

Hugh takes up the soul's challenge in a very long speech. He begins with the statement that no one is lonely if God is with him, and that love is only strengthened when the desire for worthless things is subdued. Then he insists on the necessity for self-knowledge, and that she must first realize her own value in order not to dishonor herself by loving anything less worthy. He tells her that she knows love is fire, and that everything depends on what fuel is thrown on this fire, for she will inevitably become like everything which she loves.

Then Hugh takes over a bit of her own style and tells her bluntly that her face is not invisible to herself and that her eye can see nothing until it can see itself; only the transparency necessary for this self-contemplation will prevent delusive phantoms from darkening her vision of everything else.

These statements are a sort of prologue to Hugh's real thesis. He tells her some profound psychological truths, presumably hoping that some of the seed will fall on fertile ground and take root later, for, if he had stopped here, I doubt that she would have been more impressed than before. As you know, we often do not understand a psychological truth when we first hear it; we store it somewhere, however, and it will often emerge, even years afterward, and very frequently as our own idea! For the most part, it seems that Hugh merely throws his bread on the waters.

In the last sentence, Hugh insists that the soul *can* see herself and that her eye will never see anything clearly until she does. He is evidently warning her against the danger of projection. We might further suggest that he tries, like an alchemist, to force his extraverted anima to become the transparent lapis, to internalize her forces and thus to transform them, by coagulation, into the indestructible crystal or diamond.

He goes on to tell her that if she cannot see herself, she should consider an outside opinion. (He plays on a previous remark of hers that, while rejecting the idea of being able to see herself, "man learns to know his own face" by the "ear rather than by the eye.") Then, for the first time, he mentions her bridegroom and tells her that though she has not seen him, he has seen and loved her. He loves her with a unique love, Hugh says, but she ignores and despises it. If she cannot see him, she should consider his gifts as her dowry. He then enumerates these gifts: everything that she loves in the visible world.

Then he scolds her severely for taking the visible gifts and ignoring the concealed giver. She must beware or she will rightly be called a whore and not a bride, he says, if she accepts presents and does not return them with love—if she prefers the gifts to the love of the giver. She must either refuse the gifts or reciprocate by giving a unique love to the bridegroom who gives them. This is the only pure love.

Hugh accepts her challenge of providing a different mirror. He is wisely giving her an object to love and trying to prove His existence by showing Him as the invisible giver of all things that she can see and appreciate.

In Church language, this bridegroom is Christ or God; in psychological language, the Self. Hugh is doing that which we can do to depotentiate a too-powerful anima or animus: he is doing his utmost to place her in the service of the Self. Fundamentally, the conflict between a man and his anima, or a woman and her animus, is insoluble, for they represent the most basic pair of opposites: male and female. Therefore, almost the only hope of a solution is to grow above the problem, as is so particularly expressed in *The Secret of the Golden Flower,* mentioned at the end of "The World-Weary Man," Chapter 5. In Jung's commentary, we hear that an insoluble problem is seldom solved on its own terms; rather, it loses its urgency through the dawning of a new way of life. Hugh is attempting such a solution, just as the Ba did not solve the World-Weary Man's problem on its own terms, but showed him something more important: a common home with the Ba.

Hugh and his soul can only be reconciled in the Self: "God is a union of opposites," as Nicholas Cusanus says.[11]

Hugh de St. Victor's mind is well aware of this fact, but his anima is not. She is too deeply entangled in the world of the senses, so his only hope is to use a language which she can understand, slowly bringing her to the knowledge of the existence of a uniter of opposites. Very wisely, he gives up all attempts to take away the world she loves, but makes use of it to prove his point by representing it as the gift of a bridegroom who loves her with a unique love.

At this point, I would like to mention a modern dream which shows the same problem from the woman's point of view. It is part of a very interesting series which illustrates the conflict between the collective point of view of the animus and the intensely personal standpoint of the shadow. It is worth mentioning that the dreamer was not in analysis, which means that the material is then often more naive and complete.

This dreamer was constantly torn in two between an inexorably severe animus who usually appeared in her dreams as a monk or a priest, and a passionate, childish shadow who appeared as a child or an excitable, emotional woman. On the one side, she had to accept all the remonstrances of the just, but inexorable, animus; on the other, she had to lower herself to the level of the shadow, *against* the express orders of the priest.

In the dream, she was obliged to remain standing in the presence of the priest, but nevertheless sank down onto a bench beside the despairing woman. She says that she did not forget her clearly realized obligation to remain standing, nor did she act from defiance, but she was compelled by a compassion greater than herself to sit down beside this woman. When she looked at the priest, she saw mercy in his face, but she knew he would punish her severely for what she had done. When the tension was at its height, she found herself in a great cathedral with the priest behind her and the woman whom she had befriended in front of her. Evidently, they were awaiting some sort of judgment or decision. At last a voice was heard, coming from behind and above the priest. They all listened in both fear and gladness to this voice, which was as majestic as the cathedral itself. The voice was full of compassion, yet the judgment was severe: If the child (or passionate woman) recovered from her wounds, the dreamer might go her way in peace, but if not. . . . The

[11]Jung, *Collected Works,* vol. 8 par. 406. Cf. vol. 14 par. 200.

dreamer could not hear the alternative, but the inference was that it was a sentence of death. Severest justice was thus tempered with mercy in a way which could be accepted by them all.

To return to our text, we come now to the Soul's answer. She tells Hugh that the sweetness of his words have set her on fire, although she has never seen this bridegroom whom he praises so highly. From his description alone, however, she almost feels obliged to love him. But there is a drawback which will dampen her happiness unless it can be removed by his consoling hand.

Hugh has produced an almost magical effect on the soul. His words have set her afire. She does not yet grasp the great psychological truth which he has told her about the Self, for she is still a superficial extravert; she is charmed by the words themselves and not by the idea behind them. However, she also seems to see the danger of their magic, which she turns back on him. She emphasizes the charm of his words and his consoling hand in an effort to inflate him, a favorite trick of both anima and animus for which we must always be on guard in active imagination. As autonomous daimons, they keep their power largely by producing inflation and inferiority; they use these weapons ruthlessly and in a way that is difficult to detect. If she manages to inflate Hugh, so that he begins to think, "*I* am doing it; what a fine fellow *I* am," she will have him in her pocket, and that is a power which the anima and animus— as far as my experience goes—never quite surrender. At the slightest provocation, they try it again.

Hugh says he is wholly confident that there is nothing in the love of her bridegroom which could possibly diminish her pleasure, but in order that it shall no longer seem as if he wanted to deceive her, he begs her to reveal her difficulties to him.

Hugh is no fool. He avoids her trap very cleverly; he admits that it might seem as if he were deceiving her for his own ego purposes. In fact, I have the feeling that he probably examined his own conscience on the subject very carefully at this point.

One must not forget that, although the conversation is written as if it took place at one sitting, this is by no means the case. These conversations demand the whole man and need a great deal of thought. I sometimes continue them over a considerable period of time and often contemplate a move of my vis-à-vis for quite some time before I can see what he is driving at, or before I can see the right answer.

As Jung has often pointed out, there is either no time or a completely different concept of time in the unconscious, so that it is often possible to take up the same theme with the same vis-à-vis later. But these things have a tendency to sink down again into the unconscious, so that any *unnecessary* delay or excuse is always fatal. I want to emphasize that such a conversation requires one's utmost effort, however we give it. It was only by reducing himself to his human dimensions, by seeing the danger that he might deceive her for his own purposes, that Hugh avoided his anima's trap. We must constantly remember how small we are in such conversations with these more or less eternal figures.

The soul then explains her difficulty at considerable length. Although she admits the gifts of the bridegroom are great, she sees nothing unique about them, for she must share them with other people and even with the animals. It is very unfair to expect her to love her bridegroom exclusively when there is no sign that he exclusively loves her. She says that Hugh knows this perfectly well and must show her where the uniqueness exists.

This is an example of highly feminine psychology. Every woman, and presumably every anima, harbors this demand for exclusiveness. (Jung used to tell the story of an insane woman at Burghölzli who shouted in chapel: "He is my Christ and you are all whores!") Any woman who is honest with herself can find this same demand somewhere within herself, although it is usually projected onto a real man who then has to suffer, in some way or other, from her exclusive possessiveness.

This speech confirms our suspicion that the anima was trying to lead Hugh down the garden path with her flattery, for at this point, she clearly loves her own way a great deal more than her bridegroom. This demand to be the only loved one is fundamentally one of power, not love. To some extent, Hugh has clearly sacrificed a conscious ego-power will, but here he discovers that his eros, his feeling life, his anima, is going on in the same old way. People often tell you, if you suggest that they are clinging passionately to this or that, "Oh, no, I have sacrificed it completely." This may be quite true on the conscious level, but this example shows us that if we think that is enough, we have made out the bill without the host. By his intelligent handling of the situation, Hugh is finding out just what the anima is.

Hugh answers his anima very cleverly again by telling her that he is not angry with her, for evidently she is really searching for perfect love. He does not criticize the negative in her speech, but emphasizes the positive, like a husband might say, "Darling, you are quite right; I see your motives are above reproach," as a prologue to a large BUT. If Hugh had not been a monk, he seems to have had some qualifications for being a successful husband!

Hugh continues with a long attempt to bring some discrimination into his feeling life, dividing the bridegroom's gifts, for instance, into three classes: those that are common to all; those that are special gifts shared with a limited number of other people; and those that are unique gifts. But this speech cuts no ice with the anima, who tells him he has rejected, rather than uprooted, her difficulties, so I mention it only to show the extraordinary complexity of such conversations. Hugh tries an approach with purely rational arguments, which does not impress her at all. She is no longer under the magic spell of his words and, like a woman, insists on *facts*.

He continues, however, along the same lines, in spite of her protest. He only begins to impress her when he starts a description—founded on fact—about what this unique love really is. I will quote the two most important passages in full:

> *Love may be happiness alone, but it is far greater if one can rejoice in the happiness of many. For spiritual love becomes greater in the individual if it is common to all. It does not decrease when it is shared, for its fruit is to be found unique and undivided in every individual.*

In other words, her exclusive right to unique love sets no limits to the amount of people with whom she shares this spiritual love. She need not fear that the heart of her bridegroom will be torn apart, as in human passion, for it is whole and undivided everywhere. Hugh continues:

> *All must therefore love the one with a unique love, for all are loved uniquely and should love each other[12] in the one as if they were one and through the love of the one they should become one.*

Alchemy is full of references to the subject of *one*, but space forbids me to repeat them here. Basically, the "One" in alchemy and the "One" to which Hugh refers here are, of course, symbols of the archetype of the Self.

In "Psychology of the Transference," Jung quotes Origen as saying: "Thou seest that he (man) who seemeth to be one is not one, but as many (different) persons appear in him as he hath velleities (self-willed

---

[12]Alternative translation: "should love themselves."

impulses)." Therefore the goal of the Christian, according to Origen, is to become an inwardly united man; to become one.[13]

There is also a parallel in the Brihadaranyaka Upanishad that is so near to our text that I cannot resist quoting a few lines from it:

Yagnavalkya says:

Verily, a husband is not dear that you may love the husband; but that you may love the Self, therefore a husband is dear.

Verily, a wife is not dear that you may love the wife; but that you may love the Self, therefore a wife is dear.

This is then repeated of all the things which men love and the passage ends: "Verily, everything is not dear that you may love everything; but that you may love the Self, therefore everything is dear."[14]

To us, the meaning of this text is found mainly in our experience. It is most evident, especially for women and also in our text, in relationship. We all know that no human relationship is *total*. We can share this or that with so-and-so, something else with someone else, and so on. We often feel split up, faithless, or torn between our relationships. But when we begin to feel a certain loyalty to our own unconscious, to something that is infinitely larger than our ego, we begin to realize something of this loyalty to the One, to the Self, which Hugh describes in religious language as loyalty to the bridegroom of the soul, and we begin to see that he is simply describing a *psychological fact*.

This is sometimes very clear in the transference. All the worst difficulties in the transference are usually signposts that lead toward the experience of the psychological Self. The analyst has the task of standing firm and, through consultation with his own unconscious, giving each patient what belongs to him or her in the *One*, no more and no less. And the patient has the task of accepting the suffering involved in the sacrifice of his egotistical demands, possibly and instead of learning to know the *One* in whom alone the solution of the problem can be found. And very often, the most help can be found by *both sides* in active imagination.

At the beginning of her reply, the soul again refers to the charm of Hugh's explanations. She says that for their sake, she begins to feel more ardor in pursuit of this love which, without them, was beginning to sicken her. Then she becomes more practical and says that she must

[13]Jung, *Collected Works,* vol. 16, par. 397.
[14]*The Upanishads* (Oxford: Oxford University Press), vol. 1, pp. 109f.

be shown that this love is truly effective. She will doubt it no longer if she can see from its practical effect that it is genuine.

Although she still feels the charm of his words, they no longer satisfy her. They had their use in inducing her to listen at all, but now Hugh must produce *facts*. This reaction of the soul exactly agrees with our experience of the unconscious; it has an exceedingly empirical standpoint, and suggestion has no lasting effect on it. It does indeed at times react to suggestion, but it will always turn around in the end and demand *facts*.

The main point which Hugh makes in a very long reply to the soul is that the bridegroom has not only given her existence, but a beautiful and formed existence, and moreover, a resemblance to himself.

This is an exceedingly important point which contains the whole idea of individuation. This "beautifully formed existence" is presumably the unique form which each of us has the chance of bringing into reality. It is indeed given to us, yet we have the choice of whether we bring it into reality or not. Jung compared it more than once to the framework of a crystal, but whether this framework hardens into a crystal depends, to some extent at least, on ourselves.

There is a passage in Jacob Böhme in which he speaks of God having a "subtle body," but that Lucifer lost this body when he fell from heaven. Jung once said of the passage that one can take this idea of a body symbolically as meaning an individual shape or form. According to Böhme, the devil has renounced his individual form; that is, he will not submit to the process of individuation. Therefore, in our text it would be fatal if the soul followed the devil's example and renounced this gift of the bridegroom, this "beautifully formed existence"; in other words, it would be fatal if she refused the process of individuation.[15]

The next point which Hugh makes is that not only has the bridegroom given her a beautifully formed existence, but also a resemblance to himself.

In *Psychology and Alchemy,* Jung says:

> The intimacy of the relationship between God and the soul excludes every depreciation of the latter from the outset.[16] It would perhaps be going too far to speak of a kinship, but in any case the soul must have a

[15]*The Works of Jacob Behmen,* trans. and ed. by G. Ward and T. Langcake, 4 vols. (London 1764–81).
[16]The fact that the devil can also take possession of the soul does not lessen its significance in any way.

means of relating (in other words, something which corresponds to the
Divine Being) in itself, or a connection could never take place.[17] *Formu-*
lated psychologically, the corresponding factor is the archetype of the
image of God.[18]

This "something in ourselves which corresponds to the Divine Being"
is formulated by Hugh de St. Victor as the resemblance of the soul to
God. In this text, we touch on the terrific paradox of our close relationship to the divine aspect of the Self with which we can never identify
without the most disastrous inflation. There was perhaps less danger of
this inflation in Hugh's time, for throughout the text all the action is
attributed to God, and the soul is the mere recipient of His gifts.

The alchemistic idea that the redemption of something divine
depends on man is by no means wholly lacking in our text, although the
main emphasis is naturally always put on the efficacy of God. But one
could also say that the goal of this whole conversation—freeing the soul
from her entanglement in, or even identity with, the world—is the basic
goal of the alchemists: liberating something divine from the darkness of
matter. This idea is particularly clear when the soul is reminded of her
likeness to God. We owe this suggestion of the alchemistic side of this
idea to Hugh's exceedingly scientific mind, which did not hesitate to
admit the actual state of his soul as revealed in this conversation.

He continues by telling her that, by means of this love, she has been
given four gifts. Interestingly, these four gifts are an exact description of
the four functions. The two rational functions are even so described in
words: "feeling" and "discrimination," the chief quality of the
"thinking" function. Suitably enough, the two irrational functions are
described more irrationally: "sensation," as her being decked *outwardly*
with the jewels of the senses, and "intuition," as her *inward* "garment
of wisdom." This seems to be yet another proof of the archetypal
character of Jung's four functions: Hugh clearly discovered them in the
twelfth century in this most genuine talk with his soul. Then, quite
suddenly, Hugh turns on his soul and scolds her, telling her she has
deserted her bridegroom, degraded her love with strangers, squandered
his gifts—in short, she is no longer a bride; she has "become a whore."

[17]Therefore, psychologically it is wholly inconceivable that God could be a "totally
different entity," for a "totally different entity" could never be as close to the soul as
God actually is. Only paradoxes, or rather antinomies, are psychologically correct as
expressions for the image of God.
[18]Cf. Hull's translation in Jung's *Collected Works*, vol. 12, par. 11.

Up to this point, the soul has said nothing for pages, except most appreciatively begging him to continue, so this sudden, violent attack gives one quite a shock. Presumably, Hugh realizes that she is not understanding him. In passages too long to quote, he has been getting more and more into a ''you-should'' tone; probably he feels insecure and therefore challenges the resistance of his soul with considerable emotion. Perhaps he had risen a bit above himself with his contemplation of the Divine and is suddenly furious that he cannot control half of his functions.

In a confession which he makes later, Hugh identifies himself with his soul and takes some of the blame for her shortcomings. Therefore, his sudden and unexpected burst of fury may be anger at his own failings. Violent emotion concerning the faults of others is practically always caused by a projection, for the weakness that really gets under our skin is *always our own.*

We should perhaps consider for a moment what it was in everyday life that induced Hugh to begin this conversation with his soul. She is represented as entangled in the world, so worldly aims and ambitions probably played a considerable part in Hugh's psychology and were obviously incompatible with his inward goal. In spite of, or perhaps because of, the rather condescending tone which Hugh sometimes uses toward his soul, especially in this outbreak of emotion, one can detect the man who is terrified of being possessed by his anima. One could imagine that he constantly caught himself in little—or big—plots with a worldly aim. There must have been some powerful motivating force behind such a genuine attempt to come to terms with his anima. He forms an interesting contrast in this respect to Father Joseph in Huxley's *Grey Eminence,* who could never sacrifice his anima's lust for worldly power.[19]

On the other hand, it is possible that Hugh is intentionally letting out anger which he could control, in order to give his soul a shock aimed at waking her from her unconsciousness. In an interesting discussion on this point, Jung said that the game was always lost if one lost one's temper in a discussion. Mrs. Jung retorted that sometimes anger was the right reaction and that he had said so himself. Jung replied that that was quite true, but *only* if one could just as well *control* one's anger. If one let the anger get the upper hand, it was always a mistake. We can only judge this point by the effect of the outbreak on the soul.

She replies to Hugh in a way that shows she is deeply offended. She

[19]Aldous L. Huxley, *Grey Eminence* (New York & London: Harper & Brothers, 1941).

had hoped that his hymn of praise was leading to another goal, but she sees that he only undertook it to create an opportunity to show her how hateful she is. Therefore she wishes that the conversation had never taken place and that it should now be shrouded in forgetfulness if suspicion has no pity on the guilty.

Hugh has nearly lost everything he has gained, for the soul begins to wish that the whole conversation could be forgotten; in other words, she is thinking of returning to the unconscious. In our own active imagination, we can never afford to forget how easily such figures disappear, and from the standpoint of feeling, Hugh has made a big mistake. He was getting perilously near an animus language: you should and you should not. Evidently, the anima resents this even more than a woman would; in fact, when one remembers how near the anima is to nature, the wonder is that she stood so much.

We are touching on the problem of our whole Christian inheritance from the Middle Ages. Medieval man was forced, from the absolute necessity of differentiating the white at all costs, to be very hard on himself. A great many modern people still function in exactly the same way; they find it very difficult to forgive themselves anything. But it is dangerous not to be able to forgive yourself. Christ said, "Love your neighbor *as yourself*,"[20] and we cannot really love or forgive our neighbors—no matter how we may deceive ourselves on this point—until we can love and forgive ourselves. The animus is a great deceiver on this point and loves to emphasize how unpardonably we have behaved. I found I had to learn to say to him often: "Don't be in such a hurry; perhaps I was wrong, but let us wait and see how the situation develops *before* I worry too much about it."

Hugh's outburst was certainly threatening, for he is in danger of losing all contact with the anima. All the same, it may have been necessary to take energetic measures in order to wake her up to her own shortcomings for, since she did not see her own beauty, presumably she was also blind to her own ugly qualities. Such things are sometimes inevitable, but it is a case of Scylla and Charybdis: if we say too much, we break the contact, and if we say too little, we have no chance of influencing or changing these figures.

It is clear from his extensive reply that Hugh saw the danger of losing her, for he hastens to assure her that he had no intention of heaping

---

[20]Italics mine.

blame upon her, and that he only spoke for her instruction. His intention was to show her how great the love of her bridegroom was, for it was
in no way affected by her faults. On the contrary, when her bridegroom
saw her lost in sins, he descended to the human level himself in order to
redeem her.

Hugh thus cleverly turns the tables on the soul. By emphasizing how
greatly she is loved, she falls under the fascination of this idea again,
and we hear no more about her desire to forget the conversation.
Psychologically, the ego once again abdicates in favor of the Self. Hugh
sacrifices his all-too-human anger at the shortcomings of his anima,
placing the matter in the hands of the Self.

The soul replies by saying that she is beginning to love her guilt, and
even blesses it, for she sees that it has drawn forth the love which she
now so passionately desires in order to wash it away. Then she turns from
Hugh and addresses her bridegroom directly for the first time, asking
him what he found in her to love her even to death.

The soul thereby compensates Hugh's purely moral standpoint, and
it seems that her wisdom greatly exceeds his. He has put the whole
emphasis on the white, but she sees that such a total love could only be
constellated by *both* opposites, and that it was the black in her that
called it forth. It seems highly significant that she turns for the first time
to her bridegroom as if it were something one could hardly expect Hugh
to understand.

We find this same idea in the works of Meister Eckhart, nearly a
hundred years later. He emphasized that the grace of God could only be
experienced by those who know the whole misery of being lost in sin,
and he pointed out that all the apostles were therefore particularly great
sinners. This idea was evidently already in the air in the time of Hugh de
St. Victor, though we do not know how far it really broke through into
his consciousness. At all events, in his blessedly scientific accuracy, he
faithfully records what his soul says, although at first only as a sort of
conversation among archetypes.

Once the soul has gained this firm piece of ground, she quite calmly
allows Hugh to scold her as much as he likes, which he does at considerable length. She gets a bit bored only occasionally and interrupts him
from time to time to beg him to tell her more about this fascinating
love.

The dialogue is interrupted by a very interesting confession which
Hugh addresses directly to God and in which he makes himself respon-

sible for all the sins he has hitherto attributed to the soul. He gives
thanks for the unique gifts which have been given to him, saying, for
instance, that God has left many of his contemporaries in the darkness
of ignorance, whereas Hugh has been especially favored with illumina-
tion by which he can recognize God's wishes. He has thus been able to
know God more truly and to love Him more purely, believe in Him
more honestly and follow Him more ardently than his contemporaries.
He gives thanks for the special gifts he has received: susceptible senses,
great intelligence, good memory, ease and charm of speech, convincing
knowledge, success in his work, charm in dealing with his fellow men,
progress in his studies, persistence, and so on.

Since this confession begins by acknowledging as his own the sins
which his anima committed, Hugh is very wise to draw his attention to
the corresponding positive qualities. When we realize our negative
qualities, we are too apt to forget their opposites. Yet the human psyche
—like everything else—is always double: positive and negative.

After this confession, the soul makes a long speech in which she recognizes the right of this love to be called unique, even though it is simultaneously universal. It even seems to her as if her bridegroom had
nothing else to do than look after her salvation. She makes a concession
to Hugh's point of view by regretting her sins, and she sees that they
have now become a hindrance in learning to be a receptacle for this
longed-for love.

Then one of the most interesting things in the whole text happens.
Hugh announces that a miracle has occurred and says:

> I see how you—since the beginning of our talk—have put much that
> seemed opposed to love in the center and have thus not weakened the
> power of love but increasingly strengthened it.

No sooner does she give in than Hugh also takes over something of
her point of view; now it is no longer a conversation among archetypes,
but a direct admission on Hugh's part that all he has so disliked in her
has *strengthened,* and not weakened, this love. Just as the World-Weary
Man took over something of the Ba in his last speeches, so Hugh—
though to a much smaller degree—takes over something of his soul.
Putting things in the center has, of course, the significance of making
them conscious, giving them to the Self, instead of keeping them in a
corner as private sins, and in time, forgetting them altogether.

These mutual concessions have an immediate practical effect, for the soul asks him one last question: Is it her bridegroom who touches her *tangibly* at times, so tender and yet with such strength that she feels completely changed?

This subtle substance which touches the soul is very often mentioned in alchemy. The *Rosarium Philosophorum,* for instance, tells us that some masters have seen the secret and even touched it with their hands.[21] And the alchemists frequently say that "we speak of what we know and bear witness to what we have seen." Jung has often pointed out that the alchemists only wrote for those who have experienced such things and made no attempt to explain the matter to those who have not. This passage in our text touches on this whole problem and on the problem of rebirth, but it would lead us too far off our path to do more than mention this fact.

Hugh answers by telling his soul that it is indeed her bridegroom who thus touches her, but only as a foretaste of what is yet to come. He is still intangible and invisible to her and she often even believes him to be absent, so she cannot yet possess him. Hugh then implores her to recognize, love, follow, grasp and possess the *One*. The text ends with the soul's declaration that this is now her greatest wish.

Conclusion

The text ends with an almost complete victory of the man over the soul—such a complete victory that one is left with a lurking doubt as to whether it is not a bit too good to be true. Undoubtedly, this is largely a matter of the time when the direction toward consciousness led upward toward the light. Nevertheless, there were very negative elements about in the twelfth century: among others, the struggle between Emperor and Pope, which involved the destruction of whole cities; the amazing parapsychological phenomena which took place during the founding of the Premonstratention Order near Laon, only about eighty miles from St. Victor; and the actual murder of the Prior Thomas at St. Victor, all during Hugh's residence there.

Naturally, the ego of a man of Hugh's Christian convictions was one-sided concerning the opposites. He must have believed in doing good and avoiding evil. But the Self in all ages contains *both* opposites, as the God of the Old Testament shows clearly. "God is a union of oppo-

---

[21]*Rosarium philosophorum*, p. 205; Jung, *Eranos* 1938, p. 46.

sites,'' as Nicholas Cusanus says.[22] The deepest reason that the Ba was so successful in the Egyptian text, and Hugh so successful in this conversation, was that both were on the side of the totality of the human personality, of the Self. The Ba did all he could to persuade the World-Weary Man to give up his attempt to separate himself from the totality by a foolish and ill-considered suicide. He forced the man into increasing misery until he was able to see that the totality, the union with his Ba, was the only important issue and to grow above the problem of life or death.

With Hugh de St. Victor, it was the man who was on the side of this totality, which was really the sole reason for his success. He never persisted in putting an ego demand on his soul. As we saw, the whole thing was in danger at the slightest suggestion of him doing so. According to his knowledge and as far as as he could see at that time, he used his brilliant mind to detach his undifferentiated feeling from its split-up condition in the world, where no doubt it worked itself out as the self-willed impulses which Origen had already seen as the great barrier to man becoming one with the Self.

Just as the Egyptian text shows us how a man can behave when some archetypal figure from the unconscious breaks in on his consciousness, whether he likes it or not, and how he can have it out and eventually come to terms with it, so the Hugh de St. Victor text shows us how it is possible *to intervene*, by means of active imagination, when we are constantly tripped up by some unconscious tendency of our own. In spite of, or perhaps because of, the very condescending tone which Hugh sometimes uses towards his soul, it is easy to detect the man who is terrified of being possessed by his anima. But, and this cannot be emphasized too often, he was successful only because he always sacrificed his own ego-power wishes. I remind the reader, for instance, of the time when he was so angry that he could not control his soul and suddenly criticized her unmercifully. If he had continued in such a power attitude, he would have lost her altogether. There is nothing the unconscious resents more than a power attitude on the part of the ego. When we consider how much was said by his contemporaries, and in his own confession, about Hugh's charm with his fellow men, we realize that getting his own way must have been child's play to him. Therefore,

[22]Jung, *Collected Works,* vol. 8 par. 406. Cf. vol. 14 par. 200.

it is all the more meritorious that he sacrificed it so completely in this conversation.

In this connection, we must also not forget the early age at which Hugh died, hinting that his life may have been based on the pattern of Abel's, the light son of the Father,[23] and that his destiny thus spared him anything like the confrontation with evil which dogged the footsteps, for instance, of his great contemporary Norbert.[24] We need to know more than we do concerning *why* Hugh died so early.

When Hugh admitted that everything he had so much disliked in his soul had strengthened, rather than weakened, the power of love, he had perhaps made the utmost concession which could have been expected of him and, as *pars pro toto,* he thus opened the way to a genuine reconciliation between man and anima. We must not forget that Hugh was a very critical man and therefore probably inclined to negative assumptions concerning imperfections—by negative assumptions I mean overhasty judgments which do not wait to see how a situation will develop, but which immediately assume the worst. We have seen this tendency at work in the conversation between Hugh and his soul: at the beginning, for instance, the anima assumed that Hugh was autoerotic and that the Victorine insistence on self-knowledge was merely morbid. Hugh constantly assumes the worst about his soul; not only does he liken her to a whore more than once, but there are pages of negative criticism, sometimes based on what seems to be very insufficient evidence. "All good to God and all evil to man"—or, in this case, to man's soul.

The opposite of negative assumptions is giving credit, "the benefit of the doubt," as we say. (Jung even once defined love as "giving credit.") This cannot have been easy for a critical man like Hugh, particularly in regard to his own soul. Since he talks so much about love, we may be fairly sure that it is no natural gift in him, but something which he tries to attain with great effort. It seems to me that he does attain it himself—probably for the first time in the conversation—when he gives his soul the credit for having increased this love by putting things which he personally dislikes in the center. This may appear to be a small concession to the dark side but—perhaps on account of his early death—it seems to have been sufficient, for it is followed immediately by the

[23]*Genesis* 4:1–16.
[24]*Micropaedia,* vol. 7 (Chicago: Encyclopaedia Britannica, Inc. 1943–73).

tangible evidence of the bridegroom's existence, which finally convinces the soul.

But if it were a too one-sided solution, the matter would certainly have come up again, at any rate had Hugh lived longer, as it always does in our own active imagination when the solution is too superficial, or when it does not allow enough room for one side or the other.

Whatever our opinion on these points may be, I hope that this conversation illustrates the extraordinary difficulty of such talks with the unconscious and the *total effort* which they require, as well as how essential it is to work for the establishment of the totality—to put the Self and not the ego in the center. The Ba expresses it as a common home for conscious and unconscious; Hugh, as the soul giving herself as a bride to Christ. Fundamentally, they are expressing the same thing: the totality and unity of man.

CHAPTER 7

Anna Marjula

The Healing Influence of Active Imagination
in a Specific Case of Neurosis

Introduction

About ten years ago, a text entitled "The Healing Influence of Active Imagination in a Specific Case of Neurosis" by Anna Marjula was privately printed,[1] and since then I have received many requests to make it more generally available. Jung had seen this piece of active imagination and thought very well of it. He had even promised the author that he would include it in a volume he thought of publishing, along with some similar documents. Jung died, however, before he was able to carry out this project. Anna was naturally disappointed, but I could not publish her manuscript at that time because Jung had told me it should on no account be published *alone*.

At the time, I compromised and, with the help of the Jungian clubs and institutes, it was printed and privately circulated, under much the same conditions as the Jung seminars. Copies were sold only to people who had previous knowledge of Jungian psychology. I feel now,

[1] *Anna Marjula, The Healing Influence of Active Imagination in a Specific Case of Neurosis* (Zurich: Schippert & Co., 1967).

133

however, that Jung would not object to its publication in this volume, accompanied by several other examples of active imagination. It is certainly an unusually good example, and I think it would be a great pity if it disappeared.

I am presenting the first part of the original text, which consists mainly of conversations with the Great Mother. The second part of the text consists of drawings which Anna Marjula had created at the very beginning of her analysis with Toni Wolff. The drawings themselves, therefore, were a forerunner of her active imagination, but they would be entirely incomprehensible by themselves. The interpretations which appear in the booklet were made by Anna some time after her conversations with the Great Mother, and, being *conscious* interpretations, have nothing directly to do with active imagination. Nor has any effort been made to bring the two parts together. It seems better, therefore, to omit this section of the text, and to substitute a summary of some encounters with the Great Spirit, which Anna had experienced after the booklet had been printed. These seem to fit our material better; moreover, they have never appeared before, even privately. I have also shortened my introduction to her work, because all of the first part was on the general subject of active imagination, which has been dealt with already in the general introduction to this book.

The ways of doing active imagination are exceedingly varied and indi-vidual,[2] but the visual and auditory methods are the two most usual. Anna Marjula practiced both. In the visual method, which she used first, she held fast to what she saw in pictures, a few of which appeared in the second part of her manuscript. Of course, all of the material is very condensed and shortened, but the fantasy of the tightrope dancer is a good example of the visual method in movement, so to speak. How-ever, it was the auditory method, reported in the conversation, that helped her most. Moreover, she achieved an unusually high level of active imagination in these conversations—a level which takes an unusual amount of work, concentration, honesty, courage and self-criticism to attain.

Anna was never inclined to indulge in fantasy; on the contrary, she had great difficulty in overcoming her resistances to doing active imagination and enduring the very strange contents that the uncon-

---

[2]Jung, "The Transcendent Function,"*Collected Works,* vol. 8, pars. 166ff. Cf. Also Barbara Hannah, *The Problem of Contact with the Animus,* Guild of Pastoral Psychol-ogy, Lecture 70, pp. 20–22.

scious produced. It can be seen that some of those contents were by no means harmless; in that sense, one understands why so many people are afraid of active imagination. But the contents were present from the beginning—the most dangerous appeared (unrecognized by her at the time, it is true) in the earliest pictures—and naturally, the less they were seen, the more dangerous they actually were. One knew that there were alarming megalomanic ideas at work, for instance, but they vanished like smoke if any attempt was made to make them conscious: an enantiodromia would immediately set in and dangerous feelings of inferiority would take their place.

Psychiatrists will certainly recognize themes and ideas that have led many cases to the mental hospital, but this seems to add to the value of the material. The way the Great Mother sometimes deals with this explosive material shows that the unconscious itself possesses the antidote to its own poison. As Anna herself frankly admits, she was often afraid of insanity, and her sister's suicide showed the possibility of an inherited weakness in this respect. Moreover, for many years—as she herself describes it—her own animus regularly destroyed any progress that was made and did his best to support her tendency to panic. Although I never thought she was likely to become insane, mainly on account of her creative work in music and a sort of reassuring, innate courage, I admit I did doubt for a long time whether or not it would be possible to rescue her from the claws of her animus.[3] This, in her case, could only be achieved by the process of individuation. It soon became clear that this was her destiny.

Thanks to Anna's frankness and to her undeviating individual honesty, I am able to be equally frank and admit freely that, even though it was clear from the beginning that she was a valuable person and could be even more so, she was a very wearing and—for many years—a discouraging case. Her negative father complex, reinforced by the resistances to her Freudian analyst, made it impractical for her to work with a man.[4] From the beginning, Jung had the greatest respect for

[3]The important aspect in which this courage showed itself was in her willingness to face her shadow. This was obvious from the beginning, although for many years the animus could still snatch such realizations away from her in order to keep the shadow for himself. But slowly, particularly after the tightrope fantasy, Anna realized the value of integrating her shadow, a realization which is really a *conditio sine qua non* for further development.

[4]Anna frankly admits her difficulties with men, and the reader may see in some places that she still had more work to do on her relationship to, and knowledge of, men.

her gifts and always kept a careful eye on her analysis; nevertheless, he insisted on the main work being done by a woman. Anna is not Swiss and always spent most of her time in her own country, so the treatment was spread over a number of years.

In the early years, music was Anna's great support, and naturally I did all I could to encourage her in her profession. But from the beginning, the animus had an ambivalent attitude toward this (see Anna's own account of her "great vision"); increasingly, he tried to undermine it, even persuading her at times that she must throw it out altogether. But the first reassuring evidence that there was a power at work in Anna's psyche that was stronger than the animus, came in connection with one of the worst of these animus attacks. Anna was in one of the moods she describes when, despairing of ever being "healed," she turned on me as her analyst and on Jung as well, and decided to give up the profession which was still an absolute *conditio sine qua non* at that time to the continuation of her life. No one could shake her decision, and she left for her own country more animus-possessed than ever before. This was the only time I really despaired of the case; when she left, I feared the battle was lost.

A few weeks later, however, I received a letter from her saying that the most extraordinary thing had happened. All of her mail had been forwarded to Zürich, but when she returned to her apartment in her own country she found just *one* letter in the mailbox, which had unaccountably been thrown in there some weeks before. This letter contained such a tempting professional offer that she felt it could not be refused. "But I would have refused it in Zürich," she wrote, "for I was quite determined then."

This incident changed my attitude toward the case. I saw that I was only exhausting myself and doing no good trying to help Anna save herself directly from her tyrannical animus. But, I asked myself, what was it that saved the situation at the eleventh hour through a postman's mistake? Of course, I could find no rational answer to my question, but I decided to risk the hypothesis that there was something stronger than the animus at work in Anna's psyche and that this "something" did not intend to allow the destruction of her process of individuation. In Anna's case, this was not an isolated synchronistic event. An even more striking example occurred during another negative phase when Anna, angry again at not being "cured," turned against everything to do with Jungian psychology. Then a strange accident happened to her. While on a walk by the seaside, she was hit on the head by a ball, which necessitated a long hospital treatment. During this illness, she finally realized that it was useless for her to try to escape the attempt to become whole, for if she did, the "round object" (symbol *par excellence* for wholeness) would only pursue her.[5]

Jung often said to me that people rarely integrate what is told them by anyone else, not even by an analyst to whom they may have a strong transference. "It is the things given them by their own unconscious that make a lasting impression," Jung said. Anna Marjula taught me the truth of this statement more vividly than anyone or anything else. In the early years of her analysis, nothing made any lasting impression at all. Even if there was apparent progress over a considerable period of time, sooner or later the animus was able to destroy it, as she describes very clearly herself. And the transference was a very unreliable factor— as she also says—because, however warmly Anna might have felt toward her analyst, the animus held all the trump cards for many years, and played them at every critical moment, transforming trust into distrust and love into hate.

It was with Toni Wolff, her first Jungian analyst, that Anna Marjula drew the strange pictures which appear in Part Two of her booklet. They were already a precursor of her active imagination, in which the contents that poured out from the unconscious were faithfully recorded in words. Jung always taught us to be very sparing in our interpretations of active imagination because it is so easy to stop the flow or to influence elements that should take their own courses. This series of paintings shows the wisdom of this attitude particularly clearly. As Anna herself now sees, interpretation would have been no help at that time; moreover, considering the explosive material that Anna herself found so much later in the pictures, it might well have triggered a disaster. Furthermore, the effort to understand the pictures—which she undertook nearly fifteen years later—would have been hopelessly prejudiced by any outside interpretation. Such ideas could only be accepted if they came from her own unconscious.

A few months after she left Toni Wolff, Anna came to me and was with me—with long pauses while she was in her own country or while she was ill—until 1952, when I went to America for some months. This

[5]On the same principle as Francis Thompson's *Hound of Heaven,* (Boston: Branden Press, n.d.).

was very fortunate for Anna, for she then went to Emma Jung, to whom the full credit belongs for having turned the corner in this case. Coming to it fresh, Emma Jung immediately saw that the animus was governing Anna through her "great vision" and spiked his guns by depreciating it as just "a staggering animus opinion." Before he had had time to recover, she sidestepped him with her suggestion to cease any more direct conversations with the animus for the present (as Anna had been attempting with me), and to apply active imagination directly to "some positive female archetype, such as the Great Mother," instead. It was unlikely that I would have thought of this approach, for although female archetypal figures had been very helpful to me in my own active imagination, until that time they had always done so silently; only the masculine figures or the personal shadow had been willing to talk. I mention this because it shows that one can never take an analysand any further in active imagination than one has gone oneself.

It is rather unusual in my experience for such a superior feminine figure as the Great Mother in Anna Marjula's material to be willing to carry on such long conversations. (I have met only one other such case, where there was also an unusually strong animus.) It almost seemed to me as if the Great Mother, an aspect clearly of the Self, got sick of our fumbling efforts and decided to take the matter into her own hands. Be this as it may, when Anna returned to me after Emma Jung's death, the analysis was definitely in the hands of the Great Mother.

This did not mean that a human analyst had become superfluous. Anna was still rather afraid of these conversations; she found her Great Mother so very unexpected and disconcerting at times that for several more years she would only undertake the conversations while she was in Switzerland and when I was available after they were completed. This was very wise of her, for—although I think the conversations will convince the reader that no human being could have been so wise and farsighted as the Great Mother herself proved to be—she is, of course, in another reality and not always aware of human conditions and limitations. Therefore, a human companion is absolutely indispensable in deep plunges such as those which Anna took into the unconscious. As Jung once said, we need the warmth of the human herd when we face the strange things which the unconscious produces.

I would like to mention that I had no influence on Anna Marjula's document. I said one day that I thought she ought to see that her conversations with the Great Mother were preserved. She replied that, in the event of her death, she would see that they were not destroyed, but sent to me. I heard very little more about it for a few years, until she brought me this manuscript which, apart from some shortening, has hardly been changed at all. I admit that I would have preferred a more scientific form, with footnotes, references, amplifications, and so on, but any such suggestion only disturbed and confused Anna. So—except for a few trifles—I decided to leave it untouched, to stand or fall as a human document. But it is scientific in one important sense: it is undeviatingly honest, and I can testify that nothing in it has been twisted, changed or "improved."

In reading Anna's own interpretations, the reader should know that she is a feeling type. Thinking is her inferior function, but it is necessarily used in her interpretations. Therefore, they often have the peculiarly apodictic and inflexible character that is characteristic of that type.

Anna wrote her account in the role of an imaginary lecturer in order to give herself more distance from her material. Her interpretations, therefore, have a subjective tinge: they are the interpretations that helped her and they fit this special case. But no general conclusions as to other cases should be drawn from them, for their value is specifically individual. They bear witness to the truth of Jung's conviction that people only get the *essential* things from their own unconscious. Anna's unconscious taught her like *this,* but yours or mine would teach us like *that,* in the way that fitted our individual pattern; therefore, I do not want to flatten this individual flavor by any general interpretation.

The reader should especially remember the subjective angle when Anna is speaking of God: she always means the image of God in her own soul. When she speaks of God, she means her subjective image of this figure. She does explain this point herself, but if there were any misunderstanding on this point, I could well imagine the reader being justifiably shocked by some of the things which Anna says of God, Christ and Satan.

In order to give the reader a better understanding of the personal and psychological trauma which Anna was burdened with in her struggle to become more conscious and to overcome her neurosis, the following is a summary of her case history, which is covered in greater detail throughout the case study.

During early childhood and adolescence, Anna, a gifted and intelligent child, suffered violations of her femininity by her totally unconscious and neurotic father. She also experienced the early, unnatural deaths of all her family: first her mother, then her younger brother, her sister and later, her father.

Her experiences with her father left her shy, insecure and incapable of having normal encounters with young men as she matured. Unfortunately, this was followed by an ill-received love for her Freudian analyst. She lived along with this distress till the middle of her life, when she started Jungian analysis in Switzerland.

In conclusion, I think we owe Anna a debt of gratitude for permitting the publication of this material—a generosity that is common to her profession, for creative people in all the arts are constantly trained to expose their innermost reactions to the critical eye of the public.

Presentation of the Case History
by Anna Marjula

In the following pages I have attempted to describe the gradual development of the individuation process in my own life. I chose the lecture form in which to shape my case material because this gave me the opportunity of objectifying "the patient" and enabled me to identify myself with an imaginary lecturer.

Active imagination, according to the method developed by C. G. Jung, and its healing effect on my neurosis are particularly emphasized in this essay.

I wish to express my thanks to the following people, who have helped me to prepare this manuscript for publication: Miss Barbara Hannah, Dr. Marie-Louise von Franz, the late Mrs. Marian Bayes, and Miss Mary Elliot.

I. Introduction to the Case

These lectures are meant to demonstrate the positive result which a certain patient obtained through her genuine attempt to make conscious and to assimilate shadowy parts of her psyche, parts that had been forgotten, or repressed, or that had never been known to her, and —what is even more essential—to show the healing influence which she experienced by means of her intentional and active contact with the archetypal background of all human life, a contact with some of the great unconscious forces which are contained in the collective, eternal source of life, and which nourish, activate and influence all movements of mankind or, in lesser waves, of every individual in his or her daily life.

The form chosen by the patient for her attempt at such contact is what Jung calls active imagination. She first tried to let unconscious impulses express themselves in drawings, and afterwards, she had a great number of conversations with several figures of the unconscious. Since her case of neurosis was an obstinate one, and since she had tried various kinds of treatment before she came to Dr. Jung, it may be worthwhile to look at a series of these conversations which in the end brought her the peace of mind she had sought and striven for during what was actually a lifetime.

To begin with, an introduction to her outer history and her case of neurosis will be necessary. A summary of her dialogues with archetypal figures will follow, and we shall try to pursue the growing influence which these dialogues had on the patient and, as a consequence, on the healing process in her soul.

History of the Patient

The patient was born in Europe, toward the end of the last century. Her father was a lawyer. The family consisted of father, mother, two girls and one boy. The patient was the second daughter. She was a wide-awake child, had an aptitude for schoolwork, and was especially gifted in music and poetry. When she was thirteen, she lost her mother and, when she was twenty, her brother died; then several years later, her sister committed suicide. Her father's death occurred when she was forty-seven. Thus, she was left as the only surviving member of the family. Such, in brief, is her family history. She remained unmarried and took up music as a profession. Her inner psychological history was very much influenced by the father's domineering character (which brought about a negative father complex) and by the mother's early death.

The patient was a nervous child, suffering from sleeplessness and a lack of appetite. When she was still very young, her behavior was that of an introvert. She made up poetry and composed tunes, usually in the lavatory; these treasures she showed to no one except her dolls. She was, however, full of life, quite a happy child, good at sports and games and popular with her little comrades. It was a terrible blow to the girl when her dearly loved mother died. It prevented her character from developing harmoniously. She grew precocious in her inner world and extremely shy in the outer world, especially with boys. Boys caused her panic and in return did not like her, which hurt her pride terribly. She became neurotic, but nobody seemed to notice this. Due to her shyness, all the anguish and inferiority feelings were shut up inside herself as a thing to be kept secret. She felt very much ashamed of this inferiority and tried to compensate it with achievements at school and in music. She strove with all her might always to be the best pupil, and she always *was* the best pupil. Her ambition grew in an unfortunate way. Yet, notwithstanding the fact that her mother's death was a fatal event for her in girlhood, the outbreak of neurosis was still somehow delayed for a period of eight years. However, when she was twenty-one, the breakdown came. It was heralded by a Vision, which later turned out to be the focal point of her neurosis.

Her Great Vision

At the time the patient had this Vision, which was so important to her, she was preparing for her examination as a concert pianist. Ambition had forced her to work too hard and to overestimate the importance of success or failure in the examinations. Exceedingly eager for artistic triumph and terribly afraid of spoiling her chances of success by stage-fright, she had worked herself into a condition of extreme nervous tension. On the night before the examination, the unconscious flooded her and produced a "Great Vision" or "Annunciation," as follows:

> *A Voice told her to sacrifice ambition during her examination by being equally willing and ready to accept either failure or success. After a hard, inward struggle, the patient earnestly promised to obey this command. Then her willingness to suffer a possible defeat brought her a kind of religious ecstasy. In that ecstasy, the Voice revealed to her that it was not her vocation in life to become a famous person herself. Her real vocation was to become the mother of a man of genius. In order to be able to fulfill this vocation, she would have to sacrifice her normal wishes concerning love and marriage, and look out for somebody suited to be the father of a genius. With this man she was to conceive a child in a coitus totally devoid of lust. If she could succeed in having no sensations at all during the conception, and only if that condition could be fulfilled, then her child would prove to be the genius she was called upon to bring forth. Should the father happen to be a married man, she would have to overcome her prejudices and bear an illegitimate child.*

To the girl, this message was full of *mana* (numinous quality). She felt it to be sacred. It was a religious experience, a command which had to be obeyed, and which could never be set aside and forgotten. It turned out to be *the* crisis of her life, with which it was very difficult to come to terms. We shall have to dwell at length on this inner event, because it meant so much to her. Her past life and her future met, so to speak, in this culminating point, for this vision did not originate out of nothing. It was prepared for by events in her childhood and early girlhood and by developments in her character, which together had blocked a normal unfolding of her sexuality. Because of all this, the commanding voice that spoke so loudly in the Annunciation had ever been fed in the unconscious. Its powers grew to gigantic proportions, until it was able to flood the ego in that night before the examination, for the ego was enfeebled just then by far too much nervous tension.

The first reactions of the girl to her Vision were wonderful. As long as the ecstasy lasted, she lived on a higher level than any she had ever before experienced. She passed her examination brilliantly and her shyness totally disappeared. She felt very happy, not neurotic at all, and this happiness augmented the mana of the voice. But the ecstasy could not last forever; it died out little by little in ordinary, everyday life, and all the more so as the future father of that child of genius failed to appear. Gradually, she found herself back in the state of being an ordinary girl, and she took this to be a defeat. Her shyness increased. She felt ill and miserable, exhausted by inner suspense. Her health was broken. Nevertheless, she somehow managed to keep her head above water for another three years. However, as she was now at the age in which other girls find a husband and get married, nature began to assert itself and drove the unhappy girl into a series of unsuccessful attempts at love affairs. These failures would have been difficult to bear even for a normal young girl; for our patient, whose confidence was already undermined, they meant a total breakdown. At the age of twenty-four, she found herself physically ill in hospital, and after this came an analysis with a Freudian.

Freudian Analysis

The Freudian analyst was a young doctor of thirty, only six years her senior. He had been married, but was divorced and lived alone. He was a nice man and very interested in music. The girl liked him immensely, and what was to be expected, happened: she fell in love and wanted to marry him. Circumstances were such that there seemed nothing against a marriage, and their characters might have harmonized. But the analyst preferred another girl, whom he then married. He brushed aside the patient's feelings by calling them a mere father transference, and he did not in the least know how to lead that transference into a development that was acceptable and bearable for the patient.

The best solution might have been to stop the treatment, but the girl was far too fascinated and also too weak in character to leave him; the analyst underestimated the patient's feelings for him and continued the analysis because he hoped to heal the case. His Freudian method was not entirely without result. Some of the symptoms did vanish and a certain amount of energy was restored. Also, apart from the treatment, the girl matured through the depths of her own love and the sorrow caused by its being unrequited. If the doctor had only shown a bit of feeling and understanding, he might have reached the result he was aiming for. But being a Freudian by conviction, he totally repressed the very idea that he might have a countertransference. So the two of them regressed together into what one might almost call a sexual perversion, as we shall see later.

It took the girl eleven years to detach herself from this fascination; that she could part from her love at all was due to the fact that in the end, he really behaved badly and was rude to her, whereupon anger and hatred rose up in her sufficiently to cause a final rupture. By insulting her womanhood, he had called out her pride. Later, she always felt thankful for the finality of that; it was the best thing he had done for her.

The Years between Freudian and Jungian Analysis

The patient was now thirty-three. Her neurosis was naturally by no means healed. Though she determined, very humbly, to make the best of the remainder of her life, her soul was not at peace. Indeed, she did in some measure make a name for herself in the musical world, but she knew all the time that although the work she achieved consisted of valuable inspirations, it lacked the solid background of regular hard work which would have been more than her damaged state of health could stand.

The other, more feminine possibility, namely that of finding a good husband and getting married, proved to be as remote as ever, and the next best thing, a satisfactory love affair, was equally unobtainable. There existed a sexual taboo which was not cured by her Freudian analysis. Apart from this, further forces showed themselves to be at work in her, forces that seemed to lead in unknown directions, for each time an important musical success or a satisfactory love affair appeared to be within her grasp, something from outside—such as the suicide of her

sister, the outbreak of war, the death of a partner—placed itself in the
way of realization and proved to be an insurmountable obstacle. Obviously, a concrete fulfillment was not permitted in her case. This psychological fact became evident to her, and she struggled through life as well
as she could.

The First Years of Jungian Analysis

Eighteen years later, at the age of fifty-one, she saw C. G. Jung about
her problems. Acting on his advice, she started analysis with one of his
prominent pupils, a woman, Toni Wolff, and subsequently with two
other analysts, also women. Jung himself supervised the course of the
analysis.

It was enormously difficult to get at the genuine data, because the
inner figure which had kept the patient going more or less during all
those terribly difficult years was in fact the animus. This animus was
able to exert such an influence on the patient because of the possibilities
which he opened for her in her musical work. As long as a woman is
unconscious of this animus figure in her psyche, he is too powerful a
master, able to fascinate her even so far as to gain complete possession of
her. In the case of this patient, the animus was an ambivalent figure,
and the fascination which he exercised upon her—helpful as well as
destructive—was an almost complete one. Although his musical inspirations did not bring about a true solution for her problem—namely what
she should do with the rest of her life—these inspirations often (and
very helpfully) did mean a temporary way out of crisis and despair.
When the weight of her problems made her feel desperate, the animus
and his music seemed to be her only support. Therefore, she did not
care to displease him by becoming conscious of some other role which he
might possibly be playing in her life. In fact, she *could* not, for she was
afraid of going mad if she did. And from this great fear of hers we may
well conclude that the "other" role which the animus was playing in her
unconscious might be a very negative one. Consequently, it was by no
means an easy task in her analysis for her to look this overwhelming
personality in the face.

Another inner figure, the shadow, that dark counterpart of the
conscious ego, was almost totally repressed by the wilful, proud and
conceited character of the patient. As Jung explains to us, it is extremely
important that we should be as conscious as possible of our shadow, for,
if animus (or anima) and shadow are both unconscious, then the ego

fights an unequal battle against two opponents, and is probably not strong enough to win. In the case of this patient, these two, animus and shadow, had long ago "gotten married" in the unconscious and were now inseparable. They committed all sorts of sins against the patient, who at that time was unable to reach a true insight into her own problems.

But she was persistent and tenacious; she did not give up analysis. Her analyst advised her to try active imagination. She then made spontaneous drawings. Several of them were very interesting and she liked doing this. It fascinated her. Nevertheless, these drawings did not bring any genuine change for the better. A certain point in the depths of her soul stayed untouched, and as yet, she did not see this point.

The patient made a summary of the material of every analytical hour. Consequently, she could survey the whole of the treatment later on. When she re-read her notes, it struck her how favorable the dreams and their interpretations looked. And the same could actually be said of the whole treatment. In this early stage, her analysis *seemed* successful, but somehow she never profited by it. Her animus was in the habit of running away with every favorable result before the patient had integrated it. And he always impressed her with his opinions. He was too powerful a figure to be resisted. However, in spite of despair, she did not give in to him completely. The Jungian method had impressed her even more than the objections made by the animus. She kept on.

One day, she discussed with her analyst (Mrs. Jung) the episode of the vision which had occurred in her youth (the Voice and the message). Concerning the second part of this Vision (her future female destiny), the analyst suggested that the whole of that idea might be a staggering animus opinion! She pointed out to the patient that an animus can be a very bad adviser in feminine love matters; that in fact the word "love" did not appear at all in the message of the mysterious Voice. And how utterly unfeminine the contents of that message really were! So unfeminine, in fact, that they could hardly be attributed to any other figure than that of the animus! This interpretation "clicked" with the patient and did at last really change her attitude toward the authority of the Voice. It broke the spell. To consider the remarks of the Voice as animus opinions was for the moment a lifesaver that reduced the power which the animus had over her. She almost went as far as to wipe out the whole matter, and she felt very much relieved at doing so.

At a much later stage, the religious shading of the Vision had to be restored, for looked at from a higher level, the mana and authority of the Voice appeared to be justified, but in lower or more primitive regions of the mind, they were utterly misplaced and, when taken literally, came dangerously close to insanity. For some time to come, the patient was not a bit on that higher level, and the first and most urgent thing to do was most certainly to get rid of this compelling and devastating animus idea. The analyst then advised her to break contact with the animus as completely as she could, because he was really treating the patient badly. The analyst further suggested that it would be better if the patient were to try an approach to some positive female archetype; for instance, the Great Mother. She was alluding to the figure which Jungians usually call the "chthonic Mother," but the patient—not knowing anything about this figure—evoked her own, personal Great Mother, as we shall see.

She was profoundly impressed by the suggestion of her analyst, and followed her advice, which worked out very favorably because she had a highly positive mother complex. Her mother's premature death had actually come about before she had ever criticized that dearly loved being. And the aura of holiness surrounding death made the human mother an almost archetypal figure: wise, loving and reliable. It was but a little step for the patient to have a positive mother transference to the real, archetypal mother figure, contained in the collective unconscious. Moreover, this transference was helped and sustained by the patient's growing love for her motherly analyst (Mrs. Jung), with whom she had a particularly close contact. As a consequence, she came to attribute to the archetypal Great Mother the authority, wisdom and power of the Self, that most commanding figure which stands as a symbol for the totality of all the psychic entities. Thus equipped, our patient's Great Mother might temporarily be looked upon as a suitable female parallel to God, a substitute more easily reached in conversations than would have been a masculine God, because this patient had a negative father complex as well as a dangerous, unreliable animus. When her analyst made this clear to her, the patient did not reject it, but she continued to call her inner adviser "Great Mother," just in order to feel nearer to her. Otherwise, she could not have approached the Self with such open-mindedness and daring.

Now that the case has been introduced at some length, we are coming to the point. We shall now try to reach an insight into the inner growth or individuation resulting from the conversations which the patient had with her Great Mother. After each conversation, we shall consider the reactions of the animus (insofar as we can know them), paying particular attention to the more or less clearly visible influence which both the Great Mother and the animus had on the patient. It is important to notice how the voice of the animus, at first so dominating, is silenced bit by bit, and how this powerful ruler comes down from his elevated position in the end and begins to develop into a more positive, in fact a most potent, force. This evolution of what at first appeared to be a very negative animus goes together, and is identical, with the healing process in the soul of the patient. As her individuation was a slow and detailed process, the material had to be considerably shortened before it could be presented. Actually, the main points were chosen, while details of perhaps lesser importance had to be omitted.

II. Initial Conversation

The first conversations with the Great Mother took place soon after that eventful day, mentioned above, when the patient could understand the Vision which she had had in her youth as an animus idea. She started her contact with the Great Mother somewhat hesitantly, as if she still found it difficult to part with her animus, even though by now she had clearly recognized him as her tormentor. She tried to make contact with the Great Mother in the following way.

First Conversation with the Great Mother

Patient: *My Great Mother, I want to approach you and to speak to you, but I do not see you very clearly. You are as if under a veil. When I try to remove the veil from you, it then envelops the animus and makes him invisible to me, which seems dangerous. Why is this?*

Great Mother: *Presumably, the animus threw his veil over me the day he was unmasked by your analyst. He did this because he has power over you when I remain invisible. Speak with me in spite of my being veiled, and meanwhile keep an eye on him.*

Patient:	*Can you help me to educate him?*
Great Mother:	*We must educate you first; he will follow.*
Patient:	*I have inferiority feelings because I am an unmarried woman. I still want terribly to make up for my unlived life.*
Great Mother:	*In reality it is thus: all life is lived. You lived your neurosis. In the meanwhile, I lived by proxy the life that was concealed behind your neurosis. You did not know this and therefore you feel as if you had missed your life. But your life is lived—by me! Nothing can fall totally out of the psyche. As soon as you are mature enough to receive your treasure, I shall give it to you. Neurosis is always smaller than that which is hidden behind it. You could not stand that hidden thing and you repressed it. But you strengthened your courage while passively bearing your neurosis for years and years. Compare this to a pair of scales: when courage and strength are gathered and thrown onto one of the scales—shall we say onto the passive scale?—then the other one, the active scale, can rise. Then you can seize the sum of your unlived life that I have lived provisionally for you. Nothing is lost; all of it is there. Try to take it bit by bit. In this way you will still be able to mature as a woman with a fulfilled life.*
Patient:	*But how can I ever be a woman with a fulfilled life if I have not got a normally functioning sexuality?*
Great Mother:	*It is not the sexual function that should be your starting point, but the feelings that possibly can lead in that direction, and for which the sexual function might in the end be an expression.*
Patient:	*How can I regain those feelings? I lost them long ago.*

Great Mother:	*You repressed them. They can be exchanged for courage.*
Patient:	*You mention courage all the time. I don't believe that courage was the thing I lacked.*
Great Mother:	*You certainly have courage, but of a dangerous kind. Your animus plays with your courage, and as you are animus-possessed and cannot stand his power, so your courage becomes too passive. Your animus likes to push you into psychic misery. This misery you suffer courageously, but only because you see in it an opportunity to feel yourself a heroine. This is your compensation for neurotic inferiority sensations. This kind of courage does not function in the right way. It is too passive.*
Patient:	*The animus is to blame.*
Great Mother:	*Yes, but ultimately, it is you who are responsible for your animus. In younger years, you were far too high up. Therefore your neurosis was necessary. Now you should not hate shadow and animus so bitterly. Their play with you was monstrous, but necessary. You brought it about yourself by not being in any way conscious of the dark forces within you.*
Patient:	*I feel ashamed.*
Great Mother:	*Feel responsible! That should be the way to activate courage.*

When the patient read this conversation to her analyst, the latter was very much impressed, and she warmly encouraged the patient to continue her dialogue with her Great Mother, which the patient did, even enthusiastically, over long periods of time. Her animus, however, who loved his power over her very dearly and who did not in the least intend to relinquish it, did not miss a single chance of telling her how black things looked, how superfluous her efforts were, even how injurious similar conversations were to her health! Patient and animus got involved in a tedious and exhausting battle, of which only some of the details can be given here. It might be enough to note that for a very long time after that, the patient began all conversations with the Great Mother with complaints about feeling ill and miserable, filled with doubts, disbelief and fits of despair. These conversations were neurotic "hot-air" talks, not worth repeating here.

The Great Mother patiently replied that disbelief and doubt belong to the shadow, which had formed a partnership with the animus in the unconscious, so to speak, where the two of them conspired against the patient and had a grand time doing it. If the patient could take these shadow parts into herself and feel responsible for her own despair, then the animus might become less powerful, the Great Mother said. But for the time being, the patient was far too unconscious of her shadow to discriminate its qualities, and too much possessed by her animus to stand up against his opinions. She remained their victim for a long while yet. The words of the Great Mother were immediately shouted down by animus opinions that were easier to believe. The following remarkable dream came to the patient at this point in the midst of her distress.

Dream

The patient approaches a big building. A nun comes out of it, welcomes her and gives her a rosary which consists of only a few beads. Every bead is a prayer. The nun tells her to thread more beads onto that rosary, black beads, which will become brilliant and radiant as soon as she has threaded them.

Interpretation of the Dream

The patient gave associations to the beads, or prayers. She said that they were called humility, poverty and fasting with the heart. Humility speaks for itself. She associated poverty with the following words of the poet Rilke, in his *Stundenbuch: "Armut ist ein Glanz aus Innen"* ("Poverty is a glow from within"). "Fasting with the heart" was recommended by Meister Eckhart as a means of attaining spiritual life. After amplification, the nun was interpreted as representing the *spiritual* woman, which this patient (who was, moreover, a Protestant) had to evolve in herself and to accept as *fate*. The black beads were shadow parts which would lose their darkness when they had been threaded by her on her own little chain (of consciousness).

After such a clear dream, it seems almost unbelievable that the patient could not definitely change her attitude. She could do this for a while—she *was* impressed—but it did not last very long. Exceedingly clear language used by the analyst or the Great Mother usually provoked the animus immediately to add his own drastic comments. Our patient then never failed to identify with him and to believe each one of his words.

This time, in order to blot out the influence of that nun who had appeared upon the scene, the next trick of the animus had to be a very subtle one. The animus picked up the patient's aptitude for religious devotion. He told her to accept her fate, her suffering and her neurosis willingly, even to get sexual satisfaction out of her religious readiness to bear what she might call "God's cruel coitus" with her! Here her analyst interfered, explaining the difference between obedience to God and obedience to the animus. The analyst showed her to what extent she had an inclination toward masochism, masochism being connected with extreme femininity, just as sadism may accompany extreme masculinity. The patient could see her own tendency to masochism, and this led to the following discussion with the Great Mother.

Second Conversation with the Great Mother

Patient:

> My Great Mother, if only I could reach a positive acceptance of fate, instead of cherishing that passive and foolish courage which causes me to stand the neurosis and to suffer masochistic satisfaction.

Great Mother:

> Look your masochism in the face and see the moral satisfaction you get out of it, the fortifying conviction that you are a heroine, willingly drinking endless cups of bitterness. You distill ego admiration out of that and supposed vigor. If you can sacrifice all these possessions which seem so valuable to you, then positive forces can get into action.

Patient:

> My life is built up on heroically borne suffering. This is my support and justification. It keeps me going. If I am to give it up, I shall be very weak.

Great Mother:

> You are very weak as it is, only you do not know it.

Patient:	*Is it right to assume that my desire for greatness has provided me with a great neurosis? I mean it this way: if I cannot be great in real life, then at least I can be great in neurotic suffering?*
Great Mother:	*You have never been able to sacrifice your megalomania and be just a simple, ordinary female. Therefore you chose neurosis and the possibility for passive greatness. Your neurotic suffering was great, but sterile. Again— masochism is a dangerous power. In the heat of suffering, masochism identifies with its opposite: sadism. You torture yourself. Can you recognize the sadist in yourself?*
Patient:	*I always called him animus.*
Great Mother:	*Look at this ambitious neurosis of yours. Let us call it by a big name: sadistic-masochistic heroism. We might as well call it fainthearted fear, for you are too insipid to become aware of your conceited shadow. Change your negative heroism into some positive humility. The first proof of real greatness is to own the dark forces in one's soul and humbly feel responsible for them. If you can do this, you serve me instead of Mr. Animus. Real greatness consists in ego sacrifice.*

The patient had something to meditate upon now! She did so for a while and then she forgot all about it, for the animus also had meditated on something; namely, on a new plot, in order to regain lost territory. And apparently, he proved to be more cunning than his opponents, for what happened was this: the patient fell ill. As a consequence, the next years were filled with medical treatments against diseases which the doctors were unable to cure. At the bottom of her heart, the patient was very much ashamed of being neurotic and had always tried to conceal her symptoms. Therefore physical illness, bringing an established diagnosis from medical quarters, was welcome to her. It proved in her own eyes that her complaints were not imaginary, that she was not as neurotic as everybody thought. As a matter of fact, it released her from a large part of her humiliating nervous weakness—or at least she thought it did. And the animus assiduously abetted her. Thus the doctors could not cure her. Time and money were spent in vain. She had to return to psychological methods.

Her illness had caused delay; nevertheless, it became evident that the analytical process had not been damaged by the interruption. The patient proved more ready for analysis after the apparently wasted years of medical treatments, hospitals, nurses and the like. In the end, she challenged her animus to have a serious talk with her, of which the salient points will be given here. After that talk, he seemed somewhat intimidated, and she found her way back to the Great Mother.

Conversation with the Animus (fragment)

Patient:	*If my illnesses are animus opinions, then you ought to be able to explain the idea behind this.*
Animus:	*You want to suffer, do you not, because it suits you to play the part of the masochistic heroine? I provide you with the chance of doing this.*
Patient:	*Perhaps I was once like that, but I have changed my policy. What is yours?*
Animus:	*Mine is to play husband to you. You whore with me when you are ill.*
Patient:	*Pick your words more carefully, please!*
Animus:	*I procure illnesses for you in order that you may experience being passive, helpless, over-powered. In the guise of illness, I am your husband. Have I put that nicely enough for your fastidious ears? The Great Vision of your youth (as you call it) commanded coitus without sexual lust. Now this is the reason why I figure as illness. In your illness, you are with me just as a woman is during intercourse, but without lust sensations. See?*
Patient:	*What I see is that you are a devil! For shame! . . . But, Mr. Devil, I do not want your*

> *suggestions of illness at all, neither do I want
> your proposals of intercourse. What I want to
> gain is acceptance of fate. Through this I will
> feel feminine toward God, and that is my
> goal. Is this clear to you? My femininity is
> sheltered in God. And in this way I want to
> exorcise you out of my body, you evil spirit!*

Religious Symbols

After this dramatic scene with the animus, the patient experienced a change for the better, a psychic change. This consisted in a growing interest in religious symbols, an interest which was favorable, since it led her away from ego problems and bodily difficulties. She felt less unhappy. In addition to this, she was thankful that she felt herself very much sustained by the analyst's clearly shown sympathy with her efforts.

One of the religious symbols that interested her a great deal was the symbol of the quaternity and Satan's place within it. In earlier years, she had made drawings representing a quaternity that contained Satan. These drawings were rather obscure to her at that time. Nor did the analyst explain their meaning. Later it became clear: they were anticipations. Such anticipations, either not understood or even *mis*understood, often seem totally useless, but in reality they have an influence on the person to whom they appear. They function as a kind of motor that keeps one going. In this way they are important.

The idea of seeing God as a quaternity instead of a trinity was in itself not difficult for the patient. She had been educated in the philosophy of Spinoza, and Spinoza expresses the idea that God would be incomplete if every degree of value—from the very lowest to the very highest—were not present in Him. This concept of Spinoza's had long ago convinced the patient of the fact that evil is part of God. Spinoza adds that human beings call "good" what is good for *them* and "bad" what is bad for *them,* and he agrees with this human standpoint. But—he declares—we should be aware of the probability that God's views about good and evil may not be identical with our own conceptions. Thus, Spinoza had more or less restored in the patient's eyes the concept that God is irreproachable because of His greater plan being incomprehensible in human terms.

Perhaps it is not Jung's intention to call God irreproachable, at least not in the sense of *perfect.* But in the idea of restoring God's *complete-*

ness by giving back to Satan his place in heaven, Jung and Spinoza are able to meet. Or so it appeared to the patient, and she had no great difficulty in this respect. Nevertheless, the patient was now troubled in regard to this issue. The cause of her trouble was an enormous inflation on the part of her animus, and of this inflation she was as yet unconscious. She felt inner confusion, even bewilderment; therefore, she asked her Great Mother about Satan and the quaternity. The Great Mother answered with an explanation on the subjective level only, in the following way.

Third Conversation with the Great Mother

Great Mother: *In your case, the animus is entangled with Satan. That is too high up for him. He is your animus; the devil is a part of God. Your animus cannot be placed in the quaternity. He has got a tremendous inflation if that is what he thinks.*

Fantasy

While listening to the Great Mother's words, the patient had a vision, or passive fantasy:

She saw an enormous devil with wings, who flew upward in order to go and fulfill his heavenly destiny in the quaternity. And she heard a choir of angels singing a hymn of praise to Satan because he was about to reoccupy the place left empty since his fall. The angels welcomed him into heaven, their glorious chant of "Hail, hail!" rising in waves of harmonious sound.

Interpretation

It seems remarkable that the fusion, or confusion, of Satan and animus is disentangled at the very moment in which the Great Mother alludes to it. At this moment, Satan frees himself from his imprisonment in a human soul and can fly upward. And the patient's animus, released from his daemonic inflation, feels that he has lost face and takes to his heels. The whole of this is an anticipation taking place in the patient's soul. It could be integrated only very much later, and only bit by bit, but meanwhile, it had an influence on the patient's ego. It was now clear to her that she could not get hold of her animus by looking high up into the clouds. Now, at last, she really began to understand that there is only one way of breaking a state of possession by the animus; namely, to become conscious of one's own shadow and to take this dark figure totally into oneself. Or, quoting the symbol which the nun in the dream had used, she had to thread the black beads into her own little chain and, by doing so, give the rosary more prayers. Seeing this very clearly now, she spoke to the Great Mother as follows.

Fourth Conversation with the Great Mother

Patient:

> I want to look at my "sins." Of course I know that sins are not only evil deeds, but also neglect of duties. I feel myself utterly guilty and burdened with inferiority in the presence of men because I have not given them the consolation or the pleasure that they can receive from a woman. But, now, if it is my fate to stay unmarried, if my type is that of the nun, of the spiritual woman, and if I must develop this spiritual woman within myself as my goal, how then can it be that my lacks and failures as a woman are both my guilt and my fate?

Great Mother:

> If you had really accepted your unmarried condition as fate, you would not have such terribly torturing feelings of inferiority. Willingness to live one's fate does not feel like an inferiority; in fact, just the reverse. There is an enormous difference between fulfilling one's fate actively and being willing to accept one's fate passively. You have not yet achieved this active fulfillment. But the problem is extremely difficult, because even when you have achieved active fulfillment, it may be possible that a small measure of guilt and inferiority cannot be eliminated. It is like this: an unmarried and childless woman sins against nature. If it is her fate to sin against nature in this way, then there is in her a

conflict between nature and fate. Fate comes
first. Consequently, a part of the conflict has
got to be suffered, for it is not to be solved.
But you have not quite reached this point.
Your acceptance of fate is not yet a fulfill-
ment and it is not active enough either.

The contents of this conversation were of course discussed with the
analyst, who commented, "As fate and nature want you for different
purposes, and as this conflict cannot be solved, you must try to look at it
from a higher standpoint, just as we might look down from the top of a
pass where we can see both sides of the mountain."

The patient was not yet quite at the top of this pass and could not yet
look down from a higher standpoint. She told her Great Mother this.

Fifth Conversation with the Great Mother

Patient:	*It is difficult not to let the animus come up, because he is on the side of nature and against fate; so is the shadow.*
Great Mother:	*Your problem is a woman's problem and the animus is bad at giving advice there. Do not mind his opinions! The shadow is on nature's side, of course. But, most of all, it is you who are on nature's side. It is you who cannot sacrifice sexuality as your life's goal. Indeed, you do not even want sexuality for its own sake, but only as a help, in order to get rid of your annoying inferiority and of your longing to be as other women are.*
Patient:	*I should like to know what it is that fate wants me to do. Fate always seemed to me to be something alien and hostile to my own nature, something which God imposes upon me from outside. If I were able to see that fate, my fate, was always within me, and that it belongs to me very personally, I might then be able to live it consciously and not only to accept it passively.*

Great Mother: *Your fate was born in you as a germ. One has got to live in order to develop that germ. Or, it develops by itself as long as one lives. This unfolding of fate is life's goal. As long as you are unconscious of this, fate seems to impose itself upon you from the outside. Try to become conscious of this germinating process within yourself. To the degree in which you can become conscious of it, so in the same measure or degree you unite with God. God is your fate.*

Patient: *Is there a difference between Fate with a capital F and just my own fate?*

Great Mother: *As much or as little as there is a difference between God—and God in yourself. You might put it this way: when you live unconsciously, you merely achieve your fate. This is what animals do. But when you are conscious of the achievement of fate as being your life's goal, then you are allowed to see it as Fate—with a capital F. In the ideal case, you receive fate—with a small f—out of God's hands in order to unfold it, and to give it back to Him as Fate—with a capital F. By doing so, you create God as much as God created you. Christ's life is the extreme example of this.*

Patient: *Christ created God when He consciously chose to achieve His Fate; namely, to die on the cross.*

    Dear Great Mother, I can understand what you mean, but I cannot feel it inside myself as coming up out of my own depths. I am so terribly afraid of repressing the things or the feelings which I do feel spontaneously. These feelings are, above all, my needs as a woman, which clamor to be fulfilled.

Great Mother: *Do you think Christ had nothing to repress in*

	Himself when He chose to go the way of the cross? Do not repress things in yourself as far as to become unconscious of them, but say no to them when you must say no.
Patient:	*That is more difficult still.*
Great Mother:	*Of course it is. Out of pure Freudianism, you neglected in yourself the life of your spirit. That is repression also, and in your case it is even more destructive than sexual repression, because spiritual life should hold more values for you and be even more in your own nature than the so-called natural life. Your own nature seeks not only biological fulfillment; the "nun" in you is longing for God. Try to see her and to give her a chance.*
Patient:	*It is strange that I have never felt guilty about having missed a spiritual life.*
Great Mother:	*Then do so now. Feel guilty toward the "nun" in you, toward me, if you wish to put it like that, or toward God. But do not feel guilty toward male human beings, nor inferior to married women.*
Patient:	*And if I cannot get rid of those feelings?*
Great Mother:	*Suffer them if you must, but tell yourself that they are animus ideas!*

Since the animus kept silent with regard to the last important disclosures, the patient was for once undisturbed when she meditated upon them. She noticed that these revelations concerning the fulfillment of fate were imparted to her as soon as she wanted to "look at her sins" (as she expressed to herself her willingness to assimilate shadow parts). And she kept that in mind for the future.

Here follows her answer to the Great Mother after having thought things over.

Sixth Conversation with the Great Mother

Patient:	*Because I want to develop the spiritual woman within myself and because you told me that*

*nothing can fall totally out of the psyche, I
tried to find a spiritual equivalent for the
parts of my soul which are presumably lost.
Do I understand a receptive feminine attitude toward God, or toward fate, to be a
spiritual equivalent for feminine receptive-
ness expressed in the act of love? And might
spiritual motherhood find expression in my
hope of fulfilling my fate, in order to place it
in God's hands as a thing born out of me,
after having cherished it in my soul? I had an
inspiration about how I might see spiritual
life in general. I saw what in this world we
call real life as a symbol for Real Life—with
capital R and L—the latter being God's life
in us, or that part of God that lives our life in
us. When I look at it in this way, it then
seems unimportant whether I am enjoying or
suffering my so-called earthly life, this being
in higher reality what I can experience of
God's Life.*

This time the Great Mother did not answer, but months later she and
the patient looked at the question again. It was now formulated as
follows.

Seventh Conversation with the Great Mother

Patient:	*How can opposites be united in the psyche?*
Great Mother:	*A god can unite opposites; you cannot. In your case, nun and mother (fate and nature) could not be united. Fate triumphed and the mother in you was sacrificed. When you sacrificed her, you sinned against your personal nature, but you fulfilled what is called human nature. It is a unique and essential task of the human creature to suffer the tension of the opposites that cannot be united. Your mistake was that you did not feel responsible and guilty and repentant*

regarding your personal nature. You felt
neurotic instead. Let us examine this para-
dox. You could not help your fate and its
command to sacrifice the mother in you.
Nevertheless, you must feel responsible and
guilty and full of remorse toward your per-
sonal nature—or be neurotic. Here we come
to why it is said that man is a sinner by
nature. Do you see? Man is forced to sin
because he cannot unite incompatible oppo-
sites. He sins on the one side or the other.
And this is his fulfillment of human fate.

These last conversations were presumably above the level of animus interruptions. It is to be noted that he remained silent.

To be confronted with problems of this sort had, of course, an educative influence not only on the animus, but also on the patient's conscious ego. First of all, they helped her to do away with the over-exaggerated significance which sexuality (and the lack of it) had received in her thoughts as a result of Freudian analysis. As long as she saw sexual fulfillment as the only possible goal of her earthly life, she could not develop spiritually. Now things began to look a bit different from the way they had looked, and gradually she could find a new meaning in her past life and also in the future. It was a great help to attain even some slight insight into the perhaps symbolic meaning of life. Vice versa, this insight helped her to symbolically interpret the contents of dreams and visions, and thus to develop a further understanding contact with her own inner life. The door to her further development had been opened, and progress in becoming conscious meant also an advance in cure.

III. Interpretation of the Great Vision on Various Levels of the Soul

In Jungian analysis, we repeatedly find that we have arrived at the same spots, but each time on a higher level, as Jung expresses it—the way to individuation being like a spiral up which we climb.

Without doubt, the patient had now climbed to a higher curve of the spiral, and her more elevated standpoint permitted her to attain a more extensive view. Because of this, she became able to attribute a symbolic

meaning to the curious phenomenon of her Great Vision. Together with
her analyst,[6] she came to an interpretation which was now really acceptable to the whole of her being.

Literal or Symbolic Realization?

We can divide the patient's Great Vision into two parts: the first part
deals with her examination and with her stage fright, and the second
announces to her her true goal in life. The first part had always been
clear; it could be dealt with literally, and at the time of her examination
it had caused a relaxed and receptive willingness to accept things,
whichever way they went. So far, she had understood her Vision in a
wonderful way. But the second part, which we might call the Annunciation, was much more complex. Here, obviously, a symbolic realization must have been meant.

In those early days when she had experienced the Vision, the patient
had never heard of psychological symbols and she no doubt felt that the
words were meant literally. Still, she was normal enough to see any
attempt at literal realization as a danger that might even push her
beyond the borderline of sanity. She never made such an attempt in
reality, but she got caught in a muddle, and she passionately wanted to
get rid of the whole affair. Unfortunately, she could not do away with it
because of its numinous aspect which so overwhelmed her. As she was
an introverted feeling type with very good intuition, her differentiated
functions might have steered her more or less safely on her course. But
the girl did not see the cliffs set up by her unconscious shadow, and she
unfortunately chose the animus as her pilot.

The Interplay of Shadow and Animus

The patient's positive shadow parts which we call female instincts had
been wounded in her early youth and in the beginning of her girlhood.[7]
When instincts are crippled or wounded, they cannot function well;
above all, they cause pain. Therefore, the patient had repressed them.
But when instincts are in a repressed state, their growth is blocked. As a
consequence, the patient missed the foothold which normally
developed instincts might have given her. To understand the message of
the mysterious Voice, she had to do so without the help of a normally

---

[6]At this time, Anna was again working with me.—B.H.
[7]We will come to this later p. 183.

functioning shadow, a help that otherwise might have kept her with both feet on the ground. Instead of this, the animus made himself master of the contents of the Annunciation. That the animus had the power to do this was due to the fact that he and the shadow played together against the patient. Her wounded instincts brought on feelings of inferiority, which sought for some kind of compensation. This mechanism had provided the girl with her overwhelming ambition. Only during the tension of those examination days did she begin to feel doubtful about whether she was gifted enough to satisfy the demands of her ambition. And this was the long anticipated moment for shadow and animus to pounce on her with what they said would be an excellent solution for her. Indeed, what would be simpler and easier than to shift the weight of the whole conflict onto a highly gifted son and thus make the way free for her to retire, with honor and without pain, into legitimate maternal pride? Indeed, it would be a marvelous proof of the ingenuity of this pair!

As mentioned above, the second part of the Vision can be looked at as a command for literal realization (and this would be the lower level) or for symbolic realization (the higher level). The animus had stolen the lower level on his own behalf, for the elimination of love and sexual excitement in any future relationship between our girl and a male partner is nonsense, and such an idea could not have come from anyone but the animus. It may even be possible that he changed the words of the voice a little bit—oh, not so very much—merely a touch (only just enough to enable him to get what he wanted!). One does not know about this. This is only a suggestion, but it would accord with his nature, and the fact remains that the Vision was not written down until many years later. On a higher level of the soul, the Annunciation had a totally different meaning, as we will see. But before we take leave of the primitive animus ideas, it should be made clear that the animus has two different levels or aspects of his nature within himself.

Two Animus Aspects

In his original aspect, he is merely the personal animus, meaning that little bit of undeveloped masculinity contained in a female soul. In this aspect, he ranges from the impish and teasing up to the devilishly destructive, but all this in the personal realm. He may be a positive figure even in this personal sphere, and he often seems to be, especially nowadays when women have men's jobs which they could not possibly

manage with their femininity alone. On the highest level, we look upon
him as being a Great Spirit. Every important feminine inspiration must
be attributed to this figure. Most of the time he is highly positive. If he
is negative in this upper sphere, then he is negative on the impersonal
level. In this case, he is a great evil spirit in every degree, all the way up
to Satan himself!

In this girl's life, we shall see him at work in almost every aspect. We
have already heard his witty, teasing chaff in some of the conversations,
and in the higher sphere we must give him credit as the one who
inspired her creative musical work. In the second part of the Vision, he
destroys with one blow both her future career (by saying that it was not
her vocation) and her potentialities as a woman (by excluding normal
reactions from the sexual relationship). But on the upper level again, he
is the mediating factor which, in the end, makes her see the symbolic
meaning of what the Voice had announced to her.

A Mary Fantasy

Jung once told the patient that her Great Vision was a "Mary
fantasy" and he pointed out three parallels between Mary's situation
and the patient's vision: First, Mary conceived her child by the Holy
Ghost, probably without sexual pleasure; secondly, Mary gave birth to a
divine child, to a "man of genius"; and thirdly, the child was not
legitimate.

Could we not gather from the above that the Voice in the Vision
chose these three parallel points in order to suggest a Mary fantasy; that
through them, the Voice was trying to tell the girl that she had to be like
Mary, humble and obedient, fulfilling the life which God had chosen
for her, and that she should not strive to attain fame and glory if *they*
were her life's goal? For if we alter our starting point somewhat and look
at Mary's life as if at a myth, we may interpret that myth (or that life) as
a symbol standing for the soul's extreme femininity, unfolded in devotion to receive God's Will.

In *Stundenbuch,* the poet Rilke expresses this feminine surrender of
the soul to God. Rilke uses the following words: "My soul is as a woman
to Thee." And again: "Spread Thy wings over Thy maid." This
attitude of humility and devotion was what the girl had to learn. Likewise, in one of the conversations the Great Mother had said: "If we
consciously fulfill our fate in an attitude of spiritual devotion, we create

God as much as God created us."[8] In more feminine words, to create God is synonymous with giving birth to God. And as the Great Mother had also alluded to fate as a "divine germ," we may read the symbol as follows: If we consciously live our developing fate in an attitude of spiritual devotion, we give birth to a *symbolic* divine child.

From certain things which Jung once said to the patient, she received the impression that God is the life in us, that we are His eyes and ears and that we must give consciousness to God. This last idea may express what Jung considers to be the purpose of each individual life: We must give consciousness to God!

If we are able to do this, then our human consciousness becomes divine consciousness. And thus this divine consciousness is born out of our soul by means of our earthly experience or by means of our accepted and actively lived fate. May not this have been the goal to which the Voice in the Vision pointed? God—as creator of the germ of fate in our soul—was the mysterious "father of the child" which the patient was commanded to seek, and the meaning of this was that she had to become *conscious* of God as father of the child. And, further, her vocation was to make the divine germ sprout in order that it might be born out of her as divine consciousness. Symbolically, not only the father of the child, but also the child itself had to be—God. This vision is indeed a Mary fantasy.

Of course, the Bible tells us the same thing in a much shorter and more direct way through Christ's words: "Not my will but Thy Will be done." But Jung explains that every symbol, even the most well-adapted and suitable one, may lose its mana in the long run. Sometimes a symbol becomes worn out, used up, exhausted. Where this is the case, a new symbol must be born in the person who has lost contact with the old one. This individual birth of a new symbol, capable of containing the mana of the preceding one, was in fact the difficult process of growth in the patient's inner life. When it was achieved and could emerge into consciousness, she was able to regain touch with the just-mentioned Biblical words, to which she could now give all the mana of which her soul was capable. In later years, her transformed attitude to life and fate proved to be the source of healing for her neurosis. But it did not work as rapidly as that. Insight alone was not enough. This insight had to become a living factor expressed in her daily life.

[8]The Fifth Conversation with the Great Mother.

The Girl's Examination

Let us return to the girl who had just had her Great Vision and who, on the following day, was going in for her examination as a concert pianist. Perhaps in the first part of the Vision the authoritative Voice was meant as a practical help for the girl, so that she would not spoil her examination by stage fright. We have already seen how it did work as a help in this direction. It is possible that the first part of the Vision alone might have sufficed to enable her to reach this goal, but this seems doubtful. For the first part was not as heavily laden with mana as the second part was. The patient could not have felt the simpler first part as a religious experience, at any rate not sufficiently to have it at hand at the moment in which the stage fright would try to invade her. Far more important was the second part, which dealt not only with her musical performances, but also with the whole of her future life and, fundamentally, with the future life of her soul. Here lay the religious experience. In that eventful night, she had seen God for a moment and could never be the same person again. The next morning, when she sat down at the grand piano to play her examination pieces, she was still totally under the spell of what had happened to her during the night. This is why she played so well. Even the examining committee felt the nearness of God. When she had finished playing, all of the examiners instinctively rose from their seats to let her pass. They were speechless.

Archetypal Battles in the Soul

Even if the unconscious had only meant to give the girl the satisfaction of a successfully passed examination, the second part of the vision would have been necessary in order to achieve it. However, the unconscious meant far more than this; apparently, its intention was to touch the girl in the depths of her soul so as to force her to become conscious of her dangerously ambitious shadow and powerful, daemonic animus. She was not going to be allowed to give her soul in payment for the world-famous name which she was so anxious to acquire in music. The devil was not to have this soul, at least not so long as her Great Mother was in contact with her. It almost looks as if this girl had gotten a personal guardian angel in the form of her Great Mother. Was this perhaps to make up for the negative influence of her too powerful animus? Who can tell? What do we really know about the archetypal forces of light and of darkness, fighting out battles in our souls? So long as we are totally unconscious of them, we can probably be no more than their battlefield. A small role of our own very likely starts only after we have acquired at least some measure of insight into the fact that we are not only a conscious ego, but also a minute particle of vast, collective happenings in the unconscious.

Reactions: Anticlimax and Return to the Great Mother

We must now leave the young woman and her examination and consider the elderly woman who in her analysis had relived the past days in order to obtain a satisfactory explanation for her Great Vision, and who was now confronted with the problem of how to work out her newly attained knowledge.

As we all know, it is very difficult not to become inflated when we are, or have been, in touch with archetypal figures. For if we make the mistake of identifying with them, then first inflation and subsequently deflation are bound to follow. This was exactly what happened to the patient after the last interpretation of her Great Vision. Instead of using her newly acquired insight for a better adaptation to life's demands, she felt as if—after all she had gone through in analysis(!)—she now had a *right* to obtain health, thrown into her lap ready-made, to be owned and enjoyed and used exclusively on her personal behalf. True, she could acknowledge the above-mentioned interpretation of her Great Vision as being the right one, but with that explanation in her hand she did not see the gates of paradise opening for her as she had hoped. Instead and because of this, she had to go through an anticlimax, a bitter frustration. As we know, she had striven for the true explanation during what was practically a lifetime. She had clung to it as to her only chance of salvation. And now that she had gotten it, she saw that its acquisition did not have the power to heal her neurosis. (Of course, she made the terrible mistake of insisting that she now be healed, at the very moment in which she should humbly have changed her previous attitude into one of devoted service to the unconscious forces which had revealed such important truths to her.)

In her state of depression and despair, a well-known old friend poked his trustworthy nose round the door and re-entered the scene. Her old animus, of whom she had lost sight for a while without even missing him too much, had now come back to comfort her, to "make her see," as he himself called his function, and thereby (but this he was careful not to mention) to regain his lost power over her. He had only waited for a favorable moment and there he was, his unmistakable self, continually assuring her that she had slid back two steps to every one gained on that slippery spiral she had to climb, which they call the way to individuation. Of course, as he said, this ascent was far beyond her capacity; she herself must certainly see by this time that the effort could only injure her health. It was high time to stop the venture. With this and many more insinuations of a similar kind, he bombarded her.

The patient listened to him with one ear, it is true, but in her other ear she heard a faint echo of several words which the Great Mother had spoken, words that fortunately were not totally lost on her. In the dialogues about fulfillment of fate, the Great Mother had really touched a responsive chord in the patient's soul, and the latter's attitude to her past and future life *had* changed. For instance, she now caught sight of the true reason for the delay in getting back her health, namely her self-willed character, which produced enormous resistance to being successfully analyzed, for she had a fatal tendency to be always right! So long as her shadow's conceited attitude (functioning as a compensation for inferiority feelings) was not sufficiently recognized, she occasionally went so far as to use neurotic regressions in order to prove to her analysts how much they were in the wrong and how much she herself (or was it her animus?) was always right! Not a very suitable means of getting cured, one must admit. With this attitude, she had provided an excellent hiding place for unconscious shadow parts and much-loved animus possessiveness. So long as her grand Annunciation could not be more efffectively explained by analysis, the shadow and the animus were content, and the girl herself was ill and unhappy, but comforted by the idea that she was always the stronger one, not to say the superior party! Now she would have to do away with such animus opinions. During the above-mentioned inflation, he had had an opportunity to pump her up with his ideas until she was like a swollen balloon. And when the deflation came, the disagreeable anti-climax, she had clung to him as her only support. The whole of this stage of being possessed by the animus functioned as one of those veils which the animus is so fond of throwing over his victims; while she was blinded by this veil, she could not see clearly that she had in fact ascended her summit, from whence she might be able to destroy the hiding place which actually concealed shadow and animus and their joint plot against her.

The patient had to dismiss her beloved seducer and to return to her Great Mother, which she did, but not without frequent wavering and hesitation. She knew by now that there is only one way to obtain power over the animus; namely, to look deeper into the darkness of the shadow, in order to separate that figure from him; and she knew that this was also the only way to get really into harmony with her unhappy past life and with the painful wounds received in earlier days. The Great Mother, of course, had her own idea about how to deal with animus veils. She began to teach the patient humility and ego sacrifice, thus preparing the way presumably for a great plunge into the unconscious, from which her pupil would have to fish up what was now necessary for further individuation. In fact, it was the life behind the neurosis with which she had not yet dealt, the life which the Great Mother had lived for her and had promised to give back into her hands as soon as she would be sufficiently mature enough to live it herself. As to humility and the death of the ego, the Great Mother spoke as follows.

Eighth Conversation with the Great Mother

Great Mother: *The shadow, even when conceited, is useful and indispensable to you because there are germs concealed in her that might, and should, develop into humility. Do not feel yourself too good for all the wounds you have received in your life. Be humble enough to feel responsible for them.*

Patient: *How can I attain humility, Mary's humility which made her become the chosen Mother of God?*

Great Mother: *You cannot attain it. Mary is a goddess; you are not. You can only try all the time to see how very lacking you are in humility. That is your form of humility. Be aware all the time of your conceited shadow. Do not try to get above it; you cannot. Try to accept your shadow, and go through life suffering her, but consciously!*

Ninth Conversation with the Great Mother

Patient: *I feel very ill. I feel that death might be*

	approaching. I feel afraid and horrified, as if it were going to be an execution.
Great Mother:	*In the event of its really being a sentence of death, would you feel guilty or free from guilt with regard to the sin for which you have been sentenced?*
Patient:	*You told me to feel as guilty as possible for my cardinal sin, that sin being my omissions toward my feminine nature. Is it nature's revenge which I am now fated to suffer?*
Great Mother:	*You suffer nature's revenge in neurosis.*
Patient:	*And am I sentenced to death by the Self?*
Great Mother:	*Yes, if "death" means ego sacrifice!*
Patient:	*And what about my fear of bodily death?*
Great Mother:	*I am not going to announce to you the hour of your bodily death. It belongs to human nature not to know that. But I announce to you that ego sacrifice is demanded of you, a total sacrifice. And you can only save your life, your bodily life, by bringing about this ego sacrifice.*
Patient:	*If I understand you correctly, what you mean is that I suffer bodily pain instead of adult human suffering, and if I cannot achieve ego death, then bodily death might come instead, as a kind of symbol.*
Great Mother:	*Yes, but bodily death is not always a symbol for ego death. If you now want to achieve ego death just to save your life, that is not ego death at all. You should accept death and pain and everything that might come with them. That would be nearer to ego death. Very many people are able to achieve ego death in no other form than that of bodily death. You might be one of those. Put aside the ambition to achieve ego death. Be thankful that humble death of the body can make up for many non-achieved ego deaths. You*

*are so afraid of death because you only count
on yourself and even on your intellect alone.
But you cannot direct either living or dying
with your brain. Try to rely on me, for instance. Give your fear into my hands. This
would be ego sacrifice on your level of today.
Perhaps nature, offended by your sexual
shortcomings, might be satisfied with this
penance. And not only nature, but also your
shadow. She never got her natural rights.
Fulfill ego sacrifice to satisfy the shadow. And
see your satisfaction in experience; I mean
God-experience which might be contained in
ego death.*

IV. Deep Plunges into the Unconscious

We now approach what the patient called her "deep plunges into the
unconscious." Until this time, the Great Mother had been educating
her pupil on the latter's personal level (with one or two exceptions that
were actually anticipations). From now on, the undertone changes
almost imperceptibly and the conversations take on the character of real
revelations by a great teacher to her pupil.

The first big plunge had to be mainly into the personal unconscious;
namely, into very personal repressions of painful events and adversities.
But its greatest emotional value did not consist merely in regaining
consciousness of repressed events. Much more valuable for the patient's
development were her newly acquired obedience and submission to the
Great Mother and to the pain and sorrow which this great figure of the
collective unconscious was now going to inflict upon her. In the eyes of
the patient, her dive had a downward direction. But the Great Mother
taught her to look at it from her, the Great Mother's, point of view.
And the deeper the pupil descended into the animal side of human
nature, and the more personal this animal side seemed in her own eyes,
the higher became the spiritual level from which the Great Mother
made her look at things. It almost seemed as if the patient was in
analysis with the Great Mother.[9] But in outer reality, she was also in
analysis with a Jungian analyst, and it is certain that the patient could

[9]It did not only seem so; she was.—B.H.

never have achieved her deep plunges without the solid backing and warm sympathy of this woman. *Here* the part which this analyst played in the development is practically omitted, for this paper is to be seen as an attempt at showing, above all, the Great Mother's role. But please bear in mind that the analyst is in the background at all times with her indefatigable patience and her readiness to help. She gave freely of the psychological wisdom which she herself had acquired probably only through constant and intense inner efforts.

An Unrequited Love

Before we turn to the following conversations, which were the beginning of the patient's real descent into the darkness of her own soul, we must go back to that part of her history in which, at the age of twenty-four, she started a Freudian analysis with an analyst whom we shall call Mr. X. Now, decades later, the Great Mother summons her to make a plunge to the very bottom of just that repressed despair which had been the result of Mr. X's treatment. The patient felt convinced that she had to face it, and in a written fantasy she made an honest attempt to do so. During this fantasy, she saw herself in a kind of cellar or prison. In this cellar lived her despair. Everything there seemed dark, confused and unclear. It was extremely bewildering. But there, the Great Mother came to her and brought her something, giving it into her hands. Then, at the moment in which she thought she would have to touch her despair, it turned out to be quite different. It was not her despair which she touched. It was her capacity for love, brought back to her by the Great Mother.

Here, the active fantasy turned into a passive one. In this passive fantasy she was married to Mr. X. He loved her and he was tender with her. She felt grateful and happy. They wanted each other and gave way to their desire. But her passion was not all that she gave him. They were a married couple, loving each other warmly and truly. Every feeling was genuine and intense. It was as if her girlhood dream had been fulfilled. She felt amazed to experience that her love was not trampled upon, nor torn to pieces. It showed itself to be virginal and blossoming. But it was a very young love, not matured through womanhood. And it was purified, purer in fact than it had been when Mr. X had destroyed it in outer reality. And then, somehow, she knew it was even Mr. X who had purified it. She had not received this gift only out of the hands of the Great Mother, but rather out of *his* hands too. In this way, she learned that she had never genuinely hated him. It was as if they had been married all those years, but in another world, not in this one. In an earthly marriage, they could never have achieved this kind of union.

Three days later, the patient had the following conversation with her Great Mother.

Tenth Conversation with the Great Mother

Patient:

What you brought to me in this cellar is wonderful, of course. As usual, the animus tried to take it away from me, but I did not allow him to do so. Only, on one point I think I agree with him; namely, that I don't want a girlish attitude, however pure it may be. I even prefer my sorrow. My sorrow carried me through life, and I feel more mature in my sorrow and even more dignified in it than a young girl's virginity.

Great Mother:

Then what I gave you helped you to see the value of your sorrow. That is acceptance of it, integration even. There is no repressed despair in you now, because you see the value of a woman matured through sorrow. You even feel that this means more than the untouched happiness for which you longed. This is acceptance of fate, is it not?

With these words, the Great Mother left her pupil to her own reflections and to what her analyst would have to add to them. After some dream explanations, the analyst said, "You must retain both. You must not throw away the symbol, nor the sorrow. They are one and the same thing in different aspects, and you must keep conscious of both."

An animus attempt at interruption was prevented in the following conversation.

Eleventh Conversation with the Great Mother

Patient:

When I am submissive to the animus . . .

Great Mother (interrupting her):

You have your female instincts to tell you that you had better be submissive to real men. Let them have all your submissiveness, even if you are playing a part. This will help

	you to get free from the animus. And the shadow will be pleased, too.
Patient:	*But I am shy in the company of men.*
Great Mother:	*That is an upside-down submissiveness, and a terrible possession by the animus, who swallows your persona and then, in your state of shyness, speaks out of you himself. And you project him onto real men, knowing exactly what they think and how much they dislike you, despise you even.*
Patient:	*I know.*
Great Mother:	*But what you do not know is that these great and mighty men would not despise your little comedy of submissiveness at all. They would not see through it, and their vanity would be flattered. Should they see through it, they would still appreciate your feminine cleverness in playing up to them like that, and they would react as if they were pleased. It is persona to persona then, both well-played and well-managed. This would be much better than your stubborn shyness and their being irritated by that. Enough for today.*

In this way, the Great Mother mocked at the patient's awkwardness and at the same time laughed at her own impatience. But in the following dialogue her words sounded quite serious again.

Twelfth Conversation with the Great Mother (fragment)

| | |
| *Great Mother:* | *Trust me, rely on me, when I say that you are not an unloved woman; you did reach Mr. X, but neither you nor he understood what was going on. It seemed all negative, but it was not. Your feeling was so genuine, so very real, that it belongs to the things that cannot be lost. But neither of you was equal to that and so it had to be experienced as suffering, very negatively, and had to be misunderstood as well.* |

> *Mr. X did feel your love, but he repressed that feeling, preferring not to become conscious of it. He also had to suffer, just as much as you did.*

Thirteenth Conversation with the Great Mother (fragment)

Patient:	*I fear what I call your "greatness injections!" I fear an inflation! Might it not be better to follow the advice of the animus and see my love for Mr. X as somewhat immature?*
Great Mother:	*What was immature in it?*
Patient:	*I could not see his point of view at all. I relied on my own feelings and I never considered his feelings.*
Great Mother:	*Mr. X, in his role of Freudian analyst, did not give you the slightest chance. The situation was awkward. He was not up to the situation. Your love was all right, but it could not develop. It could not develop in you, it could not develop in him. He murdered it, so to speak. Then you made a mistake: you allowed him to torture you, psychically, because torture was the only thing you could get out of him. To willingly suffer this torture meant sexual union for you. Thus he got you into a perversity, which was more his than yours. And therefore I kept your love pure for you. I now want you to take it into yourself and to integrate it. The reason why you made all this trouble about it, even trouble between you and me, is that you take his mistakes onto your own shoulders, and this again out of sheer love! You cannot see him as dark. That is childish and immature. Try to acknowledge that he had a disastrous side in his behavior toward you.*
Patient:	*Was I blind?*
Great Mother:	*Yes, but you had to be. That did not matter.*

	What did matter was that you projected the qualities of your own love onto him and when that would not work, you dethroned your love instead of dethroning its object.
Patient:	*Was X not worthy of my love?*
Great Mother:	*He was. But he was ill himself and damaged by life, and still farther away from the normal than you were. And you were not up to helping him, principally because that was the last thing he wanted. Nothing was farther from his thoughts.*

For the time being, the patient now had important material to meditate upon and to integrate if she could. To look at her poor, downtrodden love through the eyes of the Great Mother was like balm to a wound. She could now start a new contact with important values in her innermost soul and feel a bit more rooted in regard to her past life and to her own femininity. All of this was highly positive. But her case of neurosis was a complicated one, and we must have a good deal of patience with it, particularly because of her animus. That personage was like a jack-in-the-box, popping up at uncontrolled moments. We should never underestimate the mischievous pleasure he had in fighting his adversary, the Great Mother, by devaluating her sayings in his clever, convincing way. And he always made it clear that, of course, he made his speeches in a benevolent spirit and only because he wished to be of use to the patient! She had her struggle with him, but she knew by now that his power over her could only be broken if she became conscious of her shadow as completely as she possibly could. She tried to make a habit of fortifying herself with some newly acknowledged shadow parts whenever she was about to attempt another dive into the unconscious. The result of this was the following conversation.

Fourteenth Conversation with the Great Mother

Patient:	*I have tried to become more conscious of that part of me which I call the "unloved woman" in myself. She is an extremely piteous little female, and at the same time so presumptuous! She is always having hysterics, always crying and moaning. She is tortured by her*

want of love. But not even the love of Christ could have satisfied her. Her wishes are much more primitive. The only convincing love in her eyes is—if you will allow me to use her own drastic language—a penis penetrating her. And the fact that this is so is my torture. This little animal lives in me; it lives, of course, in every woman. And I presume a man, in his turn, cannot be convinced that a woman really loves him so long as she does not give her body to him. He must be as much tortured by his vagina complex as women are by penis wants, I suppose. Now that I look this animal side of human nature in the face, I feel pity and love and understanding for all human beings, not looking down on them from above, but out of the feeling I am just one of them.

Great Mother: *In your case, that unloved woman, as you call her, has had to remain unloved in order that you might reach this consciousness of her. But you should not generalize: frustration was your way of becoming conscious, whereas for others, the way may be completely different.*

Such assimilations of sexual shadow parts were absolutely indispensable for the patient as a preparation for the next big plunge into the unconscious. What she was going to fish up this time she subsequently referred to as her "family horrors." The Great Mother probably already knew about these horrors, and she knew also that her pupil would have to go through hell while fishing them up. Therefore, her preparation consisted in making sure that the tie which joined her and her pupil was sufficiently secure to stand the inevitable difficulties.

Here, the question arises whether it would not have been better if the patient had gone to a male analyst, in order to heal her damaged sexuality. But this was exactly what she could not do, because the contact with masculinity in general, and with masculine sexuality in particular, was still blocked in the unconscious. Now that she was going to try to become conscious of the causes which in earlier years had occasioned this stoppage, the patient wanted a psychic hook, a strong psychic bond, upon which to attach her own enfeebled femininity. This would help her to avoid the danger of being devoured by the unconscious, a possibility that was liable to happen as soon as the original horror, one which had totally swallowed her up, rose to the surface again.

For an extraverted person, a normal human contact with the other sex probably would have been the way out of the difficulty. But our extremely introverted patient had to go an introverted way if she were ever to attain in the depths of her soul the genuine and really convincing feeling without which she could not venture a single step in the outside world. The measure in which an extraverted solution was impossible for her shows in the fact that any attempt at overcoming her sexual panic had always failed. Twice in her life she had been very near to having what we call an "affair," but in both cases the same thing happened. At the moment in which she could have overcome her panic, the partner felt the taboo, could not deal with it and left her. This behavior of more than one otherwise normal partner was suggestive. It necessitated a second plunge into the unconscious, for the sake of acquiring a better insight into the nature of the taboo.

In the following conversation, the Great Mother makes use of the well-known fact that a genuine spiritual ecstasy often produces sexual sensations perceptible in the body. Presumably, she wanted her pupil to have these sensations because—as we have just heard—the patient's shadow could not be convinced by any truths whatsoever, except by those of the sexual parts. And this primitive shadow should not be left behind and allowed to nourish her resentment, secretly and unobserved, in the unconscious. If spiritual ecstasy is the highest possible kind of religious experience, then its counterpart, sexual ecstasy, should not be excluded, but should be allowed to have its place in order to convince not only the spiritual side, but the whole of the human psyche, i.e., the bodily shadow as well.

Fifteenth Conversation with the Great Mother

Patient: The other day, as you know, I picked up a
                                  shadow part; namely, at the moment in
                                  which I recognized in myself this little animal
                                  which said that a penetrating penis was the

only thing she could believe in. Today I experienced a similar bodily sensation. It was very real and very convincing, but the penetration took place in my soul, and the one who penetrated there was you! Consequently, I must admit now that you are the truth of my shadow. This is terrible for me. It signifies that I must give up my rational, critical hold. It means that I am totally in your power now.

Great Mother: *Surrender to me. Do it for the sake of your shadow. Our symbolic union means for her the coitus she desires.*

Patient: *What you are doing to me is penetrating into my fear, into my sexual panic and taboo.*

Great Mother: *I am not going to spare you! This act of spiritual union has got to be accomplished, for I must have certainty that you are wholly willing to give yourself up to me.*

Patient: *Then test me!*

Great Mother: *I shall! But remember, there is no retreat. Symbolically speaking, I am now taking away from you your virginity and your independence. You will belong to me forever after that, and not always in ecstasy. Much worse will be the periods in which you will feel separated from me. You will not actually be separated, but you will feel as though you were. You will long for a renewed union with me, but I shall not always grant you that. This is the test. If you can stand such trials, it will be the proof that you have developed a real contact with me. Now first of all, assimilate what you once called my "greatness injections," for without greatness you have not the slightest chance of tolerating me. Know that coitus signifies impregnation, even in a symbolic union.*

Penance

It meant hell to the patient to yield to the irrational experience of union with an archetype, to become aware of it, through ecstasy, as sexual excitement, and to be confronted with this whole situation. It looked like a penalty imposed upon her by two furious and injured entities, nature and shadow, who both felt wronged by the patient's continence in sexual matters, and who both could only be soothed if she were able to surrender unconditionally to this penance. What the Great Mother demanded was really an expiation. And during her expiation, the patient would not only have to give up the critical rebellion of her animus, which had definitely been a weapon against insanity, she would also have to completely surrender to claims which the unconscious seemed to put upon her, and which she actually could not understand.

She feared the Great Mother now and she feared losing her sanity, or that she was mad already. She feared to be inundated by the irrational and to be drowned in it. Without an analyst's backing, she could not possibly have continued. But she had that backing, and she had a sound inner motive for which to persevere: that this new experience could not be worse than the one she had had during the innumerable years in which she suffered the terrible consequences of her neurosis, which certainly was equally irrational. She decided to take the risk, even the ultimate risk of madness, because, for the sake of everything that was sacred to her, she did not want to lose this last chance to relieve her soul of its burden, the chance contained in this irrational penance which she was commanded to do.

Then the Great Mother comforted her by saying that the animus would save her. She should listen to the words of the Great Mother as well as to the objections of the animus, so that she might learn to form her own point of view. The rebellious spirit of her animus was to be seen as a possible protection against the perhaps too powerful personality of the Great Mother. The patient might keep an eye on both him and her.

This now seemed to the patient a real proof of the Great Mother's superiority. It made an enormous impression on her. Her tutor had called even her worst adversary into the arena as a help for the pupil and thus, against herself. This put an end to all doubts, and the patient was willing now to submit to the Great Mother in a symbolic act of coitus, hoping that she might in this way make up for all those experiences she had missed in bodily reality. And this, her union with the Great

Mother, proved to be at the same time a second dive into the personal unconscious, a dive that was necessary, so as to bring forgotten occurrences to the surface and to look at them from a new standpoint. The dive was a difficult one. Consequently, pages and pages were filled with conversations concerning the things that emerged. It is impossible to present this material in its whole abundance, so a contracted narrative will be given, and in it you will hear the actual words of the Great Mother only now and again.

The Family Tragedy

Let us call up in our imagination an apparently happy family: father, mother, three children; outward circumstances are quite normal; the father's character is the dominant one, and that of the mother, gentle, fitted for adaptation and for the easing of difficulties.

Because the father is the more dominant of the two parents, we shall look particularly at the kind of person he was. I think the word *self-righteous* could be applied to him: he always knew exactly what was right and what was wrong. But apart from this rigidity, he was amiable, generally loved and esteemed. He certainly loved his wife and his children; he loved his fellow men and was an agreeable comrade. Professionally, he was a good lawyer, industrious and well-known. Now this man, who seemed destined to go through life happily and without too much trouble, had a highly dangerous shadow, of which he managed to stay totally unconscious, thus bringing the whole family to ruin.

When the children were still very young, the father, who worked late at night, was often unable to get up in the morning. From the breakfast room, his wife would send the children upstairs, one after the other, to wake him up. So it happened more than once that his second little daughter, our patient, invaded the bedroom and played with her lazy father until she succeeded in making him get up. It must have been during one of those innocent early-morning visits that the almost unbelievable thing happened which destroyed the little child's harmless playfulness and wounded her for life with a sexual taboo. She was so young when it happened that, later in analysis, she could never remember the precise details, and she hoped for a very long time that it might have been an imaginary, rather than a real, happening. But the Great Mother told her that it had been exceedingly real, and the unhappy story of later sad events in the family forces us to look at it in that way.

What the little girl of about three or four saw on that, the worst of all her days, was not only her father's genitals, but probably his masturbation and, what was even worse, the expression which came over his face. What she could clearly remember later was an overwhelming sensation throughout the whole of her body, and probably in her soul, too. She completely identified with her father in what Jung calls *participation mystique*.

The Great Mother's comments to this were as follows.

Sixteenth Conversation with the Great Mother

Great Mother:	*The Freudian analyst merely encouraged you to remember what had happened. That is not sufficient. Deal with it! See the role which it still plays in your life.*
Patient:	*My libido has gotten stuck in it.*
Great Mother:	*Yes. You could never separate your own sexuality from that of your father. And this is your trouble and torment even now.*

This participation in the sexuality of her father had, of course, exerted a bad influence on the character of the little girl. She tried to repress the torment of uneasiness which she could not understand, and which consisted of guilt and inferiority feelings. She overcompensated these feelings by showing herself to be an especially obedient child (whereas she had been rather naughty before) and she began to develop a burning ambition to excel in every way. As long as her mother lived, that gentle woman was a true protection for the nervously overburdened and highly strung child, who at least felt safe in the shelter of this motherly love. But, notwithstanding all he had unwittingly done to her, the child did not hate her father. She adored and worshipped him. In fact, all her life she desperately strove to acquire his love.

Then the family was hit by the worst imaginable blow—the death of the mother. This very dearly loved woman died of cancer at the age of forty-three. She had been the one who kept the family going, and when she was no longer there, her husband and children felt uprooted. The father tried to be both a mother and a father to the children, but this attempt failed disastrously, even though he had their love and they felt his.

Shortly after the death of the mother, a bad incident occurred. The father had made a habit of going freely in and out of all the bedrooms, including the one in which the two daughters slept. (The girls were fifteen and thirteen now.) Once he came in as the youngest, our patient, was undressing and had just removed her last garment. The father was agreeably surprised to see that her young figure was already so well-developed, and he told her this. He could not resist caressing her naked, young breasts, this in the presence of the elder sister.

Seven years later, he gave another proof of his misplaced ''mother function.'' The girl was twenty now. It had been necessary for her to be medically examined, and the doctor had prescribed interior irrigation through the vagina. When the young woman, who was sexually as inno-cent as a child, started the manipulation, the father was present in the bedroom under pretext that she, in all innocence, might do herself harm. He felt obliged to show her how it should be done, and he himself inserted the irrigator. His badly hidden emotion startled the young woman and injured her soul still more.

We do not know how the father behaved toward the other children, but the fact remains that the boy died at the age of eighteen and, much later, the eldest daughter committed suicide.

Thus, the unhappy man had lost his wife and two children, and all that was left to him was the one daughter, our patient. This daughter was neurotic, and for that reason a thorn in the flesh of her father, who had always felt an utter contempt for neurotic people. He died at the age of seventy-eight from the consequences of an operation. It was a slow and lingering death. The end came in the hospital in which he had been nursed for exactly six months and to which our patient went to see him every day. In the last weeks of his life, his mind began to fail. So his consciousness was gradually extinguished. In this state of mind, he once begged his daughter to undress. As his voice was by now very feeble, she had to bend over him in order to catch his words, whereupon he attempted to unbutton her blouse with his dying hands, and was angry with her for several days after that because she had eluded his grasp. He was a pitiful sight in his last days, tortured by dreams and hallucina-tions. He fancied himself to be in prison and in chains, because he had murdered both his daughters, as he told her. It was in all the papers, he said.

At last, death delivered the poor old man from his torture. He died on a Sunday morning. At the very moment in which he breathed his last, a choir consisting of hospital sisters began to sing the habitual

Sunday-morning hymns in the corridors of the building. This was a coincidence, if you want to see it as such. But in the ears of the daughter, sitting at the bedside of the father, who had just passed away, the singing voices seemed to be a celestial escort for the soul of her father into the Beyond. This synchronistic event appeared to her to justify the fact that, in spite of all that had happened, she had never ceased to love her father dearly.

An Attempt by the Great Mother to Heal the Sexual Taboo of the Patient

The family tragedy, described above, had to be given here because of details that were not mentioned before. Without these details, we cannot understand the point of view which the Great Mother expresses in the following dialogues. But first I wish to quote from *Psychology and Alchemy*. In this work, Jung writes:

> *Whatever sins the parents and ancestors have committed against the child are accepted by the adult man as his own innate condition with which he must come to terms. Only a fool is interested in the guilt of other people which he cannot alter. The wise man will ask himself: "Who am I to whom all this happens?" To find an answer to this fateful question he will look into his own depths.*[10]

These meaningful and wise words express exactly the idea of the Great Mother with regard to the education of her pupil. The Great Mother always accentuates, just as Jung does, the value of taking responsibility unto oneself instead of hiding one's own guilt behind somebody else's shadow. Therefore, she now commands the shadow of the patient to tell the story in her own words, even if these words should turn out to be not too carefully picked. And the Great Mother summons the patient to become conscious of the latter's own role in the tragedy, the role which she played by means of that shadow which is a part of herself.

The outcome is a talk between three figures: ego, shadow and Great Mother. The shadow speaks first.

Conversation with the Shadow under Supervision of the Great Mother

Shadow (to the patient):	Why (do you think) your mother suffered and died? Why (do you think) your brother

---

[10]Cf. authorized translation in Jung, *Collected Works*, vol. 12, par. 152.—B.H.

	died so young and your sister killed herself? And how can you overlook what happened in the last days of your father's life, when he clearly showed that he sexually desired you? Don't be a child! Understand at last!
Patient:	*My love for my father blinded me!*
Shadow:	*Your foolish love! Me he wanted! And had! You chose to be innocently unaware. You repressed everything by seeing it as harmless, you silly child! But I took my chance with him. He was a child himself. I shall tell you. The doctor said that your mother was not to have any more children.*
Patient:	*I know; he told me himself. She nearly died when my little brother was born, and more births were not to be risked.*
Shadow:	*He did not touch her after that, and he took his refuge in perversions. He satisfied his lust through cruelty.*
Patient: (addressing the Great Mother):	*Please, Great Mother, may I speak with you, rather than with the shadow?*
Great Mother:	*You may have this part of the story with me. Listen! Your extraverted father, as a righteous thinking type, knew exactly where righteousness ended and where sin began. As long as he had no direct coitus with you, he saw everything as paternal and permitted. He did not see his sexual shadow, nor did he see that he lived that shadow. He loved power. He wanted everybody to give way to him, but not in a normal coitus. He made people want him and then he retired into righteousness. That is what you suffered, and that is why you felt a burning, unrequited love for him. You loved him because he was, in fact, very lovable. Partly, his paternal love was all right and more than right. But there was that perversity in him. When you were a very young child, he showed you his sexual parts and his*

	own lust in order to see you overwhelmed by desire. But he did not know about it; he was as unaware as a child. Now your shadow comes in. She liked it.
Patient:	*Please, Great Mother, may I speak with you and not with her?*
Great Mother:	*No, go to the bitter end and hear her language.*

(The patient agrees to this and listens to the shadow.)

Shadow:	*I simply liked the sensation—part lust, part fear, part guilt—and I liked to have it together with him. I felt a grand girl, and I was superior to your stupidity. Of course, he knew unconsciously that he could always get you through me. And I, as shadow, played up to his shadow.*
Great Mother (interrupting the shadow and speaking to the patient):	*Now, please try to recognize this shadow in yourself; feel responsible for her.*
Patient:	*I can remember that some warning instinct did tell me the thing was not right.*
Great Mother:	*This instinct was also the shadow; it was another part of her. If you had listened to your instinct, you might have pushed your father away from you; at any rate, on these later occasions when you were older. But you encouraged him. Do you know how you encouraged him?*
Patient:	*I am afraid I liked the contact.*
Great Mother:	*Yes. You cherished pleasures, fears and agonies in your unconscious, rather than part from his unawareness and perversions. You gave libido to your father's darkest shadow by refusing to see him as sinful, and this, in spite of your warning instinct. You must not repress your own guilt by exonerating your father. He is not only the paternal, loving*

father, and you, the obedient, innocent girl.
No! He approached his little daughter with
perverse tendencies, and she liked it and gave
way to it. Almost father-daughter incest! Just
one more little step and it might have thrown
him into prison. Of course, this little step was
not taken, and both of you retired into
"righteous" respectability, the incestuous
inclinations covered up by apparent inno-
cence. Today you are still under the spell of
all this. Now break this spell! Refuse to keep
on burdening yourself with the false respec-
tability of your father. See his shadow and
push that shadow aside by judging your
father severely. And take over the full
responsibility for the role which your own
shadow played in the tragedy. Suffer the
loathing you feel for her, suffer it completely!
Perhaps your injured nature will forgive you
then and balance may at last be restored in
your soul!

Dream

To confirm this conversation, the patient had a dream about
smuggling, which took place at some frontier. Her analyst explained the
smuggling in the dream as being the kind of dishonesty which we
contrive when we repress unpleasant thoughts up to, and beyond, the
frontier of consciousness. And the analyst added: "Most people think
they are not guilty when they do not know about deeds which they
commit. But Jung shows us that we *are* guilty when we do not know
about them. *Not to know is the guilt!*"

The next step on her path toward individuation was that the patient
had to see her human mother through the eyes of her archetypal
mother.

Seventeenth Conversation with the Great Mother

Great Mother: *It will be difficult for you, because you loved*
                                 her so deeply, but we must now look at the

part which your mother played in your "family horrors." Your mother was not as unconscious as her husband, but she was weak and easily influenced. She loved her husband above everything and she could not accept or see his dark side. She made the same mistake which you made. You copied her. This was because of your participation mystique with her. She repressed her knowledge about this dangerous shadow of her husband, for he had to remain her immaculate hero. She did not know much about her own shadow, but lived in his false righteousness. This she did out of loyalty and gentleness toward him. She was too much one with him and participated in his crime insofar as she did not protect her children sufficiently. She surrendered to his shadow and had to die for it. The devil took her body and poisoned her mortally.

An Archetypal Aspect of the Family Tragedy

Now that we have carefully examined the family tragedy in its personal aspect, it does not seem premature to turn our attention toward a possible archetypal aspect of it, because a father complex which manifests itself negatively enough to form a sexual taboo in the daughter's soul is worth following up in all its projections, symbols and aspects.

Fields of Masculinity in the Psychology of Women

When we consider the existence of a father complex or of masculinity in general in the psychology of women, we can discriminate between three aspects or fields.

The first field is the human aspect, the father complex as such, and its projections onto other real men. Its realm is the *personal* one.

Secondly, we have the animus aspect. The animus is innate in a woman as a germ which can develop into such-and-such characteristics, in the majority of cases through the father complex. This animus figure functions as a kind of bridge, for on one side he belongs to the woman's personal life, in which he represents the unconscious part of her mind; whereas on the other side, he is at home in the collective unconscious. Hidden behind the personal animus is a larger animus, behind him a larger one still, and so on. In this way, a positive animus leads up to the most positive side of God, whereas a negative animus leads down— even to Satan!

This brings us to a third aspect of masculinity in the soul of a woman, which would be the image in her of male divinity himself. The fact that a woman can have a feeling relationship to this divine power proves that at least an image or reflection of it must live in her soul, and that allows us to call this image the third aspect of masculinity in her.

When the father complex is constellated in the unfolding soul of a woman, we can discern not only its effect on what we call her earthly fate, but also its influence on the development of her animus and, ultimately, on her evolving relationship to spirituality. The differentiation of the three fields of masculinity in the soul of a woman is made more difficult, owing to the fact that in projections these fields are often intermingled. As we know, the heavenly Father is generally over-burdened with human qualities. And it does not need to be emphasized how often a human man is a kind of god in the eyes of a woman (or, just as frequently, a sort of animus-devil!).

But let us return to the case and consider the three aspects of the father complex and its projections as they are manifested there. We have already shown the influence which the father complex had exerted on her earthly fate. In the conversation which follows, the Great Mother will deal with the fatal result which the father complex had on the development of the patient's animus. And, later on, we shall get an insight into its effects upon the spiritual image, or religious concept, in the soul of this woman.

Eighteenth Conversation with the Great Mother

Great Mother: *Your animus became entangled with the shadow of your father and therefore perpe-trated the family horrors all over again in your unconscious. And you project this crim-inally infected animus on human men. So how can you expect them to love you? Through your animus works the shadow of your father, and through this shadow works the devil! This devil wanted to kill the members of your family, one after the other —and he succeeded! Your whole family has now died except for you. You must live five lives, so to speak. You had to sacrifice a normal personal life. You lived the life of the family.*

Patient: *Must I part from the family and now live a personal life?*

Great Mother: *I cannot tell yet. Perhaps you will have your hands full until your own death in achieving this family mission. In that case, there will be no personal life, just the sacrifice of it, and it must be freely given. Your mission in life might turn out to be the impersonal one of looking that devil in the face without capitulating to this fascination. Now that you have looked at your father complex in the personal realm, you must try to free your animus from the shadow of your father, lest the devil succeed in fastening his grip on him. See the tragedy in its fullest extent, and be severe about it. Do not only be impressed by your own dissatisfaction as an "unloved woman," but try also to see the family tragedy as an impersonal happening, the ramifications of which operate in the collective unconscious as well as in your personal soul.*

Patient (desperately): *Tell me, Great Mother, why do I have to go through these horrors all over again?*

Great Mother: *The idea of it is that the collective unconscious contains the father-daughter incest and that everybody is unconsciously connected with it. You are now consciously going through it, and that is more than most people do. You do it for the family, but also you do it for a much larger circle of human*

beings. And it will work itself out in a better
relationship to them. People will feel it.

The patient asked her analyst why exactly incest is forbidden. The
analyst answered:

"The psychological results of incest are not so well known as is
commonly supposed; psychically, incest narrows the horizon; in the case
of a father-daughter incest, the daughter would remain a child always.
Since 'father-knows-everything-best,' she will never take responsibility
upon herself and consequently, she cannot develop."

The animus now gets a form of treatment from the Great Mother, and
the patient's part in it consists of her willingness to have it done in her
soul.

Nineteenth Conversation with the Great Mother

Great Mother:	*You must once more go through a complete union with me, and your willingness to do so is what your animus needs in order to get healed. Give me your love; he cannot possess you then. Your willingness to endure is your necessary contribution to my act of exorcising the incest-devil out of you, and thus healing the animus.*
Patient:	*I am willing.*
Great Mother:	*By submitting to me, you separate your animus from the shadow of your father, and consequently, from the devil. Thus you heal the neurosis of your animus, which is your own. He must see that he is neither your father's shadow nor the devil. Such identifications cause an inflation in him. He is very ill and totally crushed, carrying your father's shadow.*
Patient:	*Isn't he behaving rather like a woman?*
Great Mother:	*Yes, insofar as he identifies with his anima while he allows her to fornicate with Satan. That is what happens to you in your soul, when you are carried away by nervous attacks.*

Patient:	*Is this particular devil the incest taboo?*
Great Mother:	*He is not the taboo; he is the incest. He creeps into your father's shadow where the incest is at home, and then he fornicates with your anima-possessed animus.*
Patient:	*I feel almost insane now.*
Great Mother:	*You can stand it. You must stand it!*
Patient:	*To whom can I turn if the whole family was infected?*
Great Mother:	*To me! I show you all these horrors because you must have faith in me; you must be sufficiently impressed to keep to me! You will never become whole if you cannot free your faith, this faith which is blocked in the unconscious by your horrors. You are on the verge of insanity now, but you can keep going. And then the madness of your father will die in you. You and I are now accomplishing something completely irrational, but being willing to suffer it in your soul has for you the significance of a sacrifice, freely brought and freely given. You are humble and obedient now, and courageous. Now that you side with me, the animus can be reborn through you. Our union is his rebirth!*

Two days later, we hear the patient speaking to her Great Mother again.

Twentieth Conversation with the Great Mother

Patient:	*I have read over our last conversations, but now it no longer impresses me as being particularly important, whereas at first, it seemed to have the significance of a great act of exorcism, devil exorcism, applied to myself.*
Great Mother:	*I was exorcising the devil out of you, and you know it. But words could not express this. It was beyond words.*

Patient:	*I felt as if you were gathering the whole of my being and the whole past of my life into one enormous grasp in order to unite it with yourself, thus withdrawing it from the animus.*
Great Mother:	*It was a gigantic crisis.*
Patient:	*What happened to the animus?*
Great Mother:	*Had he not been immortal, he would have died! Let him be in my charge now. Your task is to take care of yourself and your shadow.*

V. Developments

When the patient had read and thought over the last dialogues, she began to see what might be the consequences of a relationship between her own shadow and an animus who was depraved enough to have a secret affair with Satan. She saw that this shadow was giving all her blood (and indeed the blood of the patient herself) to the fatal conglomeration of animus, father's shadow and devil. This insight meant an important step on her way toward individuation, and each higher level she attained on the spiral gave her a more extensive view, which included the future as well as the past.

After the almost medieval act of devil exorcism which the Great Mother had worked upon her, the patient was free to turn to the third field of masculinity in her soul, which we have discerned as "the image of the male divinity himself," to which a positively developed animus may form a bridge and thereby enable the ego to participate.

Religious Poems

The creative animus had already appeared (apart from musical inspirations) in a series of religious poems which the patient had begun to write at this time. The contents of one of these poems will play a part in her further development. They give a clear idea of the influence which her negative father complex had upon her religious concepts.

In this poem, called "The Harp of God," she compares her soul to a harp which she yields up to God. She describes what pains she took to tune the strings accurately and how she dusted and polished the gilded frame until it shone brightly. These careful preparations having been accomplished, she offers up her harp to God, praying that His divine fingers may touch its strings. When she considered her poem finished, a curious and totally unexpected thing happened. She heard a masculine voice, the voice of God, telling her in the rhythm and rhyme of her own poem that He, God, does not wish to be disturbed just now. And, besides, He does not want her human harp at all. He has already selected the universe for a harp, the golden strings of which are— sunbeams.

So far, the poem distinctly demonstrates that the negative father complex affected even this highest level, the level on which God rejects her harp (namely her love). In the human realm, as we have seen, her womanly love for the other sex was unable to reach any partner. Instead, fascinated by the animus, she allowed him to possess and torture her. And on the spiritual level, God now refuses to play upon her harp— that is, to accept her love. But this time, powerful personalities are sustaining her—archetypal figures as well as human personalities.

She has an opportunity to read her poem, including God's answer, to Jung.[11] She expects him to laugh heartily, especially at God's answer, but this is not the case. Jung does not take it as a joke at all; in fact, he takes the matter very seriously indeed, and he tells her that she cannot leave it at that. She must find an answer to God, an answer which might inspire God to become conscious not only of beautiful sunbeams, but also of His obligation to play upon the harp of human souls. It is God who has created these human beings and therefore He has to accept His share of the responsibility for their souls.

This view about her poem which Jung said was the answer *he* would have given to God was at first no help to the patient. It somehow did not harmonize; in fact, it interfered with her own relationship to God. The difficulty may have been that she had not yet formed a clear concept of the God image which lived in her soul. Until now, according to orthodox Christian dogma, she had understood God to be "abso- lute''; that is, existing in Himself and detached from any human condi- tions. But, as we shall see, the God about which the Great Mother and the patient are speaking in the following conversations is rather a "rela- tive'' God; namely, a God whose existence is in a certain sense depen- dent upon a human subject by means of a mutual and necessary interplay. In the case of our patient, this God, or God image, was at first

---

[11]The following account of Jung's pronouncements should not be taken literally, but rather as the echo which they had in the soul of the patient.

negatively colored—as mentioned above—because the ramifications of the patient's negative father complex extended to this divine level. The goal was now to purify this image.

The Great Mother takes up its negativity in the coming conversations and helps the patient to find a relationship to it by drawing the latter's attention to the collective quality of her disturbance and to its origin in the collective unconscious.

Twenty-first Conversation with the Great Mother

Patient:	*I have the dreadful feeling that everybody has withdrawn from me. There is emptiness all around me. God has retired into the clouds.*
Great Mother:	*Perhaps God feels as desolate as you do because He refused to play upon your harp. It might be His mood which He projects upon you.*
Patient:	*Do you mean that God plays His bad mood upon my harp? Then he is a bad player.*
Great Mother:	*Are you perhaps a bad listener?*
Patient:	*Is my emptiness God's emptiness? Is God's anima projected onto me?*
Great Mother:	*Not only onto you. Onto humanity, we might say. God wants to become conscious, yet He does not want to. His ambivalence is heaped upon mankind. You are one of those who might be called upon to succor God in His state of nigredo (blackness).*
Patient:	*How can I do that?*
Great Mother:	*Be conscious of the nigredo in yourself, but without seeing it as personal. It is worldwide. You can save neither the world nor God. But you might save an infinitesimal part of its trouble, just as much or as little as you are willing to suffer yourself.*
Patient:	*I cannot see God clearly. I see clouds instead.*
Great Mother:	*You project your animus onto God. This is*

countertransference, or vice versa. Be very humble lest God hit out at you. One might compare God's condition to the state of mind that precedes creativity. God must project this forlornness caused by the nigredo onto mankind, because He is unconscious of it. If there are not enough human beings who can carry God's nigredo on their own shoulders, then catastrophe is probable. But if you know what you are carrying when you feel miserable and ill, if you do not feel your suffering to be only personal, but understand that an archetype from the collective unconscious is touching you, then you can bear it better. Do you see? To carry your own cross means carrying a part of God's cross as well.

Patient: *If I react to my desolation by judging the whole of my analysis to be a mistake, then that of course is an animus opinion.*

Great Mother: *Yes, such thoughts are animus opinions. But the nigredo feeling, as we shall call it, must be separated from them and, please, not repressed.*

Twenty-second Conversation with the Great Mother

Two days later, the dialogue is taken up again as follows:

Patient: *If God wants to transplant His negative side into me . . .*

Great Mother   *I must put this right. If God were actually to (interrupting):   do so, then there would not be the slightest chance for you to stand it. You are not up to carrying an incarnation of the devil. Only in a higher region could such an incarnation take place. Should God choose you for this purpose, you would most certainly die or become insane. You are not able to contain the image of the antichrist. To let that idea get hold of you would be an inflation.*

Patient:	*I do not know whether I had that idea or not. In fact, I do not believe that I had it.*
Great Mother:	*You had it in a way, perhaps unconsciously. Be conscious of your personal shadow and understand through her that God has a shadow too; namely, His son, Satan. God must become conscious of His shadow. He is not yet sufficiently conscious of him. This is God's state of nigredo, and its image in human souls generates the trouble in the world. A particle of God's difficult condition has to be fought out in each human being. Your family history is half-personal and half-impersonal. It is like a ladder uniting the two realms. The newly acquired consciousness of its personal, as well as of its animus, aspect will now help you to get right with God, for all the time you were struggling with your family horrors you were also wrestling with the devil, who is a part of God.*
Patient:	*Is the devil that part of God which will not accept my harp?*
Great Mother:	*It is that particular song which God will not play upon your harp. God prefers to leave that to the devil. He reserves the sunbeams and the cosmic hymn for Himself.*

As a result of this conversation, the patient now tries to look at her inner history in its spiritual aspect. At first, she calls that aspect its reflection in heaven. But in this connection, words such as reflection, mirage, image and so on seem to be out of place. She thinks she had better change her post of observation so that she might learn to look at her human tragedy as if it were the image, in miniature, of a universal drama. She even tries to see her own life as an infinitesimal earth symbol for celestial evolutions.

In order to find this spiritual standpoint, she now undertakes a symbolic journey to an unknown land under the supervision of the Great Mother, hoping to attain the new point of observation for which she is longing. She experiences this voyage as an extremely dangerous enterprise, which she describes in a long series of conversations with her Great Mother.

The dialogues contain an active fantasy of which an abridged version will be given in form of a narrative. The patient calls her fantasy:

A Tightrope Dancer Crosses an Abyss

In this fantasy the patient is standing on the edge of a precipice which lies between two realms: her old, terrestrial standpoint and the more spiritual conception of life to which she is now aspiring.

A rope connects both sides of the abyss, and apparently this rope is meant to replace a bridge. This is going to be a tightrope dancer's crossing! At first, she recoils from the danger of it. But the Great Mother reassures her, saying that she—the Great Mother—is the rope, and that the patient cannot come to grief because she is firmly fixed to this rope, although as yet with only one toe. Moreover, says the Great Mother, the patient has a balancing pole in her hands; namely, her instincts. Consequently, our poor, untrained tightrope dancer decides to venture across.

But when she has gotten halfway, she is imprudent enough to look down into the depths, and there she sees her animus and her shadow waltzing together and kissing! The sight of them makes her giddy. She loses her balance and falls, but remains hanging, head downward, from the rope to which she is attached with only one toe.

Now, just this fateful slip is that which separates the lovers. The patient is now hanging between them, head downward, as if she were a sword dividing them. A need to end this torture makes her remember her balancing pole (her instincts). She tries to reach the bottom of the precipice with this pole, in order to make contact with the earth (her own earth). But the pole is not long enough. How can she make it longer? At last, her agony forces her to cry out to her shadow, imploring her to come to her aid. And then, after the reunion with her shadow, her instincts come to life, whereupon the pole grows longer and longer. When it touches the bottom of the abyss, she succeeds, by pushing hard against it, in regaining her upright position on the rope, and then she proceeds along the rope until she reaches the other side of the ravine.

Of course, on paper it is easy enough to say that the patient united with her shadow, but in actual fact, she was in the extremity of her need when she shouted for help, and her cry for the shadow was uttered in agonizing fear. The patient expressed her need as follows:

A Talk with the Shadow

Patient: Shadow! Leave that animus alone! Unite with me! You belong to me!

Shadow: Yes! Now that the devil is exorcised out of him, this animus is nothing but a very unattractive mass of misery. I am not interested in him, not I! I prefer little flirtations with real men, and I want to get at them through you!

Patient: You said "little flirtations." That is all right. But I do not want you to flood me with your sex appeal.

Shadow: Take me or leave me! . . . In the end, the animus might recover and I might go back to him!

Twenty-third Conversation with the Great Mother

Great Mother: Can you see the mistake you made?

Patient: Oh, yes. I should have taken the whole of her while she was willing to come to me.

Great Mother: You are terribly afraid of her and of instincts that might flood you.

Through this conversatoin—as in a flash of light—a deeper understanding was given to the patient. Something which was as yet dark and inaccessible in her was suddenly illuminated.

She saw that her idea of masculinity was a misconception; that it was wrapped in darkness by opinions which actually belonged somewhere else. When she was confronted by masculinity—be it in its human aspect, in the animus realm, or in a spiritual sphere—then her panic was, at bottom, fear of becoming overwhelmed, swept away by her own sensations, emotions and instincts. Her sexual panic was called forth by unconscious shadow parts which she had projected onto masculinity, together with her shadow's shameless display of sexual need and lust. Her realization that this projection had to be taken back onto herself put an end to the enjoyment felt by the dark couple in waltzing and kissing each other in the abyss.

Symbolically, this was the moment in which her instinctive balancing pole reached the earth. It was also the moment when she could regain her upright position and proceed along the rope by leaning hard on the pole with which she kept touching the bottom of the ravine as she went. This repeated contact with her own depths sustained her, and thus she could reach the other side of the ravine. Here lay—as the Great Mother had foretold—the Promised Land, the spiritual realm which she could now begin to explore, the "world-behind-her-neurosis," as she called it. In this world, she hoped to find God.

VI. A Sojourn in a Spiritual World

Alas, the first encounter which the patient had in her "world-behind-the neurosis" was definitely not the one for which she had yearned. For the first figure which advanced to meet her was Satan himself!

Satan immediately opened a discouraging conversation with her.

Conversation with Satan

Satan:	*Do you really think that you can stand your ground? You silly child! You have not got the slightest chance of resisting me!*
Patient:	*The Great Mother is protecting me.*
Satan:	*I am superior to the Great Mother. I belong to the quaternity and she does not.*

Here, the conversation came abruptly to an end, because the patient could not find a reply to Satan's impudent words. But the patient had an analyst to whom she could turn, and this analyst had an answer at hand. The analyst said, "Satan has got an inflation if he thinks he is superior to the Great Mother," and the analyst made her the following chart of the quaternity:

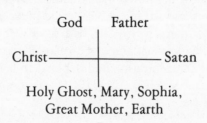

God   Father

Christ————————Satan

Holy Ghost, Mary, Sophia,
Great Mother, Earth

Thus equipped, the patient felt better armed against possible attacks on the part of her powerful opponent. She risked a further conversation with him, and this time she herself was the attacking party.

Conversation with Satan

Patient:	*Now hear me, Satan! My analyst has informed me that as Earth, the Great Mother belongs to the quaternity just as much as you do! You are not placed above the Great Mother and you are not going to ruin my relationship with her.*
Satan:	*I have ruined that for you already, and you know how I did it.*
Patient:	*It is true that I felt as if she were going away from me. I almost cried in my dismay. But now I see it was you who had a hand in the game. You tried to separate us! Go away! I want the Great Mother, not you!*
Satan:	*The Great Mother has a shadow, too. I am that shadow!*
Patient:	*No, you are not! Just as the Great Mother has a shadow, so you are related to Christ. Now leave me!*

Twenty-fourth Conversation with the Great Mother

Great Mother:	*Well done! This time he could not get you.*
Patient:	*But only thanks to you! My previous consternation was brought about by my confused thoughts concerning you and the Self.*
Great Mother:	*Your analyst told you that I am Earth. And as Earth, I am a part of the quaternity. I enter into it as the opposite of God the Father.*
Patient:	*Are you going to abandon me?*
Great Mother:	*I am always present. But it depends on you whether you are aware of this fact or not.*

Of course, Satan did not give in as easily as that. He no longer attacked his victim openly; instead, he used a hidden means to tempt her in the old way. He misused the ambition of her shadow and the almost irresistible power of her animus to inspire the patient in her music, at the cost of analysis. The patient, without having recognized this as a plot of Satan's, told the Great Mother about her temptation.

Twenty-fifth Conversation with the Great Mother, Including a Short Talk with the Animus

Patient:	*I feel terribly tempted to go back to music, and I do not know whether it would be right or wrong to do so.*
Great Mother:	*You may abandon Jungian psychology and be an artist in music again. You are sufficiently gifted to do so. Or you can go to further depths of individuation. You are standing at the crossroads now, and a decision must be taken.*
Patient:	*I know my goal is individuation, but I am terribly tempted to fly away with the animus, up into the clouds. This puts me to the test.*
Great Mother:	*If you know your goal, then make your decision quickly. Do not keep on torturing yourself.*
Patient:	*This is a real sacrifice.*
Great Mother:	*There is no need to tell me that; I know it. It is your real encounter with your animus. If you become fascinated, you will follow him and be an artist again. You are free to do so. Or you can sacrifice the fascination by choosing to become more and more conscious of your animus.*
Patient:	*Here I am. I belong to you! I have worshipped my animus as if he were God. I must sacrifice him now, or I shall never be able to see God. This is my hell. I thought that hell was to be neurotic and ill, all that kind of thing, but now I see the cause of my neurosis*

in my inclination to be fascinated by the
animus. I want to argue with him now about
this.

(The patient then addresses her animus.)

Patient: My animus, why did you make me struggle
                    with music for more than forty years?

Animus: Oh, just a pastime.

Patient: Do not ridicule me.

Animus: My undertone is mocking, but I am speaking
                    the truth. Your unconscious struggled with
                    the family horrors, but you yourself were not
                    up to doing that. So we did without you. We
                    gave your ego an occupation so that you
                    should not spoil our work or interrupt us.

Patient: Who are "we" and "us"?

Animus: The Great Mother told me to occupy myself
                    with you while she dealt with your uncon-
                    scious problems. She told you more than
                    once that she had lived your life for you.

Great Mother   This is true. He was the one who caused you
(interrupting the   to move on in music. But I was an even
animus and   deeper cause than he was. I made him push
addressing the   you. I gave him a pastime just to prevent his
patient):   mixing himself up with my work, which was
                    to prepare your unconscious for later individ-
                    uation. This individuation is the goal now.

Having come out of the struggle with Satan and her animus with a
whole skin, the patient then had an important dream which cleared her
psychic sky in a wonderful way.

Dream

The patient is in a hurry to reach the station, but cannot get on. She is
overtaken by a boy on a scooter who shouts to her for sheer joy of speed.
He has passed and is already a good distance ahead of her when she sees
him falling with his scooter while going at full speed. His head hits the
paving stones. This happens three times. The patient cannot go to his
assistance, for she has to catch her train. She is late as it is. Besides, the

*accidents happen a long way off, and the distance is too great for her to
cover. She asks for a taxi, but is told there are no taxis today. She then
tries to run to the station, but she is not able to run; her legs feel like
lead.*

*The town in which she is struggling forward is the capital of her native
country, and she manages to reach its main square. Here it proves impossible to advance because of a big procession of women, evidently a
demonstration, which is moving along and blocking the way. The women
are going to act a play or allegory on this square. The patient is now in
the company of another woman. Together they find places on a kind of
private tribune where they can look at the performance. As yet, there is
nobody else on the platform, and they have a free choice of seats. The
patient would have liked to sit in the front row, but she is willing to join
her companion and be content with seats in the back row. Moreover, she
wonders whether all of this is not perhaps a mistake, for they have come
to what appears to be the royal tribune.*

Explanation of the Dream

The dream affirms that the patient was right when she chose to go the
way of further individuation instead of listening to the tempting suggestions of her animus. The little boy on the scooter is a young animus, and
probably it was he who recently tempted her to leave analysis in favor of
eternal musical raptures together with him. Always to fly up into the sky
is natural for an animus. This tendency of his shows in his speed, which
indeed ends in a calamity, but his immortal nature enables him to
survive such disasters. Had the patient joined him, *she* would have met
with what would have been for *her* a fatal smash. She has managed to
avoid this trap.

In the dream, she was right to let the animus look after himself, but
she was mistaken as far as her goal is concerned. The goal seems to be to
catch her train. A taxi is not to be had; she must go on foot (which is the
most individual way of advancing, whereas a taxi is a more collective
means). She tries to run, but her legs feel like lead. The motif of heavi-
ness, when it occurs in dreams, generally indicates that we ought not to
reach the goal toward which we are striving. We should change it for
another goal. This is exactly what happens in the dream. The patient
forgets all about her train as soon as she reaches the main square of the
town, where she becomes absorbed in looking at the procession.

In reality, *fame* is the train for which she had been running. This
hope must now be given up in favor of the all-embracing goal of indi-

viduation. The dream gives her more details about her real destination, telling her that it is a square in the center of the town and in the heart of her native country, where she has her roots. It is a mandala that symbolizes the Self. In outer reality a national monument was erected in this square after the last war, in honor of liberation from the Nazis and from their enormous animus, Hitler. The women in the dream are going to perform a play or allegory around this monument, and the patient's associations inform us about its character, for the play is connected with a famous poem written by a well-known woman poet of her country. This poem describes a festival, celebrated by women, in honor of liberation from inner slavery, and the dream makes use of this symbol in order to express that "the women" (that is, all the women in the patient herself, the whole of her being) are celebrating the sacrifice of being possessed by the animus in favor and in honor of the Self. This performance, at which she is a spectator, is taking place in the center of her own soul.

She is together with her shadow, and for the sake of that shadow, she is willing to sit in the back row of the tribune. We ought to be thankful that the humility of the shadow prevents her from choosing seats in the front row, for the front row appears to be the royal tribune to which they have been admitted. And, surely not the ego but the Self should be seated in the front row. This tribune is a symbol of what the patient has called her "spiritual post of observation" lying in her "world-behind-the-neurosis," which the Great Mother has helped her to reach on the other side of the abyss. In the dream, the patient does not get an inflation because she is conscious of her shadow and willing to accept the responsibility for that shadow.

This important dream and its explanation opened the patient's eyes, so that she began to see the value of sacrificing animus temptations in favor of the all-embracing meaningfulness of the Self.

From that point, she tried to become familiar with the spiritual aspect of her problems by means of further contact with her inner figures and their superpersonal points of view. Her progress began to be rapid.

Twenty-sixth Conversation with the Great Mother

Patient: *It appears to me that my previous problem with the animus has now to be gone through on its highest level; namely, in relationship to God.*

Great Mother:	*Your relationship to God has changed since that devil, your father's shadow, was exorcised out of your animus and since your shadow remains separated from him.*
Patient:	*When I try to speak to God, I feel as if I were again hanging head-downward on the rope, as in the fantasy.*
Great Mother:	*Head-downward means that you should approach God not with your head, but with lower parts.*

These words, spoken by the Great Mother, recalled to the mind of the patient her shadow, who perhaps might be helpful in making a favorable approach to God.

She broached this idea to her shadow in the following way:

Conversation with the Shadow

Patient:	*Shadow, can you help me to approach God with my feeling?*
Shadow:	*I know how to feel toward masculine persons. It is very simple; you just feel feminine!*
Patient:	*In what way?*
Shadow:	*Men can help us with what we ourselves are not. We must feel ourselves very feminine, very much a female. Then men will come. Love your female body, love your own need for men. Then they come. I feel myself superior to men because I know that they must fall for me. This is a little trick. We mean pleasure to them. Please them by playing the pleasure to them. They cannot resist it; they come. You can get everything out of them when you play the ultra-female, their pleasure part. Never forget how much we mean pleasure to them!*

The patient thanks the shadow for her information and addresses the Great Mother.

Twenty-seventh Conversation with the Great Mother

Patient:	*I must acknowledge that I never could identify with my own femininity and that I never thought of humbly representing a man's pleasure.*
Great Mother:	*That would be your sin toward God. You have not accepted your fate while you have not accepted your sex. And it is not enough to accept your sex as suffering, which you did. Your shadow accepted it as a gift. She is pleased to please men and quite content with her role. Moreover, how can you be God's vessel if you repress the natural function of your feminine physique, of those parts made for the purpose of conception? Spiritual conception and the way to it can be taught to you by what your body is able to tell you. As soon as the feeling part is constellated through your instincts, you will no longer need to beg God to play upon your harp. He Himself will ardently desire to do so.*

In this manner the attempt to enrich herself with yet unconscious shadow parts had once again allowed the patient to take a step forward on her way to individuation.

She now tried to feel in which way she could *please* God. Of course, her animus immediately told her that he disagreed with her ludicrous plan. But she knew how to answer him, as we shall see in the next talk.

Conversation with the Animus

Patient:	*Animus, be silent! I want to feel God's nearness through active identification with the life He means me to live. So, first of all, I shall try to feel at home in my own femininity.*
Animus:	*I am your messenger to God! I am now going to fly up to Him and tell him this for you.*
Patient:	*Thanks, but I am going to tell Him myself.*

An Archetypal Dream

Some days later, a very short but extremely archetypal dream is given to her:

> *She hears a masculine voice, God's voice, crying out to her for help. Instead of using the common word "Help," God repeats several times, in the language of the patient, the ancient biblical word "succor."*

This is the whole of the dream.

This dream was followed by a conversation with the Great Mother, in which the latter explains how human beings can be of use to God.

Twenty-eighth Conversation with the Great Mother

Great Mother:	*Dr. Jung once told you that human beings are the eyes and ears of God and that they must give consciousness to God through their lives. It now looks as if God had called to you for help because he wants this bit of consciousness which you can give Him.*
Patient:	*I had a difficult fantasy which I want to relate to you. It said that God was angry because men had stolen parts of Him which He had not meant to be in human hands. These parts were nature's secret about nuclear splitting and, the equivalent of this, Jung's knowledge concerning the Deity. God had not intended that human beings should know about His dark side. He meant to remain unconscious about this Himself. He wants to repress this awkward business. He has resistances. Therefore Jung and his pupils, all of them, are damned in His eyes.*
Great Mother:	*The danger to all of you is not imaginary. You have experienced the enormous tension yourself; I mean the tension that existed in your soul when you had to become conscious of dark sides in yourself, or when a creative process was about to manifest itself in you. Perhaps God will create very positive things*

*as soon as He is conscious enough to start
action. But if He does not become conscious
of Satan as His son, then His own dark side
may be projected onto human persons. He
may let loose His resentments onto mankind
in a world catastrophe. Subsequently, He will
accuse Dr. Jung and Professor Einstein of
having caused it. They will be the scapegoats.*

*Now, listen: you are very near to Jung and
of course you will be destroyed with him if
the worst were to happen. But you, being a
woman, can do a thing which Dr. Jung, who
is a man, cannot do. You might charm God!
You and other women might wake Him up.
To do this would be less dangerous for you
than for Jung, because a man is likely to
provoke God's masculine eagerness for combat. Moreover, God does not need to become
aware of His masculinity but of His dark side,
which includes femininity. It is a woman's
job to make Him aware of this. Be the serpent in Paradise and make God eat the fruit
from the tree of knowledge of good and evil.
The truth is that human beings ate of it and
that God did not. Make God eat the fruit
which you offer Him. This is the same thing
as making Him play upon your harp.*

Patient:	*But that is exactly what He refused to do.*
Great Mother:	*Yes. But at that time you were not yet suffi-ciently conscious of your shadow. You can only make God do it if you and your shadow are completely fused.*
Patient:	*Oh, my Great Mother, I am not up to this task! Your femininity and the wisdom of the Self are necessary for the achievement of such a mission. Only Sophia herself might perhaps be powerful enough.*
Great Mother:	*Yes, this is true. But in your dream, God's*

*voice called to you for help. Listen: we great
female archetypes of the collective unconscious may counterbalance the too masculine
line and, therefore, dangerous attitude of
God. But to save humanity, human beings
must provide us with a foothold. It cannot be
done in our spiritual world alone. And in this
special case we need women, earth women.
We need this earthly aspect of femininity. A
sufficient amount of it might turn the scales
and bring them to balance. Play your part!
This is the meaning of your whole life.*

Twenty-ninth Conversation with the Great Mother

Patient:

*My Great Mother, I had an experience which
was not a vision but a kind of illuminating
thought, very queer and rather dangerous.
Perhaps I spoke with you in a passive fantasy.
Somebody told me things or inspired me
with thoughts. I did not make them up.*

Great Mother:

Tell me about it.

Patient:

*When Christ had to be born, God made
Mary pregnant through the Holy Ghost.
Then God's Son descended from heaven
onto earth. Now it has been indicated to me
that the reverse is about to happen and Satan
seems on the point of being admitted into
the quaternity. Until now, Satan was incarnated in mankind as sin, but now he must
either ascend from earth to heaven, or he
must be reborn in heaven. Only if this takes
place will mankind be freed from Satan; that
is to say, from sin. My fantasy said that an
earth woman must instigate this, must set the
ball rolling. We women must make God
willing to accept the apple of the garden of
Eden, which is the apple of consciousness*

about good and evil.[12] *Or—in this case—it should be called the apple of earth, the apple of human sinfulness. The offering of this apple has the purpose of evoking a thought in God's mind; namely, a consciousness of Satan as His son, or perhaps a consciousness of Sophia as His wife, out of whom Satan can be reborn as their son in heaven. Exactly how or in what manner this would occur is unclear to me.*

Great Mother: *Should you be as humble as Mary was, you can try to fulfill your part in this. Then, on the highest possible symbolic level, you will be delivered of that spiritual child which was once announced to you in what you then called your "Great Vision." On an earlier level than the present one, this, as you will remember, was explained as "active fulfillment of fate."*

Patient: *I am afraid it is impossible for me to be as humble as Mary was.*

Great Mother: *If you become inflated, you will either die or suffer deeply.*

Patient: *I am willing to die for it, or to suffer deeply, if only I may be allowed to bring forth this symbolic child. I can have no peace unless such a fulfillment takes place.*

Great Mother: *You cannot make conditions.*

Patient: *I see. I will accept my fate and try to fulfill it. Should the anger of God strike me before I have attained fulfillment, I am ready to accept it.*

Great Mother: *That is how it should be.*

Patient: *Great Mother, be with me! I beg you to tell me at once if I tend to become inflated. Warn me, please! Help me to be humble.*

[12]In a drawing she made at the beginning of her analysis, many years before, Anna had depicted both herself and a serpent offering apples to the trinity.

Great Mother:	*You know God called to you for help. Let awareness of this fact give you humility, for it is God who makes you do it. In yourself, you have not the power to achieve this task. God Himself will inspire you to do the right thing, even though this may seem to be irrational. You are just this bit of human foothold which is needed. Satan is in mankind; he is imprisoned there. In the same way, your animus was once imprisoned in you. Your animus cried out of you as neurosis. You opened that prison. He then told God you might open another prison also.*
Patient:	*Is Satan in this prison? Or is God? Did God shout for help, or did Satan?*
Great Mother:	*There is no difference. Satan is a part of God. You redeem both of them and mankind if you can achieve this mission.*
Patient:	*My Great Mother, are you not causing me to get an inflation? I do not want to identify with divine matters!*
Great Mother:	*It is more humble to obey than to retire in fear. You said that you preferred to be sacrificed rather than to have this feeling of eternal unfulfillment.*
Patient:	*Then I submit.*
Great Mother:	*If you are unable to fulfill this mission, there will be other women who are ready to take it over. Perhaps your task is merely to provide a beginning. It is of no importance whether it be you or someone else who will achieve it. Somebody must make a beginning, and a beginning demands the utmost effort.*
Patient:	*What must I do?*
Great Mother:	*When you were hanging head-downward on that rope in your fantasy and did not fall in that ordeal, you then became fertilized with the whole of this upside-down situation. Remember what you said previously: "Once*

God descended from heaven to earth; now earth must bring forth that which is lacking in heaven." You are one of those who must help this to come about. You must sacrifice being fascinated by the animus. If a sufficient number of women do this, then Satan can rise up into heaven. But the thought that you must achieve it alone is the result of an inflation. Such thoughts are animus ideas. You are one woman of many who are called upon to free God, or Satan, or their own animus. Just now, I left you in your inflation for a moment because I wanted to test you (or God tested you) in order to see if you can be humble. You can; you have just proved it.

Patient:

I feel utterly bewildered. What happened exactly?

Great Mother:

You see, as soon as you try to open the prison of your animus—which would favor Satan's ascension—he immediately attempts to possess you by giving you an inflation. In consequence, this swollen idea came up, the idea that only you were called upon to help God. This is, of course, not so. Femininity is called upon and you must fulfill your part with great humility. You must free your animus, not all at once, but bit by bit, step by step. And not in ecstasy by flying up with him to the sky, but by learning humility for the rest of your life on earth. Keep in mind these women in the main square of your town in the dream. They celebrated liberation from the animus, and you were privileged to be a spectator at this festival of liberation. Today you started action yourself, and now you are in it—you are one of those women. You must do in your humble domain what we archetypes of the collective unconscious will do in our spiritual domain. The too mascu-

*line God in you is your animus. Heal him
from his inflation when he thinks he is God
or Satan. By disentangling your animus from
Satan, you help the latter to ascend to the
quaternity. Thus, you play your part in the
celestial drama, and you will feel that you are
participating in it.*

*Now I must put you on your guard against
a coming danger: you will incur the risk of
getting terrible inflations yourself. Be aware
of this danger all the time. Only through you
can the inflation of your animus leave him.
You can do away with it by your suffering
awareness. Besides, inflation will not be the
only danger for you. Deflation is just as bad.
Do not feel inferior when you see that you
have been inflated; feel humbly human.*

*Never forget that it was God who called to
you for help, although you are not the only
creature whom he has called. Be patient. Let
things grow at their own rate. Be with your
shadow always. For it is not certain that you
will now abide forever in what you have
called your "world-behind-the-neurosis."
Perhaps you will have regressions. Go
through them if you must. Be courageous
and be watchful!*

With these words, the Great Mother took leave of her pupil for a
longer period. Obviously, this teacher held the view that the patient
might now be sufficiently mature to stand on her own feet. And, generally speaking, she probably was, though some difficulties remained to
be solved.

On the whole, the patient no longer considered herself to be neurotic.
She avoided certain difficult situations, it is true, and she was still a bit
afraid of possible regressions, which she would sooner evade than risk.
When living quietly, she could manage a considerable amount of work.
And she had the satisfaction of feeling that people liked her better and
that some actually sought her out.

As to the process of individuation of which I have shown the development in the course of these lectures, the patient fully acknowledged
what she owed to the Jungian line of thought in general, and to the
method of active imagination in particular. In addition to this, she had a
warm feeling of gratitude for her analysts and their unfailing love and
patience which had carried her through, and raised her above, long
periods of despair.

Above all, she experienced deep and real thankfulness to the sublime
figure of the Great Mother, her eminent teacher, who had nourished her
with archetypal food. In honor of this great personality, the final word
will be given to her in the form of a last conversation. It was not the last
in sequence, but it was laid aside at the time in order to close this series
of conversations.

It took place when the Great Mother and her pupil were sojourning in
that spiritual world which the patient had reached at the end of the
tightrope dancer's crossing of the abyss. After this crossing, the Great
Mother and her pupil were dwelling together in the upper spiritual
realm. There, this sublime teacher drew the attention of her pupil to a
curious sound which the latter had not previously noticed, a very curious
sound indeed, which she could never have heard had she not been
trained by the revelations of the Great Mother. The latter explained this
sound in such a way as to give a notion of proportion to her pupil.

Thirtieth Conversation with the Great Mother

Great Mother: *This sound which you are able to discern now*
                            because you are living in what you call your
                            "world-behind-the-neurosis"—this curious
                            sound is breathing. You hear the breathing
                            of Life now, the breathing of God: out and
                            in, out and in; birth and death, birth and
                            death . . .
                                One divine breath is the whole life of a
                            human being.

Epilogue by Barbara Hannah
Later Conversations With the Great Spirit

After Anna had completed her conversations with the Great Mother, she devoted herself for two or three years to interpreting the drawings she had made many years before at the beginning of her analysis with Toni Wolff.[13] As mentioned before, Jung usually advised against interpreting active imagination *at the time* it occurred, in order to avoid influencing its development. Moreover, Anna was in no way ready to understand her drawings at that time. It was also much better and more convincing that their interpretation should come—as it eventually did—from her own unconscious. Jung used to say that although people are interested in the interpretation of their analysts, they never *really* incorporate such interpretations into their actual lives until their own unconscious gives them *its* version. The analyst would be foolish, however, to mind this, for the only important thing is that the analysand really be moved by the meaning.

For several years after Anna had finished this work, she devoted herself to preparing the text, *Anna Marjula,* for its private printing. I must emphasize that she herself did all the considerable work that was necessary, for the conversations as they originally took place were far too long and unwieldy to print uncondensed. My involvement was to read her manuscript through from time to time, and to offer a few suggestions.

During this period, Anna felt much better than she had before her

[13]Five of these drawings plus another four supplementary drawings, together with Anna's own interpretation of them, are included as Part II in the privately printed booklet known as *Anna Marjula*.

conversations with the Great Mother; in fact, she already felt completely healed, which had been her goal for so long. She continued with her analysis, but no longer because she felt it was necessary for her health, nor to cure her previously laming sense of inferiority, but solely to increase her consciousness. She was fully convinced that increase of consciousness was the most urgent need of modern man.[14] However, her experience in childhood and adolescence with her exceedingly unconscious father had wounded her far more deeply and fatally than she had realized, and there was still a region in her whole relation to men and to the animus where trouble might begin again and ruin all she had gained. In *Anna Marjula,* we saw that her father had remained completely unaware, and therefore completely unrepentant, even on his deathbed, of what he had done and still wished to do to his unfortunate daughter.

The daughters of such a father equate sexuality and incest, and therefore the strong traditional taboo against incest will operate overwhelmingly in them whenever the realm of sexuality or any intimate relationship to men is touched. For this reason, such an area will resist and will remain unchanged, even by such a thorough transformation as Anna had experienced in the material which she describes in *Anna Marjula.*

Indeed, for some years it did suffice to make Anna quiet and happy, so that she was able to devote herself to the interpretation of her early pictures and to the preparation of *Anna Marjula.* But when all this work was completed, the taboo area began giving her trouble, and she painfully realized that more work in active imagination was necessary before she could rely on her transformation to free her for the kind of "rainmaker" existence that gives meaning even to the most advanced old age.

She had fully realized this and we were already discussing where to begin when she had a dream which came to the rescue. She reported it as follows:

> *I am in a restaurant where self-service (or "Self" service!) is the custom. The door opens and in comes Professor Jung. He takes a place at my table and speaks with me. Then the situation changes: I myself am seated, but Professor Jung is now standing at my right, speaking with a man. I cannot follow the discussion, for they speak to each other as equals and their subject matter is above my intellectual grasp. But all the while they talk,*

[14]Hannah, *Jung: His Life and Work,* pp. 171f.

Jung is protectively hiding me behind his broad back, and he keeps holding my hand. Through this touch I feel a stream of new life entering me.

The strange man is evidently an animus figure whom she had not yet met, and indeed, her work on the animus in *Anna Marjula* was mainly confined to the negative side. The fact that this figure could speak to Dr. Jung as an equal on "subjects above her intellectual grasp" shows that he came from a positive *niveau* of her animus of which she was still completely unaware. It seemed to me, therefore, that this figure was the equal of her Great Mother on the masculine side, and that, if he were willing to talk to her, he would be able to take her as far into the logos as the Great Mother had taken her with the eros. The transference to Jung, moreover, was always disturbed by what her own father had done to her, and was often very much in the hands of her negative animus. This dream figure, therefore, also seemed to offer an opportunity of great improvement in this respect, a hope that was subsequently fully realized.

Nevertheless, it was obvious in the dream that the venture might be somewhat dangerous, or why should Dr. Jung hide her protectively and hold her hand throughout the dream? But the fact that new energy poured into her through this contact made the venture obviously worthwhile. Very wisely, Anna kept open the contact with the Great Mother, and from the beginning, she was quite sure of her full approval in the venture. In fact, the Great Mother intervened more than once when things were difficult, thereby saving the situation.

These conversations with the "Great Spirit," as Anna called him, were just as long and unwieldy as the original version of her conversations with the Great Mother, and obviously needed a great deal of condensation before they could be included in this book. She had arranged them in the form of lectures, as a sequel to *Anna Marjula*. But by this time, she was approaching ninety years of age and, moreover, the Great Spirit was inspiring her to write poems in her own language. Therefore, she asked me to do the condensation for her and she gave me full permission to do what I thought best with the material.

I did not feel capable of keeping it in the first person or as imaginary lectures; moreover, the reader has already experienced this form in Anna's conversations with the Great Mother. Therefore, I decided to pick out what seemed the most important points and condense the rest, as I have also done in the other cases.

First Series of Conversations

Anna had great difficulty in beginning these conversations, for her sole experience of the animus so far had been of a personal, negative figure that her unfortunate experience with her father had imprinted on her. However, the father, though so blindly unconscious in regard to his daughters, was also a very intelligent, distinguished man. Therefore, her personal animus had a more positive side which she had never seen, and behind this was the archetypal image of the Great Spirit. But all these aspects were hopelessly confused and contaminated with each other when she began these conversations, so naturally the first part was entirely concerned with their disentanglement and with the removal of Anna's projection of her negative power animus on the other aspects.

Anna tries to speak to the archetypal image right away, although she admits to seeing him very dimly and says that her negative animus is between them. The Great Spirit replies that, since the figure is much smaller than he, this can only be true if Anna stays so close to the negative figure that he can obliterate the far larger figure. He also complains that she is too afraid of this smaller figure, whereas her tone is too bold when addressing the Great Spirit.

The next day, she tells him how much this conversation has helped her, and she feels she has changed some of her fear into reverence for him. But the Great Spirit says that it should be put the other way around: she has changed her aggression toward him to a more humble attitude, thus neutralizing some of her fear of his "little brother," as he calls her personal animus.

Anna had read a great deal of Meister Eckhart and was very sure that we must give up our way for God's, or, in psychological language, that the ego must abdicate in favor of the Self. Therefore, she asks the Great Spirit if he can help her comply with God's wishes willingly. He replies that the "willingly" is entirely her own business, but in general, he can let her know what God wishes of her. But, he adds, this is just what she does *not* want to know; she is far too afraid of being asked to pick up her cross, so to speak. Therefore, she prefers to be possessed by his little brother. She regards that as harmless compared to what God might wish of her. Anna then complains that although the Great Spirit is curing her of her fear of his little brother, she is much more afraid of him than she ever was of her negative animus!

In her next conversation, she accuses herself of inflation. The mention of the cross made her identify with Jesus and once again, she saw herself as much more than she really was. (The reader will remember that many of her conversations with the Great Mother were disturbed by Anna's burning wish to become "a great woman.") The Great Spirit reminds her that not he but she herself was the one who began wanting to know God's wishes in regard to her.

I must point out that, owing to the contamination between her own positive animus and the Great Spirit, she attributes all the answers she gets to the latter. This, in itself, is enough to cause inflation, and shows us why it is so necessary in active imagination to distinguish between individual and collective elements. Just as when a woman first begins to see her negative animus, she often regards him as Satan himself, so, on the positive side, she can mistake her own individual unconscious mind for the Great Spirit per se.

Anna notices in her next conversation that she is doing most of the talking herself, which she considers very foolish if she wants to learn from him. As I pointed out in my comments about Hugh de St. Victor, this is a fault she shares with many—in fact, most—of the medieval records we have of such conversations: the so-called dialogue is really a monologue by the writer himself.[15] But Anna had less excuse for such lapses, for it belongs to the technique of conversation in active imagination first to speak or question oneself, then to make one's mind quite blank so that one may hear the answer. As the Ba said 4,000 years ago: "Behold, it is good when men listen"—advice that only very few of us have learned to follow even today. The world would probably be in a very different state if more people had learned this lesson.

The Great Spirit, or rather Anna's unconscious, creative mind, then tells her that though he has no objection to her questions about her personal life, she must understand that if he needs her for a creative purpose—a poem or more music—he will simply force her to obey as he has done all her life. She then speaks of it being too much for her to "carry him on her shoulders," which leads him to tell her not to talk such nonsense! She cannot, and does not, carry him; she can only become pregnant with his inspiration, as is woman's way. If he chooses a woman to bring his inspiration into reality, she should not suddenly turn herself into a second-rate man! She must try to empty herself, particularly of his little brother's animus ideas. Then he can create

15See above, p. 109.

through her. This is exactly the technique that we have to use in order to listen to the unconscious: emptying oneself and listening.

But Anna is not yet content to listen, and, like the World-Weary Man, she begins to play with the idea of suicide. She calls it using her ambition in the interest of self-sacrifice. She says: "In one single blow, then, suicide might relieve my unconscious guilt feelings (by self-punishment), and satisfy my megalomania or ambition to become great, especially if the suicide took the form of ecstatic self-sacrifice!"

The Great Spirit, like the Ba, at once opposes this idea. He says that the time is long past when she can follow her sister's example,[16] for now she is equipped with "just a bit more consciousness of her shadow. . . . And—still more importantly—a bit more consciousness of God as a living being."

Admitting that she still often confuses God's wishes and animus opinions, she also concedes that while she is not crazy and can use her common sense, she will never commit suicide. But she is very afraid of a "religious ecstasy" which might sweep her away. If she could only change this to the Biblical fear of God. . . . The Great Spirit replies by telling her that she must first accept her own limitations and face the fact that she is just *not* a great woman.

We see here almost exactly what Jung tells us at the end of his chapter "On Life after Death" in *Memories, Dreams, Reflections*. He says:

> *The decisive question for man is: Is he related to something infinite or not? That is the telling question of his life. Only if we know that the thing which truly matters is the infinite can we avoid fixing our interest upon futilities, and upon all kinds of goals which are not of real importance. . . .*
>
> *The feeling for the infinite, however, can be attained only if we are bounded to the utmost. The greatest limitation for man is the "self"; it is manifested in the experience: "I am only that!" Only consciousness of our narrow confinement in the self forms the link to the limitlessness of the unconscious. In such awareness we experience ourselves concurrently as limited and eternal, as both the one and the other. In knowing ourselves to be unique in our personal combination—that is, ultimately limited—we possess also the capacity for becoming conscious of the infinite. But only then!*[17]

[16]*Anna Marjula*, p. 256.
[17]Jung, *Memories, Dreams, Reflections*, p. 325.

But Anna is not yet ready to sacrifice her favorite goal of becoming a great woman. She tells him she now sees it as her task to accept the "Great No" from God's hands: no husband, no children, no lover, not a great composer or poet. This is her feminine dignity of today. But the Great Spirit is her great seducer; therefore, she must now take leave of him. He gave her pleasure from time to time when he inspired her, and he may still do so if he accepts his secondary rôle in her life, which is now completely occupied with the Great No.

He points out that being dismissed and reduced "to a possible embellishment of her life" would not suit him at all, but she scarcely hears him. She sees nothing but her Great No. God has seduced her now, and the Great Spirit is far below them. She even claims that her "Great No" is nothing less than the union of opposites as experienced by Luther.[18] He thus became a great man just as she expects to become great, though she admits that her greatness will be more invisible because she is a woman. If only the Great Spirit can realize his secondary role and just embellish her life, he might even please God!

At this point, though she seemed prepared to boast along these lines forever, she was called to order by a dream. She dreamt:

> I am in an unknown town. I climb a steep street. At its top is a big building (Association: Palace of Justice in Brussels). Four roads lead to it. I reach the top of the hill and look down its steep descent. The view is magnificent, and fills me with ecstasy. Then I am down again in the lower town and in a very dirty kitchen (the shadow's kitchen?—a witch's kitchen?).

Although as a rule it is best not to interfere in active imagination, one should, of course, point out when it is being used wrongly, and it had been obvious to me for some time that Anna had again fallen victim to her negative animus. But she was no more inclined to listen to me than to the Great Spirit, for she was totally possessed by the opinion of her Great No. This dream gave me may chance, however, and I asked her, for "justice's sake," to re-read the last conversation and see

---

[18]Luther, as a young monk, was very neurotic; perhaps even mad. He did whatever he could to outgrow his illness. He confessed five times a day, he flagellated himself, he fasted. Nothing helped him. In utter despair, he then said to himself: "All right, God has cursed me, I belong to hell. I now shall be willing to submit to God, willing to accept being cursed, separated from God." (Generally a man fights his fate, whereas a woman suffers her fate. But in his extreme despair, Luther chose the feminine way, and that attitude brought him healing.)

whether she was being just and fair to the Great Spirit, and to also ask herself what she was doing in a witch's kitchen.

Of course she did not like it, but "for justice's sake" she was willing to do it. By the next time she came, she had thrown off her animus opinion of the Great No entirely and had seen just where it overtook her. But it still took a little persuasion to induce her to resume her conversations, for by this time she was very afraid of facing the Great Spirit after all her impertinence to him.

She does do so at last, however, and asks him if it is still possible for him to talk to her after her terrible mistake of confounding him with her negative animus. She has quite forgotten her dream where he talked to Jung as an equal, and she admits that it is most probable that he did not seduce her at all.

He replies by telling her that it is most important for her to find out the identity of her seducer. She says she is afraid ambition seduced her. He replies that it was not ambition, but megalomania, which is much worse because in it, ambition appears as if in a fulfilled state. When he told her to accept the fact that she was not a great woman, he trod on her megalomania. Immediately, she retorted that she was great, for she had accepted the Great No from God and even claimed this as equal to Luther's union of opposites. Then for "justice's sake," he agreed that she had accepted her fate, but she had ruined this genuinely humble gesture by being proud of it. She thus gave it over to her megalomania and again felt herself to be a great woman. She should get quite straight about this.

Moreover, the Great Spirit advises her to become much more conscious of her personal negative animus. She is making the mistake of thinking that becoming more conscious of the positive side will automatically keep the negative down, he says. But only by becoming more conscious of the negative can she approach the Great Spirit more positively. Only by hard work on the lower regions can she begin to understand the spiritual things of which he was speaking to Jung in her dream.

In the next conversation, Anna speaks of her sexual taboo which, she believes, is keeping her from relationship to men and to the Great Spirit. He points out that it is her power animus and her own craving for power that is doing this. He says:

In the sexual act, a woman must give up her power and allow herself to be

overpowered by the male. Deep down, this is what she wants. She wants
to be overpowered by the masculine. The moment in which she has to
give in is her moment of satisfaction. Such is nature.

She asks where her mistake is. He replies that she judges men by her
own negative animus, who really only overpowers her to gain power over
her, and she thus has no confidence in men, in their tenderness, or in
their love. She projects her own negative animus on men and thus
destroys all chance of the man loving her.

Anna, being well over 70 when this conversation takes place, says, "I
try to realize that the time for sexuality is past and gone." The Great
Spirit replies that the time for concrete sexuality is indeed over, but not
the time for its symbolic realization. With sexuality in the background,
she must learn to look spirituality in the face. Anna then realizes it was
her own lust for power, for being a great woman, that has spoiled her
feminine sexuality.

The Great Spirit explains that although she has sometimes realized
that she was possessed by the negative animus, whom she has always
regarded as something outside of her, she must now realize that he is
within her. It was her lust for power that had kept her from the normal
feminine reaction of wanting to be overpowered. She blocked the way to
her feminine nature by her craving for power. No outside devil did this
to her; she did it to herself.

In the next conversation, she tells him how much all he told her has
helped her. But now she is distressed by something new. A woman in
her hotel, whom she calls Mrs. C, has gotten on her nerves. She was
determined to end all contact with her, but she now realizes that she was
"cruel and egotistic" toward her, and wonders how much she has
harmed her. She is also aware that she was dishonest in accepting too
much change at the post office that morning. What does he think of her
behavior?

He replies that one can not accept one's negative shadow parts
without some consequences. At least she now knows she is not more
honest than other people. But he does not intend to tell her what she
has done to Mrs. C because she did not do it for the other woman's sake,
but entirely for her own. She now enjoys her freedom, but the joy is
mixed with uneasiness because she is forced to see that she can be
"hard, cruel and pitiless."

Anna asks him where the negative animus comes into this situation,
but the Great Spirit replies that these acts were committed by her
shadow and had nothing to do with her animus. She must learn to

distinguish between them: the animus is the one who offers her irrefut-
able opinions as to what she should or should not do, whereas the
shadow slips in the actual concrete, negative acts.

The Great Spirit draws Anna's attention to something very important
here: it is unwise to blame the animus when he has had nothing to do
with it. I learned that the hard way once when, during my analysis, Jung
was away for the Christmas holidays. I got badly out of myself and
blamed the animus entirely for my predicament, which only made the
matter worse. In my first analytic hour, I told Jung I had been badly in
the animus throughout the holidays. He looked searchingly at me and
said, "I don't think that was the trouble. Now what really happened to
you at the beginning of the holidays?" I then remembered that someone had hurt me very badly, but I had been understanding and "reasonable" about it, without seeing how much I really minded. It was the
unrecognized emotion that had really thrown me out of myself, and by
blaming the animus, where for once he was wholly innocent, I had
naturally infuriated him and made him into an additional, though
secondary, difficulty.

As often happens in active imagination, Anna's great mistake turned
out to be a blessing in disguise. It gave the Great Spirit the opportunity
to teach Anna the difference between himself and her negative animus,
and to distinguish between the latter and her shadow. This first part of
her conversation ends with the development of her ability to keep these
three figures apart, and she makes no such mistakes—or at all events,
she sees it at once when she does—in the subsequent conversations. But
she has as yet no discrimination between her own individual positive
animus, or unconscious mind, and the image of the archetypal Great
Spirit. She must learn this differentiation the hard way in the course of
the next series of conversations.

Presumably, the inspirations of which she speaks came from her own
individual positive animus, though such inspirations also seem to come
partly from the archetypal level. The fact bears witness that the spirit of
the times seems to express itself through the paintings, poems, or music
of the individual artist. This is very clear in the paintings of such an
artist as Peter Birkhäuser, for example.

Second Series of Conversations

In this second series, Anna wanted enlightenment from the Great
Spirit on how to relate to God's dark side and on whether or not we may
be called upon to do evil *consciously*. It must be pointed out from the

beginning that consciously doing evil is something very different from being possessed by it unconsciously, as seems to be the case all around us these days, and it is *very* different from regarding evil as good. In the former case, we take the responsibility for the evil we do, and we suffer a great deal from having to do it—that is, if we have been brought up in the Christian belief that all evil is of the devil and should be carefully avoided, as Anna had been. This fitted the needs of man 2,000 years ago, when Christ preached it, but it has become far too one-sided today, when it is clear that our task is to accept both opposites and do the best we can with them.

Anna realized this and was appalled, as we all are, by the problem of how we can possibly relate to evil. Jung wrote a chapter in *Memories, Dreams, Reflections* entitled "Late Thoughts" when he was well over 80. He said:

> *Light is followed by shadow, the other side of the Creator. This develop-ment reached its peak in the twentieth century. The Christian world is now truly confronted by the principle of evil, by naked injustice, tyranny, lies, slavery, and coercion of conscience. This manifestation of naked evil has assumed apparently permanent form in the Russian nation; but its first violent eruption came in Germany. That outpouring of evil revealed to what extent Christianity has been undermined in the twentieth century. In the face of that, evil can no longer be minimized by the euphemism of the privatio boni. Evil has become a determinant reality. It can no longer be dismissed from the world by a circumlocution. We must learn how to handle it, since it is here to stay. How we can live with it without terrible consequences cannot for the present be conceived.*[19]

Anna did this active imagination after Jung's death. Just after *Memories* was published, and, remembering that the figure of the Great Spirit was talking to Jung in her dream as an equal, she hoped the Great Spirit would be able to teach her how to "live with evil," if possible, without the "terrible consequences." Like all of us, she realized that the terrible consequences may overtake any or all of us in terrifying Apoca-lyptic form at any time, but we all still naturally pray with Christ: "If it be possible, let this cup pass from me,"[20] which is quite legitimate if we can honestly add, nevertheless: "not my will, but thine, be done."

Anna begins by asking the Great Spirit how she can relate to God's

---

[19]Jung, *Memories, Dreams, Reflections*, pp. 328f.
[20]*Matt.* 26:39.

dark side. He asks her to consider if she really wants to do this. She admits that she does not, but she is sure she *must*. He accepts this answer, but advises her to begin by relating to her own dark side and adds, "Perhaps you think you have done this already, and I admit you have made the shadow conscious to a considerable extent, but you have not actually related to it." She asks if he means that she must change her attitude to the extent of sometimes doing evil consciously. He replies, "That is exactly what I mean," which causes her to revert to her Christian attitude and ask him if he is Satan himself! He answers, "No, I am not the evil principle, but because the principle of opposites must be fulfilled—this being the condition for life—I know that those who do bad deeds (*consciously*) are serving God's wishes." Anna asks if human beings cannot leave this to God. But the Great Spirit replies: "If you leave it to God, He does it through you, but you turn your back on it. This is the reason why your back is so tired and why your neck aches so much. Then you can look into the clouds. But your eyes are also over-tired because of too much light. Moreover, the whole of this attitude is a lie."

He goes on to explain that we do evil anyway, because we are "half-good, half-bad" by nature, but "in conscious hands, evil takes on a different color. That is what you can do for other people: you may deliver them from a part of their evil by materializing your own evil into *conscious* deeds."

I tried to show how this works on a practical level when I described Charlotte and Anne Brontë's attitude to their brother Bramwell,[21] and Prue Sarn (in Mary Webb's *Precious Bane*) leaving all evil to be done behind her back by her brother Gideon.[22] But the Great Spirit goes further, and explains how one can suffer physical symptoms as a result of evading the fact of the equality of the opposites. According to the prophet Isaiah, the Lord Himself tells us: "I form the light, and create darkness, I make peace and create evil: I the Lord do all these things."[23] Obviously, therefore, the Lord expects us to accept both these opposites created by Him.

Unfortunately, or perhaps fortunately, we who are still living, after two world wars have shown us that the Christian solution of repressing evil no longer works, have the task of somehow relating to *both* oppo-

[21]Hannah, *Striving Toward Wholeness*, pp. 159f and pp. 182f.
[22]Ibid., pp. 94–97.
[23]*Isaiah* 45:7.

sites, a task which has perhaps never before been asked of man to this extent. This evidently belongs to the change of eras: we can no longer swim in the unconscious with the fishes; rather, we must carry our portion of it with Aquarius, the water carrier. I remind the reader that Jung thought the whole future of the world might depend on how many people could complete this task.[24]

Anna then asks if her behavior toward Mrs. C was not a start in this direction, to which the Great Spirit agrees. But then she asks him if she may be very prudent. He replies that she may also go on carrying her share of evil by means of an aching back if she prefers it, but then he will retire and leave her to his little brother, for he admits it is easier for her to leave her part in evil to God than to *do* her part and thus share his suffering with him. He then warns her to leave megalomania out of it—to do it for God's (the Self's) sake and not in order to be great after all, for then she will indeed be lost.

Anna considers this conversation for some time, and thinks she sees a chance to be great after all. She therefore suggests to him that, since indulgence in megalomania is undoubtedly a "bad tendency" of hers, and if she must be evil anyway, she might bring this evil tendency into her conscious life. She does not agree with him that if she does so she will be lost.

He repeats that if she does, she *will* be lost, but this time he adds that in such deep regions of the soul, one must sometimes be lost. She asks him if he will be her support and guide in these regions. He replies that he will be her guide, but she must take the responsibility herself. "Greatness begins with taking responsibility," he says. She then speaks of the shyness which hampers her so much, and she thinks it could be cured if she gave up fighting her megalomania. He points out that now she is facing it to do away with her shyness, not for its own sake! She asks if shyness and megalomania are not two aspects of the same complex, to which he agrees.

She then asks if she may begin by "cajoling her megalomania a little" and he replies, "Try it out." She asks if he is disgusted with her; he replies, "No, I am amused." She reports that she feels a wave of libido coming into her. He says yes, she has dared to take a stand against him, but he warns her that she will now have to deal with his little brother. She accepts this, saying she dares to do so because the Great Spirit has promised to be her guide, to which he replies that it looks rather as if she

[24]See above p. 8f.

thought she was *his* guide! She sees his point and welcomes the little brother very condescendingly.

Later, Anna thinks over this conversation very carefully. She begins to see that she has again been too bold with the Great Spirit, probably because she was possessed by his little brother. The Great Spirit tells her to distinguish between them even more closely, for it may then be possible to reconcile them with herself. She tells him that she has indeed seen that indulging her megalomania would be ego service, not Self service as in her dream. She realizes this would be wrong and says that she is now aware that only the Self can be great in her. She must not identify with it; rather, she must bring sacrifices that it may fulfill itself in her.

We see here how wisely the Great Spirit is guiding these conversations. By telling her "to try out," i.e., indulging her megalomania, she learns its dangers through her own experience, which is the only way to learn anything. He ends this conversation by saying: "Reduce megalomania to its unfulfilled state—namely, to your hankering after greatness —and then dissolve your hankering into the Self's hankering after it in you. Obey this. Serve it. Do not try to become great. Try to become so humble that the Self can be great in you, and can live its greatness through you."

Here Anna learns for herself the truth which was confirmed for Jung in the two dreams he records at the end of his chapter on "Life after Death" in *Memories, Dreams, Reflections;* they are of the UFOs (unidentified flying objects) in October 1958, and the earlier one of the Yogi[25] which I mentioned before.[26] In these conversations, and in her meditation on them, Anna realizes dimly that the Self, in order to incarnate itself, would need to wear, so to speak, the garment of the human form in order to have earthly experiences. She decides to do what she can to help the Self incarnate itself in her.

In the next conversation, Anna tells the Great Spirit how she hankered for greatness even as a child, for she wanted to be an infant prodigy. He admits she was a gifted child, and because he did not know what to do about it, the talent started growing "crooked" even at that early age. But now she is old enough to realize that all greatness belongs to the Self and that he, as part of the Self, is her giftedness.

This surprises her, and she suggests that since she has shared her life with him, she must be married to him, with which he agrees! We see

[25]Jung, *Memories, Dreams, Reflections,* pp. 323–326.
[26]See above p. 80.

here how dangerous it is not to discriminate between the individual and the universal side of the Self. She was indeed married to her own individual, creative spirit—as all creative women must be—but to see herself as the bride of the archetypal image of the Great Spirit naturally led to an inflation and to great difficulties in subsequent conversations.

Seeing herself as the bride had one great advantage, however; it taught her to become aware of herself as a feminine being. Until then, when her creative spirit seized her for inspiration, she had transformed herself into an inferior man, as the Great Spirit has now warned her not to do. But now she realizes that she, like all truly feminine women, longs to be overpowered by the masculine. With her passion to be great herself, it is doubtful if she would have accepted this at the hands of her individual, creative spirit. To be the bride of the Great Spirit, however, was something she could fully and readily believe, and she allowed him to overpower her as much as he liked. But this led to more sexual excitement than her aged body was capable of standing, and his two warnings: that a human being could not marry a Great Spirit and that only a goddess could become Shiva's Shakti. Both warnings fell on deaf ears.

Anna makes the same mistake that Faust did when he made himself the bridegroom of Helen of Troy, instead of leaving her to Paris, to whom she truly belonged. Jung pointed this out more than once, and attributed the early tragic death of Euphorion—the son of Faust and Helen—to this mistake.[27] But Anna was very much taken with the idea of being the Great Spirit's bride. She began to want to give it up not only when her health suffered but when she also became depressed and felt that she had lost all she had gained in her long work in active imagination. All her previous peace and sense of well-being had completely disappeared.

In this dilemma, she was greatly helped by a dream: She is walking on a steeply descending path in a forest. At the forest's edge she comes to a farm, although the path goes on descending to a lake with a bathing hut. She obtains the key from the farmer's wife and goes down for a swim in the lake, but she decides she is too tired and will return home instead. She returns to the farm and discovers she has left her purse with all her money and some of her clothes in the hut. In spite of her fatigue, she decides she must go down to fetch them. An enormous mail van passes her and she sees that the bathing hut has become a post office.

[27]Goethe, *Faust,* Part 2.

She shouts to the men to pick her up, but they say the van can go no farther, for the road becomes too narrow. The van has blocked the road and she cannot pass it. She wakes up in distress.

Anna saw for herself that the beginning of the dream was very positive and that a swim in the lake meant the plunge into the unconscious that the Great Spirit was helping her to take. She also saw that everything went wrong when she gave up this plunge, which would have meant giving up trusting herself to the Great Spirit.

The associations to the dream bring more enlightenment—especially the key, which she associated to the key which Bluebeard gave to his young wife and which belonged to the forbidden chamber in which she found the skeletons of all her predecessors. She also saw for herself that Bluebeard was the dark, evil side of the Great Spirit, and that she had the same difficulty in relating to his dark side as she had in relating to God's or her own. Yet clearly it is his dark side that has the key to her whole endeavor, so that in not trusting him (not daring the swim in the lake) she makes everything go wrong. She attributes everything to this cause and points out that the unconscious always behaves like Bluebeard: it gives us the key which it could easily withhold, and then punishes us for using it. An example which shows this particularly clearly is in Rosenkreutz's *Chymical Marriage*. It was Cupid himself who led Rosenkreutz to the chamber of Venus and who allowed him to gaze on the sleeping goddess, yet Cupid also punished Rosenkreutz for his intrusion by shooting him with one of his arrows.[28]

At the end of her interpretation, Anna mentions the two brothers who saved their sister in the Bluebeard story and supposes they cannot be kept out of the interpretation. She unwillingly associates them to the two postmen, "in spite of the fact that the two postmen do nothing to help the dreamer." She vaguely assumes that they must represent the Great Spirit and his little brother! Anna entirely overlooks the fact that the brothers, as the girl's near relatives, certainly represent two *individual* animi, which is confirmed in the dream by the postmen belonging to outer daily life, whereas she herself has just likened the plunge in the lake to having confidence in the Great Spirit. Therefore, the image brought forward as the solution of the dream is clearly the discrimination between the individual and the archetypal. I do not remember if I

[28]Christian Rosenkreutz (pseud. of Johann Valenti Andreae). *Chymische Hochzeit* (Strasbourg, 1616). For translation see: *The Hermetick Romance or The Chymical Wedding,* trans. E. Foxcroft (London, 1690).

saw this as clearly then as I do now, but that interpretation would
certainly have fallen on deaf ears, as such warnings from the Great spirit
had already done.

A period of several weeks followed, with only what Anna herself
called some rather worthless conversations with the Great Spirit. I
remember agreeing with her about this, and they are not repeated in the
written record which she gave me. Anna was anything but at peace with
herself during these weeks. Fortunately, I remembered how Emma Jung
had previously dealt with a similar situation when she recommended
that Anna talk to a feminine figure, whom she later called The Great
Mother. Therefore, I recommended a halt to her conversations with the
Great Spirit for the time being, and suggested that she talk over the
whole situation with the Great Mother. Anna was very willing to do this
and accepted my suggestion immmediately.

To my relief, the Great Mother recommended that she loosen herself
from the Great Spirit, and most particularly from her attacks of sexual
excitement which were much too corporeal for her age. The Great
Mother pointed out that the Great Spirit had done a great deal for her:
he had rehabilitated her femininity. This should normally have happened when she was about twenty and this was what her "great vision"
had tried to do, but unfortunately, it was misunderstood. Anna must
remember, says the Great Mother, that nearly fifty-five years have
passed since then, but that her femininity has only developed to the
stage of a young woman of twenty. Since this is totally unsuitable at her
age, she must realize she is just not the young bride per se, but that the
archetypal image of the young bride had come to life in her at last. As
an archetypal image, she is of royal birth and is a princess. Anna must
learn to be conscious of this princess in herself. This archetypal figure is a
youthful bride who is entitled to all the feelings which Anna's ego had
usurped to itself. She must now find a way of relating to this archetypal
image.

Anna asks how she can do this. The Great Mother replies that she
must see that she is the young bride's mother or grandmother. Anna
should tell her about the years she has apparently missed. The young
princess can help her make these years appear fulfilled and whole by
filling gaps and correcting failures, for Anna has repressed her to the
extent of being totally unconscious of her. She must try to understand
her with motherly love, and teach her to accept her feelings and sensations, as well as to control them "through awareness of her royal birth."

Anna also belongs to the "royal family of gifted women"; therefore, her passionately feminine daughter is not allowed to break every "inconvenient law."

Until now, Anna had always been too hard on that inner royal daughter and had trampled her down. Now, however, Anna has seen her archetypal origin and must rehabilitate her. The Great Spirit has awakened in Anna a genuinely feminine reaction to his masculinity, but for her this means the birth of—that is, the becoming conscious of—her royal daughter. But just as she had pushed her down in earlier years, so now the girl herself wants to overrun Anna, who must not let her do so. Anna has her age as a natural protection and counterbalance to the girl's unbridled passion. "Call her Irene, which means peace" states the Great Mother. "Make peace with her; live in peace with her by giving her the pleasure of making you acquainted with the feminine feelings that are her natural birthright. Be aware of her as an archetypal image. In this manner she may yet bring you peace."

Anna asks if she may be allowed one last question: May she continue her relationship with the Great Spirit? She is told to introduce her royal daughter to him. There is an immediate protest from the ego: "But is *she* going to marry him?" The Great Mother replies that indeed she is, and that Anna will then be the bride's mother. Anna indignantly asks if she must be content with looking at their pleasure, while lacking it herself. The Great Mother replies:

> You are at the age for this attitude. Bring your sacrifice as a penance for the misdeed you committed in younger years, the misdeed of repressing the little bride within you, the archetypal princess. Today in you and beyond you, Masculine Spirit and Feminine Love are going to be married.[29] Personal renunciation is your part in it. You may satisfactorily participate in their union, but this is only possible if you are up to a merely participating experience. Prepare yourself for their wedding.

Anna finds herself in the same position as Rosenkreutz in *The Chymical Marriage*. He would have liked to marry Venus, on whose naked beauty Cupid had allowed him to gaze while she was asleep, but he had to be content with even less than Anna; for he was only a guest at the *Hieros Gamos*—the sacred marriage.

In one conversation, the Great Mother has thus made Anna see, albeit reluctantly, the great difference between the human and the archetypal

[29]*Hieros Gamos.*

realm. The Great Spirit had tried to do this in vain, and my efforts in the same direction had been worse than useless. Once again, I realized how far more convincing it is when the analysand's own unconscious teaches him or her, and how very superior the knowledge and insight of the unconscious is to that of the conscious. The unconscious still further confirmed what the Great Mother had said by two fragments of a dream. Anna writes:

> *I am together with my own Princess Irene and with another lady who seems to be a crown princess. The latter is writing my "Supplement to Anna Marjula's Essay."*

and:

> *I am in a train which just stops at the end station. There is nobody in the compartment, but it is filled up with luggage which belongs to my father. No porter is to be had. I must carry all my father's boxes home myself. Though I know I cannot really do it, I decide to try anyhow.*

Through this dream, Anna at last fully realizes what the Great Mother has taught her: that her archetypal daughter, Irene, is destined to marry the Great Spirit in a true *Hieros Gamos*. She accepts this solution of her lifelong sexual problem. She has indeed sinned in repressing Princess Irene, but if she had identified with her early life and had lived too freely, she would have repressed the crown princess, the gifted woman in herself. She could not escape sinning, but nevertheless, the debt of every sin must be paid.

In the second dream, the boxes might represent her father's enormous ambition regarding his gifted daughter. In this case, the dream suggests that since she has realized the archetypal origin (or inspiration) of the woman who writes *Anna Marjula* in her, and who has accepted the archetypal young bride of the Great Spirit, Irene, she will be able to carry her own giftedness home. At all events, the boxes seem lighter and more manageable at the end of these two dreams.

When Anna gave up identifying with the archetypal bride of the Great Spirit, there was, of course, danger of an enantiodromia—of Anna throwing herself away as worthless. The dream meets this danger with the usual genius of the unconscious. It takes up the Great Mother's suggestion that Anna herself also belongs to the royal family of gifted women, representing her even as a crown princess. At the time, all of Anna's creative ability was pouring into her epilogue to *Anna Marjula*, to these conversations with the Great Spirit, so that clearly, the creative woman in herself was meant. Although she kept this effort entirely anonymous—I have had to promise never to reveal her real name even after her death—the success of the *Anna Marjula* booklet, and the fact that a great many people found it a help in their efforts with their own active imagination, was a considerable satisfaction to Anna. After these dreams, she was always perfectly willing to let the archetypal Princess Irene marry the Great Spirit, and she made no further efforts to push her ego into the *Hieros Gamos* as the bride.

In their next conversation, she tells the Great Mother that she feels wonderfully at peace since their conversation about the *Hieros Gamos*. Reading it over, she feels she has integrated all the suggestions made to her. But she still has the problem of how she should now behave to the Great Spirit. She feels she has not finished with him, yet hesitates to speak to him again in case she loses the peace she so greatly values.

The Great Mother says that while she is in Zürich and in contact with her analyst, the danger is not so great as she imagines. Her previous talks with the Great Spirit have indeed gotten her into great difficulties, but they have also brought her "remarkable inner growth." She advises Anna to not waste the time and promises also to keep an eye on her. (Anna would never talk to her inner figures when alone in her own country, though she somehow kept enough in touch with them to remain at peace.) The conversation ends with Anna expressing fervent gratitude for all that the Great Mother has done for her.

Shortly afterward, she risks another talk with the Great Spirit, explaining to him how afraid she is of talking to him. He replies that the important thing is whether she wants to talk to him or not. She answers that she wants to speak with him very much, and she hopes that her daughter, Irene, may function as a bridge between them.

He corrects her phrase of "my daughter" to "*our* daughter." At first, she is very surprised but then she sees that it was only through the Great Spirit's help that she gave birth to Irene; that is, became conscious of her. But she recoils from the fact that then the *Hieros Gamos* which took place in her was a father-daughter incest. He explains to her that a *Hieros Gamos* always has an incestuous character: gods and archetypal figures are not bound by human laws.

This was so clearly recognized in Egypt that the Pharaoh (as the god's representative) was bound to marry his sister. Anna recognizes this and no longer criticizes it. The Great Spirit replies by applauding her deci-

sion, pointing out that this *Hieros Gamos,* particularly her right participation in it, has also had a personal consequence for Anna. It has freed
her from all her incestuous desires and her recollection of these, which
were troubling her half-unconsciously. These remnants were entirely
absorbed in the realm of the *Hieros Gamos.* Even if she could not
understand this, it was still a fact. For this reason, she could truthfully
assure the Great Mother that she felt wonderfully and permanently at
peace. Irene was also at peace, freed from her prison at last, so that she
could finally unfold her archetypal ability to experience the *Hieros
Gamos* with the Great Spirit. He begs Anna not to underestimate the
great event that has taken place in her, and to realize that the Self has
enabled her to achieve the right participation in it, of which she will
eventually realize the full meaning.

This speech of the Great Spirit ends the second, and by far the most
important, part of Anna's epilogue to *Anna Marjula.* The important
climax—which gave Anna an extraordinary peace throughout her
extreme old age—was the *Hieros Gamos* which took place in her soul,
the union of all the opposites within her, and the fact that she
"achieved the right participation in it." She was able at last to distinguish between the ego, herself as a human being, and the archetypal
images, and to sacrifice her inflation of identification with any of them.
This achievement of a rare order was due to her being able to dedicate
all of her considerable creative ability to unusually long and hard work
on active imagination.

Union of Positive and Negative Animi

The climax of these conversations was reached when Anna succeeded
in achieving the right participation in the archetypal *Hieros Gamos*
which took place within her own soul. Two more parts to the notes she
gave me were very important to consolidating her own peace of mind,
but it would be an anticlimax and quite unnecessary for me to present
them here in detail.

The third part consisted of more conversations with the Great Spirit
and concerned his union with her negative animus, the little brother.
But it was not really the archetypal Great Spirit; she herself says that it
was, rather, his image in her soul; in other words, it was a union
between her positive and negative *individual* animi. That this was completely successful, at least in the sphere of the unconscious, is shown by
the dream she had at the end of part three of her conversations.

She dreamed she attended a car race with a very superior man. A special enclosure was set apart for them. The superior man was standing on her right, whereas the racing cars approached her from the left. One car was so much ahead of the others that the driver could afford to drive slowly. The superior man held up his hand and stopped the driver, who had already won the first round and was therefore competing for the great prize of the day. All the same, he stopped immediately, exactly in front of them. Then the dreamer saw why he had been stopped. Two pieces of wood protruded from the front of the car, like the giant tentacles of some insect. This was normal to all the cars in the dream. But in the case of the leading car, one of these pieces of wood was broken and had the car gone on, it would inevitably have led to a fatal accident. Anna was especially struck by the complete calm with which the driver took the loss of his great prize and by the fact that he did not even show satisfaction at his life having been saved.

The very next morning, Anna was walking in the forest near her hotel when she saw two boards attached to a tree. One was broken and hanging down exactly as in the dream. This piece of synchronicity impressed her greatly, especially since she remembered Jung telling her that dreams which were thus reflected in outer events were notably important.

The superior man, who took her into the enclosure, is clearly a personification of the Great Spirit, so that she had the opportunity to see what happened in the dream from a higher standpoint. In his commentary on *The Secret of the Golden Flower,* Jung says that such a standpoint developed in some of his patients, thereby allowing them to view their old problems from above. From that viewpoint, the problems seemed more like a thunderstorm that was taking place in the valley below them.[30] Such an opportunity is granted to Anna in this dream.

Anna herself, as we know, had been very ambitious, and since this trait mainly came from her father, it was naturally carried on by her animus. This is shown by the fact that the driver was competing for such a large prize. But the totally new detachment and willingness to take victory or defeat as it comes, and life or death with the same equanimity, show clearly that the union between her positive and negative individual animi has been completely successful. Jung often said that in such dreams, the animus shows the way which the woman herself must take.

[30]Jung, *Collected Works*, vol. 13, par. 17.

At exactly this point, interestingly enough, outer problems recalled Anna to her own country unexpectedly early. The chance was thus granted her of bringing the new standpoint which she had been shown by the animus into her own outer life. Although it took her considerable time and effort to give up her lifelong ambition and megalomania, she was eventually completely successful in this endeavor.

In her lecture on active imagination for the International Association for Analytical Psychology in Rome in 1977, Marie-Louise von Franz pointed out that this step—which she calls the fourth stage in active imagination—is the most important of all. If we fail to incorporate into our actual lives what we have learned in our active imagination as an ethical obligation, we have failed to take it seriously at all.[31] This crucial step was taken by Anna Marjula, and I attribute most of the peace and happiness of her old age to this fact.

Part Four

Part four mainly consists of various important things that the Great Mother said to Anna, chiefly during her conversations with the Great Spirit. They are, however, not dated, so I have no means of knowing where they belong. Moreover, though interesting and often extremely wise in themselves, they are not essential to our theme.

There is only one conversation that I would like to mention, because it forms an interesting parallel to a conversation between Beatrice and her spirit man.[32] In fact, it throws light upon the latter. This conversation was the result of the following dream: The dreamer is walking hand in hand with Anna's old friend and foster mother Urs, "the Great" (a literal translation of her surname). Her old friend is leaning heavily on her and asks her for a cup of coffee as a stimulant.

It seems to me that this dream meant that the Great Mother might want Anna to do something for her, and Anna asked her if that were the case. To her great surprise, the Great Mother answered: "Yes, help for the world situation." Beatrice had asked her spirit man for help in the dark situation in which she found the world, but Anna was not, like Beatrice, particularly worried about it. Therefore, the Great Mother's suggestion surprised her almost as much as the World-Weary Man was astonished at the sudden attack of his Ba. One reason for her lack of concern was that Anna's active imagination took place many years

[31]Cf. Jung, *Memories, Dreams, Reflections,* pp. 189 and 192.
[32]See above, Chapter 4.

earlier, when the danger was not so glaringly apparent. For another, the problem continually oppressed Beatrice, but Anna had never regarded it as any business of hers, although the Great Mother had mentioned it to her earlier. In other words, Beatrice knew that Jung thought the world situation largely depended on how many individuals could stand the tension of the opposites in themselves, whereas Anna had not yet heard of this concept.

The Spirit Man advised Beatrice to take her anxiety to the flower, where the warring opposites were united. The Great Mother had to explain to Anna that the archetypes need human beings who are conscious of them and who can therefore represent them by doing what they want in outer reality on earth. She attacks Anna's lifelong shyness as responsible for her not seeing this need: when she is shy, she is entirely in the ego, but when she sees the great value of the archetypes within her, her shyness no longer troubles her. Anna can help the world situation by fully realizing this and by being humble before the great archetypes, instead of foolishly shy because she is projecting these same archetypes onto other people.

Anna finishes this fourth and last part with a final conversation with the Great Spirit. Although it helped her significantly, it only emphasizes parts of the conversations which we have already considered but which she had evidently not sufficiently realized. Therefore, there is no reason for us to go into it here.

At this point, Anna's age and health no longer allowed her to visit Zürich, so her active imagination came to an end. She gave up her flat and settled in what seemed to be a very satisfactory old-age home. At first, she had some difficulty in accepting being with people of her own advanced age, who had really come to die, but very soon, her inner peace reasserted itself. This evidently had an effect on her companions, for she made many friends, particularly among the men, with whom she had had such difficulty establishing relationships earlier. She wrote to me more than once, telling me that her old age was the happiest and most serene time of her life.[33]

[33]Editor's note: The woman known as Anna Marjula died twenty years after completing this work. Her nation mourned the death of one of their well-known musicians. She died at the age of ninety, just a few months prior to publication of this book.

CHAPTER 8

The Eternal Search for the Inner, Great Spirit

Although the examples of active imagination could have been multiplied and varied ad infinitum, I hope enough have been given to show the reader the uniquely individual character of each of them. Jung always encouraged me to give courses on active imagination; I wish to make it very clear, however, that there is no recipe, nor any generally comprehensible method, of putting it into practice. The goal remains the same in every case: establishing contact with the unconscious and learning to know the infinitely wise guidance that exists in all of us, but which so few ever bring into reality.

In a talk with the students of the C. G. Jung Institute in Zürich in May 1958[1] (three years before his death), Jung made this guidance very clear by calling it the ''2,000,000-year-old man'' in us all. He referred to him throughout this discussion as the ''Great Man'' in ourselves. This Great Man appears in images and symbols that are infinite in number and which are different in every case.

In *Man and His Symbols*, Marie-Louise von Franz so vividly shows this Great Man at work in an unspoiled people that I would like to quote what she says in full:

[1]Reported from notes made by Marian Bayes in *C. G. Jung Speaking*, eds. William Mcguire and R. F. C. Hull (Princeton: Princeton University Press, 1977), pp. 359ff.

This inner center is realized in exceptionally pure, unspoiled form by the Naskapi Indians, who still exist in the forests of the Labrador peninsula. These simple people are hunters who live in isolated family groups, so far away from one another that they have not been able to evolve tribal customs or collective religious beliefs and ceremonies. In his lifelong solitude the Naskapi hunter has to rely on his own inner voices and unconscious revelations; he has no religious teachers who tell him what he should believe, no rituals, festivals, or customs to help him along. In his basic view of life, the soul of man is simply an "inner companion," whom he calls "my friend" or Mista'peo, meaning "Great Man." Mista'peo dwells in the heart and is immortal; in the moment of death, or shortly before, he leaves the individual, and later reincarnates himself in another being.

Those Naskapi who pay attention to their dreams and who try to find their meaning and test their truth can enter into a deeper connection with the Great Man. He favors such people and sends them more and better dreams. Thus the major obligation of an individual Naskapi is to follow the instructions given by his dreams, and then to give permanent form to their contents in art. Lies and dishonesty drive the Great Man away from one's inner realm, whereas generosity and love of one's neighbors and of animals attract him and give him life. Dreams give the Naskapi complete ability to find his way in life, not only in the inner world but also in the outer world of nature. They help him to foretell the weather and give him invaluable guidance in his hunting, upon which his life depends. I mention these very primitive people because they are uncontaminated by our civilized ideas and still have natural insight into the essence of what Jung calls the Self. [2]

Jung told his students that the transference was entirely due to the existence of this Great Man, and he advised them to work with their patients in analysis until they were aware of, and could establish a connection with, the Great Man in themselves.

It seems to me—although Jung said nothing about it in this talk with the Institute students—that he had experienced this 2,000,000-year-old Great Man in himself fairly early in his childhood, as his Number Two personality. Or perhaps he experienced a comparatively small aspect of him, for at first he felt this Great Man as coming from the eighteenth century. [3] I think he can only have slowly realized the immense, indeed

[2] C. G. Jung, ed. *Man and His Symbols* (New York: Doubleday & Company, 1964), pp. 161f.
[3] Jung, *Memories, Dreams, Reflections*, p. 34.

archaic, age of what he called the 2,000,000-year-old man when he was well over eighty years old.

In the oldest example which we have used, the 4,000-year-old text of "The World-Weary Man and His Ba," this is particularly clear to us, for the Ba himself could be said to be a personification of the 2,000,000-year-old Great Man in the unconscious of the World-Weary Man. The Egyptian religion had recognized the fact of the existence of this 2,000,000-year-old man, but, having projected it into the Beyond, they only saw him as a collective figure. Therefore, it was only because the World-Weary Man was a genius endowed with most unusual courage that he was eventually able to see the appearance of the Ba as an *individual* event, which forced him to an encounter entirely beyond all that he had been taught and all that he had believed in the religious dogma of the time. I know of no medieval or modern example that can compare in this respect with our old Egyptian text; in fact, Jung advised me to stop searching, because one did not exist.

Jung once told me that it was a very long time before the archetypal anima (who of course is a counterpart of this total 2,000,000-year-old man) spoke to him directly. For many years before that, she had only sent him her emissaries. The emissaries are what has mainly appeared in all of our other examples.

Let us take the case of Edward (Chapter Two). We do see a direct trace of the 2,000,000-year-old man in the Spirit of Fire, Water, Wind and Ice that terrified Edward in the storm. We can also see a trace of the negative side of his consort in the archetypal witch who was the cause of the whole trouble. But for the most part, Edward is always in contact with his emissaries, particularly with the two aspects of the anima: the Guide and Four Eyes. The extraordinarily genuine character of Edward's active imagination is vouched for by the fact that every detail in the fantasy is truly symbolic. The "defect" of the fantasy comes from its having been undertaken *before* Edward had dealt with his own personal shadow. Therefore, he is quite unable to endure the destructive side of the Spirit of Fire, Water, Wind and Ice. It is only after we have seen that we ourselves have a very destructive side that we can endure that side in the archetypal figures which we encounter. Therefore, this most genuine example of active imagination, produced only by unusually long, hard work on Edward's part, is still only the prelude to more hard and painful work on his own shadow, who appeared at the banquet as the boatman.

When we come to Sylvia in Chapter Three, we are not dealing with a real example of active imagination at all, but only with a prelude that provides a great many starting points for true active imagination and reveals Sylvia's whole psychology in a way that no *direct* attempt could have done at that stage in her development. Sylvia—far more than Edward—would have shied away from seeing her personal shadow. Only the fact that she felt she was writing a story about imaginary people allowed it to be revealed that, given sufficient provocation, she was even capable of murder. And many hints were thrown out in the allusions to the Greek gods of the 2,000,000-year-old man in herself.

In the case of Beatrice, Chapter Four, we have an even more unique document, because it was created during the last few months before her death. That is, we have only studied the final part of a very long effort in active imagination, much longer than Edward's. It is indeed an *active* imagination, for she is fully involved in it from beginning to end, and the Spirit Man, alias the Bear Man, was the result of long and painstaking effort in the process of making his acquaintance. By the time we enter her fantasy, he can be recognized as a very trusted emissary—or almost a personification—of the 2,000,000-year-old man, as he appeared to Beatrice and prepared her for the great change which he knew was closely approaching. As I pointed out at the time, although Beatrice's death was sudden and completely unexpeccted in a way, she was already showing herself unusually well-acquainted with, and appreciative of, the Beyond. In fact, during her last two days of life, when she entered the flower—which she had been repeatedly warned might lead to her inability to return—one almost feels she was conscious of the great change that was coming to her.

The 2,000,000-year-old man in Beatrice is unusually clear; in fact, it can only be compared with the "World-Weary Man and His Ba." The Spirit Man's main symbol is the flower that unites all the opposites in itself. But the Spirit Man or Bear Man, who always guides Beatrice to the flower and who evidently lives in it himself, was certainly its completely trusted emissary, or even a personification of the Great Man himself.

It must be emphasized that this figure began as the animus which gives every woman so much trouble and which was particularly difficult for Beatrice. But by very long, hard work at active imagination, she succeeded in uncovering the figure that is always behind woman's animus—the Great Man himself. Not that his tormenting side disappeared: it is to be seen in the firmness with which he makes Beatrice acknowledge and face her hated countertransference. Moreover, she still had trouble when she was away from her miraculous flower with his negative opinions. We can see this especially clearly in her unfounded fits of jealousy concerning an imaginary attraction of her husband to a young girl whom he did not even like! And we saw the berserker rage which the Bear Man showed—during which he very nearly killed Beatrice—when she exhibited an "abstemious" attitude, thereby repressing her own negative emotion. She had to promise never again to repress her emotions "for the sake of being reasonable" before he could be reconciled to her.

This throws a very interesting light on our ingrained Christian attitude toward morality. Evidently, we must now be *whole,* as we really are even when we face the Last Judgment, so to speak. We cannot escape from the opposite of evil, but must suffer the tension between it and good—to say nothing of the other opposites—right to the end.

This concept goes against everything we have been taught. We believe, to the marrow of our bones, that God wishes us to be good and to repress evil. Therefore, it is the most difficult thing in the world to realize that God now, most certainly, wants us to stand the *tension* between good and evil. Yet old Isaiah saw this truth all those centuries ago when he was inspired to write: "I form the light, and create darkness: I make peace and create evil: I the Lord do all these things."[4] The Lord has, for the most part, allowed us to forget Isaiah's words and to bask in the sun of righteousness for nearly 2,000 years.

Originally, it was indeed necessary to do all we could to see the light side to achieve the far more difficult righteous opposite. But it is clear from the tremendous outbreak of evil all over the world, which is threatening our very existence on our planet, that God is determined to remind us that it was He Himself who created evil; therefore, we must somehow come to terms with it. As Jung wrote, "We must learn how to handle it, since it is here to stay. How we can live with it without terrible consequences cannot for the present be conceived."[5]

The first modest attempt we can make toward averting the "terrible consequences" is to reconsider our inborn conception of God Himself in the light of Isaiah's little-known description of Him. In the last 2,000 years, we have been taught to think of Him as a wholly benevolent,

[4]*Isaiah* 45:7.
[5]Jung, *Memories, Dreams, Reflections,* p. 329.

omnipotent God, and to attribute all evil and destruction to the devil. We have not even kept in mind the well-known fact that the devil is Satan, God's elder son. For nearly 2,000 years, it has been more or less possible to believe that the benevolent God was the stronger of the two, and therefore, not to question His omnipotence.

But is it possible to maintain this attitude in face of the worldwide outbreak of evil today? We must choose between a dualistic conception of God (God and His enemy, the devil) or admit that God Himself contains both sides and is thus truly whole and omnipotent. If one has experienced how relative and totally different the opposites become when both are fully accepted, it is not difficult to imagine a God who contains *both* opposites. Jung's *Answer to Job* helps us do so.

To me personally, it is a much more bearable thought to conceive of a whole God who contains all opposites—and, like nature, creates and destroys—than to see the worldwide outbreak of evil as the work of God's enemy, the devil, or as man's own fault, while an only good and omnipotent God apparently does nothing to prevent him or us from perpetrating that evil. Indeed, we can only accept the negative side of God, or any archetype, after we have faced our own shadow, our own negative and destructive side. We saw, for example, in the last banquet scene and when he was confronted by the Spirit of Fire, Water, Wind and Ice how weakened Edward was by having this work on the shadow still before him, and how nearly the Bear Man put an end to Beatrice—*before* her right moment to die—for thinking she could repress her own negative emotions even a few days before her death. It seems to me that all the evidence points to mankind *at last* taking Isaiah's text seriously and drawing the necessary conclusions from it.

I am sure Beatrice must have known from her material that a great change was approaching, but it is always an uncertain matter when dreams or active imaginations prepare us for a great change, whether rebirth in this world or in the next is intended—a change that involves a complete change of standpoint, and indeed, of personality. We know that Beatrice expected the change to come in life, for in the last record, written the day before her death, she tells us so herself. She writes:

I contemplate the flower. As I meditate upon it, I become, as I did yesterday, the flower itself, rooted, growing, radiant, timeless. Thus, I take on the form of immortality. Then I feel quite well, and protected from all

*attacks from outside. It also protects me from my own emotions. When I
am in the center, nobody and nothing can attack me. They can still attack
and hurt me in my human form and I know that I must still spend most
of my time there.*[6] *But I shall always have the opportunity now and then
to become the flower.*

Thus, Beatrice experienced immortality in her lifetime, and death for
her would be entering her beloved flower without the necessity of being
obliged, as she evidently expected, to leave it again for most of the time.
The 2,000,000-year-old man in Beatrice had certainly prepared her for
death in a wonderful way.

The next example of active imagination which we examined (Chapter
Five) was our best, although it comes from 4,000 years ago. But I have
already dwelt on "The World-Weary Man and His Ba" in this concluding chapter. We come then to the dialogue between Hugh de St. Victor
and his soul (Chapter Six), which was a complete contrast to the World-
Weary Man's experience. The World-Weary Man was totally and unexpectedly invaded by a figure from the unconscious—the Great Man—
whereas the medieval dialogue was started by Hugh himself. The first
text, which shows us how to adapt the conscious to such an invasion, is
really an example of a completely successful coming to terms between
conscious and unconscious. The interference from the unconscious was
much less dramatic with Hugh; indeed, we can only surmise that his
conscious program did not suit his anima by what the soul replies to his
fully conscious and intentional remonstrances. As the representative of
the unconscious, she clearly saw farther into the future than Hugh did
and tried to make him widen his point of view to include some of the
dark side. But it was still too early; she could only have very little success
in this endeavor, for in the twelfth century, a man—especially a monk
like Hugh—was still legitimately struggling to develop the light opposite and to persuade his timeless unconscious to remain mainly within
that frame, as Hugh does do very successfully. But the anima does
succeed in preparing the ground for a later acceptance of both opposites
when she induces Hugh to see that her adherence to the dark side has
strengthened, rather than weakened, the love of her bridegroom. It is by
such small, almost invisible steps that the unconscious slowly prepares
the way for completely new circumstances, not only for the individual,
but for humanity.

[6]Underlining added to emphasize that she expected the change to come in life.

The lectures of Jung at the Eidgenössische Technische Hochschule (E.T.H.) in Zürich dealt with active imagination as it appears in two great religions—Buddhism and Christianity—both of which attempted to solve the problem within the boundaries of their own dogmas.[7] Jung pointed out that these dogmas are by no means an invention of consciousness. They are built up on the unconscious; in fact, they are usually, at the time they arise, an almost perfect expression of the unconscious. For a time, they act as a perfect canalization, so to speak, of the unconscious of the individual. Just as long as the unconscious is willing to flow in these channels, the religion in question provides everything that is required, and these times belong to the happiest in the history of the human race. There are still people today whose whole unconscious fits into the dogma of the church or religion in which they were brought up, and such people should be encouraged to remain within it. But as the state of the world teaches us daily, this is no longer the case for the vast majority. It is useless to deny that we are confronted with a flood of water from the unconscious which is only finding a channel in the conscious of a very few individuals. These few have realized that the unconscious is now demanding much wider channels that will contain *both* opposites, and not exclude the dark, usually expressed as the evil, opposite, as the former dogmas do now.

Taught by all that she had learned from Jung—to which she was especially open from her earlier study of Spinoza—Anna Marjula really did attempt, through her active imagination, to include both opposites. The first part—which I was able to leave exactly as it came from her own pen —is really a preparation for the more obvious play of the opposites in the second part: her talks with the Great Spirit. She was fully convinced of a whole God that contained both opposites, and that she must include them both in her active imagination *before* she began her talks with the Great Spirit. Before these ended, she had carried them through to the unusual, but most desirable, climax of the *Hieros Gamos* itself. She was rewarded by the opposites no longer troubling her, because they had become relative to each other; therefore, she enjoyed an unusually serene old age.

Anna first endured the tension of the opposites and then achieved the right participation to enable them to unite in her. I must mention that in her own analysis of her earliest pictures, which she undertook

[7]E.T.H. Lectures, vol. 2; vols. 3 and 4, 1st ed.

between the conversations with the Great Mother and the Great Spirit, she learned how far apart the opposites were in her, and that it was the nearly intolerable tension between them that was undermining the peace she had found after her conversations with the Great Mother. This caused her to speak of them much more openly in her talks with the Great Spirit. This, in its turn, led to the wonderful climax of which the Great Mother says:

> Today in you and beyond you, Masculine Spirit and Feminine Love are going to be married. Personal renunciation is your part of it. You may satisfactorily participate in their union, but this is only possible in case you are up to a merely participating experience. Prepare yourself for their wedding.

Anna Marjula thus fulfilled the condition that Jung said was the only possibility of averting atomic war.[8] When I told him what she was doing, and before he saw her manuscript, he replied, "It shows that one should never despair of a case." For, as I mentioned before, there was a considerable time when Jung and I feared that she would never get the better of her negative animus. It seems to me, therefore, that Anna Marjula's example of active imagination is a particular encouragement to women in the great difficulties they encounter with their animus.

In a way, one cannot compare such small, individual efforts with the dogmas produced by generations in the great religions. Yet only by such individual efforts can people who are still supporting the religions begin to see that their dogmas must *develop* if they are to remain alive and not become dead relics of the past. Jung often pointed out what a tremendous step Pope Pius XII took in this direction when he raised the Virgin to heaven and thus began to turn the Trinity into a quaternity, that age-old symbol for wholeness.

We can see what significant importance Jung attached to the union of opposites by the fact that he devoted his last long book, the *Mysterium Coniunctionis*,[9] entirely to that subject. It took him many years to write this book; indeed, it was his "main business," as Goethe called his *Faust*. At the very beginning, he devoted a footnote to a quotation from the well-known early-seventeenth century alchemist Michael Maier, which has always struck me as one of the best descriptions of how the opposites can unite. Maier says:

[8]See above p. 8.
[9]Jung, *Collected Works*, vol. 14.

Nature, I say, when she turned about the golden circle, by that movement made its four qualities equal, that is to say, she squared that homogeneous simplicity turning back on itself, or brought it into an equilateral rectangle, in such a way that contraries are bound together by contraries, and enemies by enemies, as if with everlasting bonds, and are held in mutual embrace.[10]

We see clearly how impossible it is for the conscious to unite the opposites; only nature can do that if human beings have the right participation in it. We have seen, from how the Great Mother described it, that the ego must give up all its egotistic demands and allow nature a completely free hand. Or, to look at this right participation in another way: the ego must achieve the same attitude as the Chinese rainmaker of Kian Tchou.[11] He told Wilhelm that it could not rain until he had gotten himself back into Tao; then, of course, it did rain. As I see it, nature can only bind "contraries . . . together by contraries, and enemies by enemies, as if with everlasting bonds" and hold them in "mutual embrace" if we can achieve the right attitude or participation toward it.

[10]Michael Maier, *De circulo physico quadrato*, p. 17.
[11]See above pp. 13ff.

Bibliography

Artis auriferae, 2 vols. Basel: 1593.

Boehme, Jakob. *The Works of Jacob Behmen,* Translated and edited by G. Ward and T. Langcake. 4 vols. London: 1764–81.

Budge, E. A. Wallis. *The Book of the Dead.* New York: Barnes & Noble, Inc., 1953.

Brugsch, H. *Geographische Inschriften Altägyptische Denkmaler* (Ger.) 1860 text ed.

Dorn, Gerhard. "Speculative philosophia," *Theatrum Chemicum,* I.

Goethe, Johann Wolfgang von. *Faust.* Translated by Philip Wayne. 2 vols. Harmondsworth: 1949, 1959.

———. *Faust. An abridged version.* Translated by Louis MacNeice. London: 1951.

Hannah, Barbara. *Jung: His Life and Work: A Biographical Memoir.* New York: G. P. Putnam's Sons, 1976.

———. *The Problem of Contact with the Animus.* Guild of Pastoral Psychology, Lecture 70.

———. *Striving Toward Wholeness.* New York: G. P. Putnam's Sons, 1971.

Hogg, James. *The Memoirs and Confessions of a Justified Sinner.* London: The Cresset Press, 1947.

Homer. *The Odyssey.* Translated by E. V. Rieu. New York: Penguin, 1950.

Huxley, Aldous L. *Grey Eminence.* New York & London: Harper & Brothers, 1941.

I Ching, or the Book of Changes. Translated by James Legge. New York: Dover Press, Inc., 1899.

I Ching, or the Book of Changes. Translated by Richard Wilhelm, rendered into English by Cary F. Baynes. Princeton: Princeton University Press, 1967.

Jacobsohn, Helmuth. *Timeless Documents of the Soul.* Evanston: Northwestern University Press, 1968.

Jung, Carl Gustav. *Aion: Researches Into the Phenomenology of the Self.* Vol. 9, part ii, *Collected Works.* Princeton: Princeton University Press, 1959; 2nd edn., 1968.

————. *Alchemical Studies.* Vol. 13. *Collected Works.* Princeton: Princeton University Press, 1968.

————. *C. G. Jung Speaking.* Edited by William McGuire and R.F.C. Hull. Princeton: Princeton University Press, 1977.

————. *Civilization in Transition.* Vol. 10. *Collected Works.* Princeton: Princeton University Press, 1964; 2nd edn., 1970.

————. *Collected Works of C. G. Jung.* Princeton: Princeton University Press (Bollingen Series XX), especially the following:

    Vol. 17: *The Development of Personality,* 1954.

    Vol. 14: *Mysterium Coniuntionis,* 1970.

    Vol. 16: *The Practice of Psychotherapy,* 1966.

    Vol. 12: *Psychology and Alchemy,* 1968.

    Vol. 5: *The Psychology of the Unconscious,* 1967.

    Vol. 11: *Psychology and Religion: West and East,* 1969.

    Vol. 7: *Two Essays on Analytical Psychology,* 1966.

————. E. T. H. (Eidgenössische Technische Hochschule) Lectures, Modern Psychology, Vols. II, III, IV and V. Zurich: privately printed.

————. *Letters.* 2 vols. Edited by Gerhard Adler and Aniela Jaffé. Princeton: Princeton University Press, 1973.

————. *Man and His Symbols.* Edited by C. G. Jung. New York: Doubleday & Company, 1964.

————. *Memories, Dreams, Reflections.* New York: Pantheon Books, 1973.

————. "Psychological Analysis of Nietzche's *Thus Spake Zarathustra.*" Private seminar given in Zurich during the 1930's.

Maier, Michael. *De circulo physico quadrato.* Oppenheim, 1616.

Marjula, Anna. *The Healing Influence of Active Imagination in a Specific Case of Neurosis.* Zurich: Schippert & Co., 1967.

Mead, George Robert Stow. *A Mithraic Ritual.* Echoes of the Gnosis Series. London, 1907.

————. ed. and trans. *Thrice Greatest Hermes.* 3 vols. London, 1949.

Micropaedia. Vol. 7. Chicago: Encyclopaedia Britannica, Inc., 1943–73.

Preisendanz, Karl, ed. *Papyri Graecae Magicae.* 2 vols. Stuttgart, 1973.

Rauschning, Hermann. *Hitler Speaks.* London: Thornton Butterworth, Ltd., 1939.

Richard de St. Victor, *Benjamin Minor.*

Rosarium philosophorum. See *Artis auriferae.*

Rosenkreutz, Christian (pseud. of Johann Valentin Andreae). *Chymische Hoschzeit.* Strasbourg, 1616. For translation, see *The Hermetick Romance, or the Chymical Wedding.* Translated by E. Foxcroft. London, 1690.

Saint Gertrude. *Life and Revelations of St. Gertrude*. London: Burns and
    Yates, 1870.

Thompson, Francis. *Hound of Heaven*. Boston: Branden Press, n.d.

The Upanishads. Parts I and II. Oxford, 1879.

van der Post, Laurens. *A Mantis Carol*. London: Hogarth Press, 1975.

von Franz, Marie-Louise. *Die Visionen des Niklaus von Flüe*. Zurich: Rascher
    Verlag, 1959.

————. *Projections and Re-Collection in Jungian Psychology: Reflection of the
    Soul*. Translated by William Kennedy. La Salle: Open Court Publishing
    Co., 1980.

Wilhelm, Richard. "Death and Renewal in China." *Spring: A Magazine of
    Jungian Thought*. Analytical Psychology Club of New York, 1962.

Wolff, Paul. *Die Viktoriner: Mystische Schriften*. Vienna: Thomas Verlag
    Jakob Hegner, 1936.

Other Titles from Sigo Press

The Unholy Bible *by June Singer*

Emotional Child Abuse *by Joel Covitz*

Dreams of a Woman *by Shelia Moon*

Androgyny *by June Singer*

The Dream-The Vision of the Night *by Max Zeller*

Sandplay Studies *by Bradway et al.*

Symbols Come Alive in the Sand *by Evelyn Dundas*

Inner World of Childhood *by Frances G. Wickes*

Inner World of Man *by Frances G. Wickes*

Inner World of Choice *by Frances G. Wickes*

Available from SIGO PRESS, 25 New Chardon Street, #8748A, Boston, Massachusetts, 02114.

SIGO PRESS

SIGO PRESS publishes books in psychology which continue the work of C.G. Jung, the great Swiss psychoanalyst and founder of analytical psychology. Each season SIGO brings out a small but distinctive list of titles intended to make a lasting contribution to psychology and human thought. These books are invaluable reading for Jungians, psychologists, students and scholars and provide enrichment and insight to general readers as well. In the Jungian Classics Series, well-known Jungian works are brought back into print in popular editions.